TRAMPS
and
REFORMERS

1873-1916

TRAMPS
and
REFORMERS
1873-1916
The Discovery of
Unemployment in New York

Paul T. Ringenbach

CONTRIBUTIONS IN AMERICAN HISTORY
NUMBER 27

GREENWOOD PRESS, INC.
WESTPORT, CONNECTICUT ● LONDON, ENGLAND

Library of Congress Cataloging in Publication Data

Ringenbach, Paul T
    Tramps and reformers, 1873-1916.

    (Contributions in American history, no. 27)
    Bibliography: p.
    1. Unemployed—New York (City)—History.
2. Tramps—New York (State)—New York (City)—History.
3. Social reformers—New York (City)—History.
I. Title.
HD5726.N5R53   362.8'5   77-175610
ISBN 0-8371-6266-1

Library of Congress Catalog Card Number: 77-175610

ISBN: 0-8371-6266-1

First published in 1973

Greenwood Press, Inc., Publishing Division
51 Riverside Avenue, Westport, Connecticut 06880

Manufactured in the United States of America

To Mom and Dad

The "tramp" comes with the locomotive, and almshouses and prisons are as surely the marks of "material progress" as are costly dwellings, rich warehouses, and magnificent churches. Upon streets lighted with gas and patrolled by uniformed policemen, beggars wait for the passerby, and in the shadow of college, and library, and museum, are gathering the more hideous Huns and fiercer Vandals of whom Macaulay prophesied.

Henry George, *Progress and Poverty* (1879)

Yet the tramp, known as he is now from the Atlantic to the Pacific, is only a part of the phenomenon of American economic growth. Behind him, though not obtrusive, save in what we call "hard times," there is, even in what we now consider normal times, a great mass of unemployed labour which is unable, unwilling or not yet forced to tramp, but which bears to the tramp the same relation that the submerged part of an iceberg does to that much smaller part which shows above the surface.

Henry George, *Social Problems* (1883)

Contents

List of Illustrations

Acknowledgments

AS ALL WHO have written a book know, completion is possible only with the assistance of numerous people and institutions. Without exception, libraries and other institutions opened manuscripts and other resources to me. Individuals who were particularly helpful included the Reverend W. Vautin of the McAuley Water Street Mission, Lt. Colonel Margaret K. Hale and Major Katherine Ruud of the Salvation Army, Mrs. Dorothy Swanson of the Tamiment Library, Mr. Henry Rowen of the Columbia University Library, Miss Virginia Downes of the YMCA, and Mr. Paul Rugen of the Manuscript Division of the New York Public Library. Mr. Haig Ajamian and Mr. Robert Fuglein introduced me to the great riches of the Russell Sage Collection at the City College of the City University of New York. Without the many kindnesses of Miss Anna Fazakerley and the assistance of Mr. Milas Nall of the Community Service Society, I could not have completed this study.

In a study of this type the unsung heroes and heroines are the interlibrary loan librarians. Miss Roberta Smith and her staff at the University of Connecticut and Mrs. Betty Fogler at the USAF Academy have my deep appreciation for their professional and cheerful disposition of my endless requests for obscure and fugitive materials.

My special thanks go to my friend, Mr. Gilbert L. Campbell of The Filter Press, Palmer Lake, Colorado, who devoted considerable time and effort in preparing the illustrations for this manuscript.

Many individuals read the manuscript in different versions and greatly strengthened it with fresh insights and perceptive criticism. Any errors that remain do so in spite of their suggestions. These readers included Lt. Colonel Monte D. Wright, Major and Mrs. David

MacIsaac, Mrs. Edward P. Brynn, Daniel J. Wacker, my Mother, Reinhold A. Dorwat, James. O. Robertson, and especially Harry J. Marks. Professor A. William Hoglund of the University of Connecticut suggested the tramp for study. His patience, assistance, and friendship made the whole project much easier.

Finally, most important was the aid and encouragement provided by my family. Kathy, Paul, Dan, and Ted with great understanding (almost always) gave up ice skating and vacations and other fun so that Dad could work on his book. And to my wife Sally goes the deepest thanks of all for keeping things happy and healthy at home while I was on the tramp.

Introduction

VAGRANTS, AS TRAMPS were once known, aroused attention in the New World as early as the seventeenth century. Elizabethan England had enforced vagrancy laws vigorously, and brutal punishments such as branding, mutilation, and death were meted out to jobless wanderers. When the English colonists came to America, they brought this predilection against vagrants with them. Laws enacted by the Plymouth colony in 1642 and 1682 insisted on land settlement to discourage vagrants and rootlessness. Strangers who could not show officials that they could support themselves had to leave town. In 1657, Boston officials insisted that jobs be found for all freed servants. While these laws reflected an apprehension that all men might not want to work, little thought was given to the problem that work might not be available.

The panics of 1819 and 1837 upset the assumption that work was always available as the relief rolls filled with the jobless. Unemployment had become a visible problem, and reasons for its existence were sought. New Yorkers blamed outside forces, especially immigration, for upsetting the economic balance, and some justification for this belief existed: some European cities paid the passage of paupers to America; most immigrants had small cash reserves and quickly slipped onto relief rolls in times of economic adversity. The increase in vagrancy also was blamed partly on the availability of relief. In the 1820s, New York State investigated relief laws and constructed almshouses. Following the panic of 1837, the New York Association for Improving the Condition of the Poor was founded to organize the distribution of relief available to the destitute. Both these actions reflected in part a belief that existing relief measures helped increase vagrancy. No real connection, however, was seen between the increase in unemployment and the numerous vagrants.

The other major cause of vagrancy was considered to be personal deficiency, especially caused by "demon rum." The morality play, *The Drunkard*, staged in the 1840s, featured a hero whose evil weakness was drink. In time, drink drove him from his family, home, and employment until he reached the depths of degradation as a city vagrant. He was saved only through the intervention of a minister. Vaudeville comedian Nat M. Wills' characterization of "The Happy Tramp" at the turn of the century still dwelled on this theme. Many of his jokes, monologues, and parodies reinforced the belief that men became tramps because of their own personal weaknesses. One of his parodies, "Old Familiar Faces," exploited the theme in the lines:

> I've just arrived this morning by the first freight
> > from the West.
> I was a member of the Spanish army I don't think;
> There's fringe upon my whiskers, and no buttons on my
> > vest,
> To feel dry is enough to make me drink.
> I'm captain of the sons of rest.
> Who vowed they will not work and swear
> > They'll keep a poorman's whiskey down.
> The Secretary sent me to see that no one breaks the
> > pledge.
> Now I'll tell you what I saw since I struck town.[1]

Following the panic of 1873, more vagrants were visible than ever before. The enormous increase in numbers and the type of jobless appearing led Americans to use a new noun when describing them—"tramps," which was probably derived originally from any one of a number of similar European verbs such as the German *trampen* meaning "to wander on foot."[2] These tramps were not the wanderers described by Whitman and Twain, but were considered by their contemporaries as a threat to American society.

This study principally explores the reactions of a group of New York City reformers to the tramps between 1873 and 1916. These "reformers" were the participants in the charity organization movement who were usually members of either the New York Charity Organization Society (NYCOS) or the New York Association for Improving the Condition of the Poor (NYAICP). Provoked into action by the appearance of the tramps who presumably challenged the established order, the reformers at first supported suppression and confinement of them. However, more tramps appeared with each economic trough in spite of the repressive measures.

The panic of 1893 proved to be a turning point in the attitudes of the reformers. The presence of huge numbers of tramps in New York City after 1893 and detailed study of them gradually led the reformers to believe that most men assumed to be tramps were, in fact, involuntarily unemployed. The tramps needed relief immediately, but in the long run they needed jobs. The reformers found that shipping tramps to rural areas to find jobs was not a solution to the problem; moreover, they found that jobs, thought to exist for everyone in America, could not be found. Their dilemma led to the recognition that unemployment was a constant problem in the United States and to eventual reform in dealing with unemployment.

NOTES

1. Nat M. Wills, *A Son of Rest* (Chicago, 1903), 16.
2. H. L. Mencken, *The American Language, Supplement II* (New York, 1952), 675-679. See also Eric Partridge, *A Dictionary of the Underworld* (London, 1949), 739.

TRAMPS
and
REFORMERS

1873-1916

Abbreviations

Annals	*Annals of the American Academy of Political and Social Science*
NCCC	National Conference of Charities and Correction
NYAICP (AICP)	New York Association for Improving the Condition of the Poor
NYCCCC	New York City Conference of Charities and Correction
NYCOS (COS)	New York Charity Organization Society
NYC YMCA	New York City Young Men's Christian Association
NYSBC	New York State Board of Charities
NYSCCC	New York State Conference of Charities and Correction
SCAA	State Charities Aid Association

1

"Hark! Hark! The Dogs Do Bark":

The Discovery of the American Tramp,

1873-1890

IN THE 1870s when tramps first appeared in significant numbers on the American scene, farm journals compared them to destructive pests like locusts. Locusts, of course, had always been a symbol of frustration, as well as danger, for the farmer. Not knowing why, when, or where the insects would appear, the farmers could not prevent them. And when the locusts did appear, they often did so in such large numbers that the farmer could not cope with them at all. Although a single locust was repulsive, it constituted a real danger only when it joined with others. In mass numbers, the insects could ravage a year's work in the fields in minutes. The *New York Times* in 1876 noted that the insects moved from place to place in obedience to hunger, but speculated also that the flights were prolonged by the "excitement which movement in great masses gives to individuals." Here truly was a "frivolous emblem of improvidence." To the harassed farmer, the American tramp was not unlike the locust; he was an "emblem of improvidence himself."[1]

Begging and stealing, threatening and cajoling, tramps became a familiar sight in America in the 1870s. Magazines and newspapers more and more often referred to "the tramp evil." Of course, vagrants

3

had always existed in the United States, but "tramp" was a new, popular word used for the homeless unemployed after the Civil War. The press used it increasingly in the 1870s; one of the earliest uses of the word as a noun in the United States appeared in an issue of the *New York Times* in February 1875.[2] While the reason for the sudden appearance of the tramps was not understood, most people assumed that men became tramps because of natural defects in their characters.

The period following the Civil War in America was still one of largely unlimited opportunities for the individual in theory. No reason existed, said the theorists, for a man to become a tramp. Hard work and diligence, combined with thrift, could make all Americans successes. In the last half of the nineteenth century, a profusion of books and articles appeared, telling the dramatic success stories of these self-made men.[3] The able-bodied lazy man who would not work by choice was a burden to society. Just as industry and civilization went hand in hand, idleness and barbarism were "invariably" linked together. The amassing of capital by thrift and saving had two important aspects: individual character was greatly strengthened by the denial of present pleasures for future security and accumulating capital enabled one to achieve greater participation in society. This might mean becoming an entrepreneur or buying property or a home, thus committing the individual to a spirited defense of capitalism. The man who did not succeed failed because of personal deficiencies.[4]

Besides seeming to reject the work ethic, the tramp was also the antithesis of another American ideal. By definition, the tramp was homeless, and the home and the family were fundamental in American ideology (or mythology). The home was "the crystal of society and the nucleus of national character," encouraging responsibility and stability in adults, as well as offering the proper outlook on life for children. Both mother and home environment were essential for the moral training of youth. Otherwise, immorality would flourish and national ruin would be certain.[5]

Books and magazines constantly repeated this theme. They explained how to make the home function properly so that it could fulfill its proper role in society. For good reason in the nineteenth century, "Home Sweet Home" was popular both in song and on samplers. And editor Edward Bok stressed the home, rather than the woman in it, in the make-up of his *Ladies' Home Journal*.[6] But the tramp apparently rejected the home, one of the foundations of America.

Living outside the pale of society, the tramp neither sought nor received understanding, but, like the locust, he moved to satisfy his hunger and to seek shelter. In the countryside in the summer, he became a familiar figure, plodding the dusty roads, standing hat in hand at the kitchen door to seek a handout, or, if necessary, to perform a chore or two in exchange for food and shelter. While the farmer's wife was often moved by pity at such a wretched sight, she was more likely to feed the tramp from fear of what the tramp might do to her or her farm.[7] One aged widow in Millertown, New York, had no time to decide whether to feed one tramp, but was pushed and bullied by the tramp until she collapsed and died, presumably of heart failure. Another rural couple fed and housed three tramps for several days and were rewarded for their humanity by the theft of $2,000 from a bureau in the farmhouse.[8] Even the idyllic country was no longer safe for leisurely walks; a group of tramps "waylaid" and "outraged" two young girls out on a stroll.[9]

Such events called dramatic attention to the tramp. While undoubtedly most tramps meant no harm and local people blamed them for crimes they did not commit, incidents of actual and suspected tramp violence received wide publicity, creating an atmosphere of fear and distrust. *Harper's Weekly* printed an engraving in September 1876, which well illustrated this fear. The artist portrayed the tramp as a humble if not pathetic supplicant; nevertheless, the little farm family saw only a threat (see plate on page 6).

As prolific and dangerous as the tramp seemed in the rural areas in the 1870s, he was also becoming a problem in the cities and on transportation lines around them. The problem of tramps in the urban areas intensified during the winter when the homeless unemployed from the rural areas followed the railroad tracks into the cities. These men, usually without money, found that riding the railroads without a ticket was a skilled, daring, and dangerous procedure.

The public attitude of different communities and the policies of different railroads made tramps unsure of their reception. Although often tolerated, they were frequently thrown off trains, and, in the process, the tramps sometimes fought back and occasionally wounded

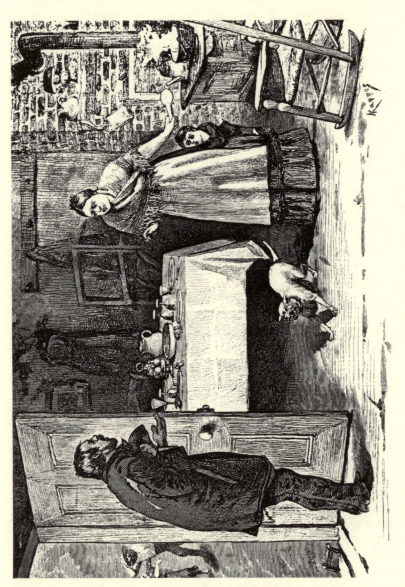

The Tramp

Harper's Weekly 20 (September 2, 1876), 720.

or killed members of the crew. Crews then responded with wanton brutality against succeeding tramps.

Jack London, the famous American adventure writer who tramped himself and wrote of his experiences, referred to a railroad line where crews had been injured by tramps as a "bad road." Tramps rode such a line only at the greatest of risks. Except for the ever-present danger of falling asleep while riding the rods beneath the cars, which raced at speeds up to fifty miles per hour, most tramps felt safe from the crew once the train had started to move. But on the bad roads, "shacks" or brakemen devised an insidious way of dislodging their unwelcome guests. Positioning himself on the platform in front of the car under which the tramp hung suspended, the brakeman fastened a heavy coupling pin to a length of bell cord. He then dropped the pin between platforms and played the cord out slowly. The coupling pin struck the ties between the rails and then the missile of death careened to the underside of the car and then back to the ties. The brakeman played the cord left and right and then back a little, over and over again, smashing every inch of the car bottom with a "tattoo of death." Only the next day might someone find a mangled body—"no doubt" a tramp who had fallen asleep on the track.[10] In revenge, tramps often wrecked trains on the offending lines. The problem of tramps on railroads grew rapidly, and railroad journals expressed concern.[11]

Upon reaching the city, the tramp was usually weary but moved quickly away from the railroad to avoid the railroad "bulls," or private police, and to seek aid. Armed with hope and usually a little cash, he set out into the city possibly to find work and certainly to find the necessities of life. He generally spent his cash quickly and had to use his wits to find bed and board, often eventually applying to relief agencies for help. During the winter of 1874 and 1875, relief applicants put such tremendous pressure on organizations and institutions that traditionally provided relief to the needy of the city that some ran into financial difficulties. For example, the Bread and Beef House, which aided the "deserving poor" of New York City, ran low on cash and had to move to the basement of the Anthon Memorial Church to reduce expenses.[12]

The hungry homeless obtained food in many ways. Perhaps the simplest was to beg small coins from patronizing passers-by. With

A Ride on a Truck

Drawn by J. Carrell Lucas   Engraved by Peter Aitken

Trainman and Tramps
Scribner's Monthly 4 (November 1888), 558

this change, the homeless could procure hot and filling, if not especially nutritious, meals at cheap restaurants and coffee stands. Another
method was to wait in bread lines established by various commercial
and charitable groups. While not exactly a meal, the day-old bread
did ease the hunger until better times came with the next meal—or
the next or the next. Still another way to secure a meal was to visit
one of the various religious missions that frequently gave out food
following services. Although city meals were bland and starchy, it
was easier to obtain food there than in rural areas, especially during
the cold weather.

To secure lodging in a city was fairly easy, although decidedly
less pleasant than in summer in the country. In the winter, however,
the city was warmer and safer. If one had money, cheap lodging
houses were numerous, and, if the night was not too cold, doorways,
empty warehouses, dock facilities, and parks provided shelter. If these
options were not acceptable because of weather, police stations in New
York City provided lodging on a one-night basis. This one-night rule
applied only in each precinct; the homeless, therefore, moved to a
new precinct each night and became known as "revolvers." In 1875,
the *New York Times* reported that huge numbers of tramps were using
the police facilities in Boston and Chicago and suggested that the numbers could be reduced by requiring work in return for lodging. In New
York City, the situation was even worse than in the cities mentioned
by the *Times*. A special committee of the State Charities Aid Association (SCAA) reported that during 1874 and 1875 over 435,000 persons
were lodged by the police in station houses in New York City, but
there was no way of telling how many different individuals were
involved because the same individuals often went from station house
to station house. Even so, the numbers were huge, and the places
lodging tramps were abominable. One lodging room at the Fourth
Precinct was fifty feet long and ten feet wide. Lodgers slept on planks
provided for beds crammed into this room. Quoting from a New York
newspaper, the report stated that the room was like the "Black Hole
of Calcutta." The presence of sixty or seventy unwashed, gin-steeped
bodies added indescribable stenches to snores, groans, and screams.
The *Herald* reported graphically that a flickering gaslight sent "feeble
rays through the laden air and every ray touches a pile of rags which
in the morning will hatch out a tramp."[13]

The foul conditions, combined with the failure to provide work for the lodgers and the indiscriminate mixing of tramps with other unfortunates, prompted reformers from the SCAA and other groups to urge the city to end police station lodging. As an alternative, they proposed that the police refer "worthy" applicants to special lodging houses and not charge the men with vagrancy. Officials would have to make the judgment whether the apparent tramp was really willing to work and therefore worthy. Reformers organized a group known as the Night Refuge Association of New York. Setting up a lodging house in the Old Strangers Hospital on Avenue D and Tenth Street, they lodged the worthy men referred to them from the police stations. While the applicant who went to the lodge would get a real cot and a small breakfast, he would also possibly be expected to work the next morning for an hour or two to pay for these advantages. Only a few of the great numbers involved had to work for their keep, the unlucky ones being selected by lottery. After the Association's Lodge opened, the use of police station lodging declined dramatically. The reason for this was that the small number of men whom the police considered worthy were sent to the Night Refuge Association. The others were no longer allowed to stay in station houses as guests, but rather the police arrested them on vagrancy charges and judges sentenced them to "shelter" in regular cells. In fact, vagrancy arrests in 1877 in New York City rose to over 1 million, almost twice those of the previous year.[14]

The plight of the homeless unemployed in the 1870s was accentuated in the cities by large numbers shuffling through the streets in search of work, bread, or rest. Harassed relief agencies, overworked police, and an anxious public tried to assess the number of destitute persons. During the winter of 1873-1874, the usual popular estimate of unemployed for the nation was around 3 million. The confusion of the involuntarily unemployed with tramps can be seen in the reports that out of a population of 40 million Americans, there were "three million tramps."[15]

The depression of 1873 had a severe effect indeed on New York City. Prior to the crash, the unemployment situation was already bad due to pilfering of the city finances by the Tweed ring, which resulted in the discontinuance of some public works. The Department of Charities and Correction's records showed, moreover, evidence of having been tampered with by the Tweed ring. The combination of the depression with other problems reduced New York City's cash reserves to a dangerous low, resulting in the cancellation of all public outdoor relief in the city from July 1874 until the end of January 1875.[16] Counting the unemployed in New York City was an impossible task. Food distribution centers could not make an accurate count because one needy individual might go to any number of centers on any given day. Employment bureau records were sketchy even when available. Counting the homeless unemployed in bed was a hopeless task because of the diversity of places in which they slept. Estimates of the unemployed residents who quietly remained at home increased the numbers of destitute.[17]

While the large numbers of tramps in the cities were of great concern to New York City officials and reformer elements, far more sinister was the increasing proclivity of the tramps to join together in committing violence. In rural Conklingville, New York, after being refused food and forced to leave town, tramps returned in the evening to burn down a woodenware factory, at a loss of $35,000. In a similar occurrence at Batchellerville, a washboard factory was destroyed. In the midwest, a gang of tramps occupied Jacksonville, Illinois, and some 200 tramps seized a train on the Rock Island Line and fomented a bloody battle with town officials in Beardstown, Illinois. In New Jersey, a group of tramps terrorized Belvidere, changing the communist cry of "bread or blood" into the cry for "blood or money."[18]

New York City newspapers expressed an uneasiness about the reported tramp and communist challenges to municipal authority in proximity to the city. The Paris Commune of 1871, which had been the subject of considerable unfavorable newspaper comment, led to predictions that a similar one would appear in New York if labor troubles did not quiet down.[19] The Tompkins Square Riot in New York City in January 1874 had shown that "communism" did have a certain appeal for some Americans. On that occasion John McMichael, the head of a "committee of safety," demanded public works and called for a mass demonstration. Mayor William Havemeyer had first approved and then had withdrawn approval for the meeting. Not knowing of the latter action, a crowd of about 3,000 formed, made up of the "lowest class" according to the *New York Times*. The police moved in with clubs, broke up the meeting, and made arrests. The

Times reported that all who were arrested seemed to have been "foreigners"—chiefly Germans or Irishmen. This was, it noted, understandable because communism was not a weed of "native growth." By 1877, the fear of "communism" and the continual use of the term "army" with "tramps" in literature and the press were suggestive in themselves of the increasing tendency of tramps to move and act in groups more militantly.[20]

In the summer of 1877, many industrial areas erupted in violence. Rail facilities in city after city were battlegrounds on which blood flowed in the glare of burning railroad buildings and equipment. So-called communists, youth labor, and tramps were aligned against the forces of capitalism—state militia, municipal police, and railroad company guards. To disinterested and interested observers alike, the clashes had all the flavor of European class struggles.[21] "RIOT OR REVOLUTION?" screamed the headline of the New York *World*. Revolution seemed just a gun flash away. The New York *Evening Mail* called for 5,000 regular troops to come to New York at once. Practical-minded William H. Vanderbilt of the New York Central and Hudson River Railroad wrote New York City Mayor Smith Ely reminding him of a state law passed in 1855 to compensate parties whose property was destroyed by riots or mobs. Vanderbilt told the mayor he feared mob action in New York City and hoped for the mayor's support in defending railroad property against any mob. When the unemployed agitated for public works on July 25, 1877, the situation looked at least as critical as it had in 1874. But it turned out that fears were not realized because a mixture of alcohol and good humor turned a combustible affair into "beer-logged" good fellowship.[22]

While tramps were not ordinarily accused of starting the great strikes and riots of 1877, magazines noted that they constituted the "very lowest layer" of the proletariat "who would gladly participate in any mob action." One New York newspaper saw tramps as auxiliaries marked by "badges of red" and stated that the tramps' role was to sever telegraphic communications when labor violence began.[23] *The Man Who Tramps*, a novel published in 1878, dealt with the relation of tramps to labor disputes. In it, a young man runs away from home and associates with tramps. He discovers that tramps have a regular organization, which is interested in something like revolution and which orders them to proceed to Pittsburgh. In that city occurs the dramatic conclusion of the novel during the great strike of 1877. The tramp leader is killed and the riot is crushed, while the boy is saved and returned to his farm home.[24]

The connection between tramps and the great labor disturbances of 1877 was pointed out to the Conference of Boards of Public Charities held at Saratoga Springs that same year. Professor Francis Wayland, charity organization president from New Haven, warned the assembled reformers that "the inner history of the recent disgraceful and disastrous riots" in some principal cities revealed how large detachments of "our great standing army of professional tramps" rather than the "so-called strikers" were mainly responsible for the destruction of valuable property. He also suggested that the tramps were at war with all social institutions and implied that they were loosely organized under a central agency.[25] His warning reinforced the belief of the New York reformers that the challenge of the tramp, the homeless unemployed, or the able-bodied pauper as he was called at first, needed more immediate attention than most other problems in the 1870s.

In New York City, Henry E. Pellew, a recently arrived wealthy British immigrant and social reformer, was the chief promoter of the privately organized Bureau of Charities, which proposed to register all persons seeking outdoor relief in the city. Presumably, by doing so, charity relief would then be administered more efficiently and sci-entifically. This was the earliest attempt by the New York City re-formers to participate in the charity organization movement and was a direct response to the unprecedented demands put on existing relief agencies during the depression of 1873. But the lack of cooperation by all agencies involved led to the failure of the bureau in 1874.[26]

In the meantime, another group of individuals in the SCAA was also working on the problem of able-bodied paupers. Possibly influ-enced by the work of Louisa Twining, who had founded the Workhouse Visiting Society in England, Miss Louisa Lee Schuyler founded the SCAA in 1872 for the purpose of visiting tax-supported charitable institutions. A woman of tremendous energy who had shown outstanding executive ability in relief activities during the Civil War, Miss Schuyler molded the organization into an efficient and influential body.[27] In a letter published in the first annual report of the SCAA, Miss Schuyler recommended the erection of workhouses for able-bodied paupers to prevent hereditary pauperism from infecting the United States, which allegedly had already occurred in Europe. The SCAA established the Committee on Able-Bodied Paupers to secure such a workhouse, ascertain the number of able-bodied paupers, promote laws for the arrest and commitment of vagrants, and do anything else necessary for the elimination of vagrancy. As the head of this committee, Mrs. Josephine Shaw Lowell achieved prominence in New York and national reform groups.[28]

The widow of a Union officer who had died in the Civil War, Mrs. Lowell devoted her life to civic causes and charity after the war. One of her principal aims was to bring together labor and capital.[29] A very ambitious and energetic woman, she plunged into the work of the committee, surveying the tramp problem in 1876. She decried the lack of uniformity in dealing with tramps in the various towns and cities of New York. Some towns kept tramps in private homes or local jails, while others sent their tramps to county institutions. Some tramps were put to work and some were not.

She noted that certain local officials received their principal income from handling the tramp problem. Some justices received a fixed fee for each tramp sentenced; one justice alone earned $2,500 in this fashion in a one-year period. Some overseers of the poor (local town officials) lodged tramps in their own homes and charged the local government for room and board. This service, in fact, provided the only source of money that the elected overseers received from their towns. By treating tramps well, the overseers of the poor could be assured of their return—and perhaps visits by their brothers of the road because of high recommendations. While this was appropriate for successful innkeeping, the system was hardly designed to discourage tramping. In Mrs. Lowell's view, the fact that these elected officials were drawn from the least educated classes only strengthened her conviction that the system had to be changed. She concluded that antivagrancy legislation was necessary and that tramps should be withdrawn from local institutions and be incarcerated in centralized institutions where they could be put to work.[30]

In 1877 members from the SCAA and other reform groups in New York, as well as other reformers from across the nation met at Saratoga Springs to discuss the tramp problem in a national forum.

The occasion was the regular annual meeting of reformers, which had begun a few years previously as the Conference of Boards of Public Charities, a section of the American Social Science Association. The parent association and its counterpart, the National Association for the Promotion of Social Science of Great Britain, held the basic assumption that the "application of science to the problem in human relations would result in significant progress in the overall field of social relationships."[31] Thus at first, it seemed natural that practicing social reformers wanted to participate in scholarly discussions, opening the way to the new practice of scientific charity. Increasingly, however, the reformers became less interested in theory and more interested in a forum where they could exchange ideas and methods. Therefore, in 1879 the Conference of Boards of Public Charities separated amicably from the American Social Science Association and eventually assumed the name of the National Conference of Charities and Correction.

At the meeting in 1877, individuals who were later to become leading figures in organized charity already held positions of influence.[32] This forum's concern with the tramp foreshadowed an interest that was incorporated in 1882 into bylaws, charters, and constitutions of social agencies such as the Charity Organization Society of New York City.[33] The participants at the conference in 1877 were no different from most other Americans in their basic assumptions regarding the meaning of America and the role of the individual in society. They were not social critics or dissidents in the usual sense, but rather were critical of elements that did not conform to their own American ideal. Their remedy for the "tramp evil" was to develop methods to help homeless individuals assume their proper role in society.

While a few radical social critics of the period noticed a relationship between the depression and the homeless unemployed, only one participant at the conference of 1877 argued that the condition of business might help explain the presence of tramps. The Rev. Edward E. Hale, while suggesting that the development of new technology or a temporary oversupply of labor in one sector of industry might cause men to become tramps, made no suggestions as to how industry should handle the tramp problem. In his view, no man with "much force of character" or with an established skill would be likely to travel looking for work.[34]

And the idea that men *could not* find work was absurd in the judgment of the delegates. Professor Wayland pointed out to the assembled that it was "very rare" when employment could not be found by someone "really anxious" for work.[35] This was a consistent theme among reformers. As early as the first meeting of the Conference of Boards of Public Charities in 1874, the Rev. Dr. John Hall of New York City stated that the huge natural resources of the country and the demand "everywhere" for labor gave no excuse for anyone not finding work.[36] The view that the tramp refused to find work was the most acceptable one in America.[37]

The Civil War was also blamed for the rise of tramping. Reverend Hale said that military life hardened men to the rigors of travel and bivouac. This life style, moreover, encouraged the habit of living off the country and the disposition to let the future take care of itself. His opinion was seconded by such public figures as Allan Pinkerton, famous as a private detective, and occasionally by the press. A poem, "The Tramp of Shiloh," published in *Frank Leslie's Illustrated Newspaper* exploited the war theme, saying:

Yes, bread! I want bread! You heard what I said
    Yet you stand and stare,
As if never before came a Tramp to your door
    With such an insolent air.
At your Shiloh—What you? You battled there, too?
    Well you beat us—That's all.
Bread! Money! and Wine! sir? Madam, I dine
    At your feet—and please, sir, I pray
You'll pardon me, sir—that fight trenched me here
    Deep—deeper than sword-cut that day. . . .[38]

In addition to the effect of the war, indiscriminate charity was considered beyond doubt as one of the major causes which made men into tramps. The reference to charity as indiscriminate reflected the growing importance of science in philanthropy. While traditional charity was based on the apparent need of the applicant, the new "scientific'' charity demanded that the real need of the seeker be ascertained before giving aid. This was, in a sense, contrary to the American self-image of generosity. Reverend Hale in 1877 told of dining with an Ohio couple who had complained bitterly about the rise of tramps. When the minister asked his host if any man ever went hungry from his door, the man "thanked God no such disgrace had ever come upon his household." This, Hale noted in his discourse, was a "cardinal difficulty which appears at the outset" in any attempt to reduce the number of tramps in America. The idea that indiscriminate charity caused tramps and attracted them to the cities was constantly emphasized by New York reformers like Dr. R. T. Davis and repeated well into the twentieth century. Even the city press reasoned that misdirected charity was responsible for pulling men away from the rural areas where their labor was needed.[39]

Another idea that received wide support at the conference in 1877 was the belief that most tramps were either recent immigrants or weak-willed Americans who gathered around a hard core of foreigners.[40] In 1875, this idea had been linked with heredity by a newspaper article published on tramps in New England. The article rhetorically asked why New England had tramps now but had none in 1845. It concluded that, in the earlier period, "the whole people of the country were of such a grade of intelligence and respectability that tramps and beggars could not come of them, more than grapes of thorns." The "Land of Steady Habits" was not changed from within by poverty or anything else; rather, the change was the consequence of introducing a new element—immigrants—chiefly concerned with factory employment, in larger numbers into the population. The tramps were only a reflection of a "radical change in the character of the population."[41]

Men became tramps, asserted Professor Wayland in 1877, because of personal deficiencies and immoral indulgence. And what was worse, the weak could transmit their unfavorable traits to their children. One reformer offered some hope, however, by saying there was one "saving grace." Even though the transmission of an undesirable trait did occur, he noted it rarely went beyond three or four generations, because physical and mental processes of those involved degenerated so rapidly that the family became extinct.[42] Although almost universally believed in 1877, the "scientific" evidence of the inheritance of unfavorable traits presented by Richard T. Dugdale on the "Jukes," first to the Prison Association of New York and then to the Conference of Boards of Public Charities, made the idea more fixed than ever. Published in book form in 1877, Dugdale's study became immensely popular and was widely quoted by reformers and authorities alike.[43]

In July 1874, while making inspections of county jails for the Prison Association of New York in rural Ulster County, Dugdale observed six blood relations in the same jail. His curiosity aroused, he traced the family (whom he called the "Jukes") for five generations and found that an outstanding percentage of them were paupers, criminals, and prostitutes, thus refuting the position that undesirable families would die out in three or four generations. To make his case even stronger, he explained that certain branches of the family were more prone to one type of degeneracy than another. For most of his readers, Dugdale showed a close link between heredity and defects of character, which led to crime, pauperism, and degeneracy.[44] Taking a cue from Dugdale, one author writing in 1878 pointed out that tramps were actually a tribe that passed "bad blood" from one generation to the next. He traced the genesis of the tramp to colonial Pennsylvania, based on a description in Crèvecoeur's *Letters From an American Farmer*.[45]

Almost no one took issue with Dugdale in the years following his disclosures on the Jukes or his ideas on heredity, including the notion that paupers and criminals were equally hereditary defectives. Poverty was degenerating and few crimes were "more reprehensible than inability to make a living."[46] The reformers and others recognized that a very small percentage of apparent tramps might be earnestly looking for work and thus urged caution. But they offered no way in which one could really determine whether a man was involuntarily unemployed. Professor Wayland defined a tramp so broadly as to cover almost any traveler: "All idle persons . . . not having any visible means of support . . . wandering about . . . and not giving a good account of themselves."[47] Unless a tramp was actually caught begging or stealing, his crime against society was a vague one.

Yet, assuming that the tramps were committing a crime against society, what approach should be taken to cure an individual tramp and to preclude tramping in the future? Practically without exception reformers, including Theodore Roosevelt, father of the twenty-sixth

President, called for restrictive laws and for confinement of the tramps with sentences long enough to assure rehabilitation. Furthermore, the tramps should not be permitted to lounge in prisons, but should be forced to do hard labor for the purposes of both punishment and learning.[48] An important by-product of the confinement, said the reformers, was to reduce the number of tramps who married and produced defective children. One delegate to the conference in 1877 supported what she called "the German restriction on marriage," concluding her discussion: "I don't think a pauper has any right to marry nor do I think the State has a right to allow him." Most New Yorkers, while willing to support confinement to restrict reproduction, rejected compulsory sterilization.[49]

The reformers decried the process of "passing on" the tramps rather than confining them. This was the method whereby local enforcement officials forced tramps to leave their area, sometimes even paying the tramps' one-way fare to the next town. Reverend Hale stated the reason quite simply. He asserted that it did not pay a town to have an intelligent and useful man spend half the day watching a lazy one to be sure that the tramp worked for a night's lodging. In "nine cases out of ten," the officer and town would rather just give the tramp a railway ticket. This only increased movements of tramps while the goal of all should have been to restrict this movement.

Charles Loring Brace, founder of the Children's Aid Society of New York City, proposed a pass system already used in England and elsewhere in Europe. Under this system, the tramp had to show a pass on demand to any law enforcement official to prove that he was indeed a man genuinely unemployed and looking for work. American societies of craftsmen or other similar groups could provide each legitimate workman a certificate or diploma to show "in what regard he was held at home." Because of the American workman's traditional freedom to move freely and seek employment at his own whim, the suggestions of passes fell on deaf ears both among the reformers themselves and the public at large. Americans apparently were unwilling to allow such social control. Reformers still believed confinement was the key to the tramp problem.[50]

For most Americans, confinement of the tramp was acceptable

A "Timber Lesson"
Century Magazine 47 (November 1893), 104

as seen by gradual enactment of vagrancy legislation. However, many proposals for punishment and prevention beyond confinement appeared in popular literature during the last half of the nineteenth century. For prevention, the *New York Times* suggested that its readers "procure a large dog who understands how to insert his teeth where it will do the most good." One gun company produced a shotgun model which it called the "Tramp Terror" for the purpose of "peppering" tramps. The *Chicago Tribune* suggested that a little strychnine or arsenic in the meat or other supplies furnished the tramp would be profoundly discouraging. Public whippings were suggested and occasionally administered. The *American Rural Home* told of a mob in Anderson, Indiana, which removed four tramps from jail. After whipping them until they bled, the mob forced the tramps to run under a shower of blows through a gauntlet to the river's edge. From there the tramps were free to swim for safety. Although the policy seemed "rough," the writer of the story nevertheless recommended the procedure, predicting that "its initiation in other places infected by the lazy predators would prove highly beneficial to the communities invaded."[51]

Another preventive measure, of course, was the proposal to end the indiscriminate relief so often pointed out as a cause of tramping. The reformers directed warnings against this practice to all dispensers of relief from the private kitchen to the soup kitchen run by secular and religious agencies, as well as by local governments. While private relief met with strong criticism, the stronger admonishments were directed toward the public agencies, which the State Charities Aid Association, among others, feared to be the most indiscriminate of all.[52]

If there was one preventive that all delegates agreed upon at the Conference of Boards of Public Charities in 1877, it was the need for antitramp legislation. Laws making criminal offenses out of begging, aimless wandering, and alms soliciting would allow authorities to jail tramps and to put them to work at hard labor. The laws had to be carefully drawn—not too severe or so complicated that communities would not enforce them, and, if possible, they should be everywhere, so that the tramp would find no advantage in moving from one area to another. To aid communities in drawing up uniform legislation, the conference published in its proceedings a copy of the recently passed Rhode Island Tramp Act.[53]

Professor Wayland stressed the importance of tramp legislation in his paper and praised the antitramp bill submitted by the SCAA during the previous year to the New York legislature. Among other things, he noted the need to separate the operating of facilities for tramps from securing facilities from contractors in order to end any conflict of interest. He also applauded the insistence on work for those confined, longer terms of confinement, and recommended maintenance of complete records on all commitments.[54]

Armed with the encouragement of the conference in her endeavors, Josephine Shaw Lowell, as chairman of the Committee on Adult Able-Bodied Paupers for the SCAA, prepared another recommendation for vagrancy legislation. Her proposal, which was forwarded to the New York legislature in March 1878, sought workhouses for such "able-bodied vagrants known as tramps" and petitioned the state not to allow tramps to be put into other corrective institutions.[55] Finally, in May 1880, the goals of the SCAA and Mrs. Lowell were realized, at least in part, when the legislature passed "An Act Concerning Tramps." Although the act did not incorporate all of their proposals, the association had at least caused enactment of an antitramp law. The law was basically a restrictive measure, defining a tramp as "one living without labor or visible means of support," and roving "place to place begging." Punishment under this measure was imprisonment at hard labor in the nearest penitentiary for not more than six months.[56]

The New York act concerning tramps was not the first such piece of legislation, but it was typical of most other antitramp measures. While many states had antivagrancy legislation prior to the Civil War, the "tramp" first appeared "legally" in a New Jersey statute in 1876, according to Professor John J. McCook of Trinity College (Hartford), who surveyed four hundred volumes of statutes for all the states. He found that the tramp laws existed primarily in the northern states along the temperate belt where the tramps could "avoid extremes of heat and cold." McCook also felt that the tramp laws he looked at had "a panicky look" which suggested "a pressing evil, real or imaginary. . . ."[57] One representative from Rhode Island substantiated this point in 1877 in discussing his state's new tramp law. He said the law was actually superfluous since few tramps were troubling Rhode Island, but felt it was enacted in reaction to "outrages which had occurred in other parts of the United States."[58]

While the New York legislation was not unique, the annual report of the SCAA for 1881 glows with success and self-plaudits. The report heralded the decline in the number of tramps in New York in 1881 with much satisfaction. The discussion of this point indicates how little credence Lowell and the SCAA gave to the connection between hard times and tramps. While the report acknowledged that the call for labor had its effect so that the tramp act could not receive credit for "all the improvement," the report smugly stated that the "general opinion" was that "the Tramp Act had done away with a great nuisance."[59]

Actually the renewed "call for labor" that the SCAA noted as America pulled out of the panic of 1873 ended the tramp problem. As the unemployment rate steadily dropped, demands on relief agencies lessened. For example, the Night Refuge Association Lodge in New York, established in 1876 to take the pressure off police station lodging, had long since closed because it was no longer needed.[60] In the early 1880s, magazines and newspapers carried few, if any, "tramp" articles.[61] Public and even voluntarist interest in tramps disappeared or at least became dormant until the depression of 1882-1886 reawakened that interest.

America had hardly recovered from the panic of 1873 when a much weaker one occurred during the middle 1880s. No great panic or market crash introduced these years, but stock values and business activity gradually declined. Most Americans felt it was only a speculators' panic, but unemployment steadily increased. In October 1884, *Bradstreets'* conducted a field survey in twenty-two northeastern states and arrived at a figure of 350,000 unemployed, or about 13 percent of the employable. In 1885, the new Federal Bureau of Labor reported 1 million unemployed in the United States, or about 7.5 percent of the labor force. Presumably the unemployment rate was higher in the Northeast because of the concentration of industry there. The New York Commissioner of Labor noted that it was almost impossible to ascertain the true number of unemployed in a city like New York.[62]

During these years of mass unemployment in New York City the

SCAA became interested principally in children, while the NYCOS, founded in 1882, became the new leader in dealing with the homeless unemployed. Among those responsible for the establishment of the NYCOS was Josephine Shaw Lowell who had been appointed the first woman member of the New York State Board of Charities in recognition of her efforts to reduce tramping. Using this position, Mrs. Lowell was influential in prompting the introduction of a resolution into the state legislature to charter the new society. Thus, the New York society was established as a result of the dedicated efforts of a few New York reformers with the aid of the Rev. S. Humphreys Gurteen who established the first successful American COS in Buffalo.[63]

While the charity organization movement as a whole had grown slowly at first in the United States, by 1893, 55 societies were participating in the national forum of the movement, the National Conference of Charities and Correction. By 1907 more than 150 groups were participating in the conference. The NYCOS, acting as a clearinghouse for relief in 1907, held nearly 100,000 case records of individuals who had sought relief in New York City. Some records spanned twenty years and contained forty to fifty thousand words. The NYCOS kept these records to aid cooperation between relief agencies and to prevent individuals from receiving relief from more than one source.[64]

Besides its function as a clearinghouse, the COS tried to prevent willful idleness and to expose imposters. Amos Warner, reformer, lecturer, and author, said that many people looked at the COS as an "anti-mendicity league" or a "detective society for preventing imposition and bringing swindlers to justice."[65] However, the COS also included in its responsibilities preventing pauperism, finding adequate relief, encouraging inspection visits to workhouses, and investigating requests for aid. One leader of the Philadelphia COS added another responsibility which was never listed on charters; he felt that the charity organization societies were the only "real answer to the Socialistic and Communist theories being energetically taught to the people."[66]

The question of tramps arose again on the national level at the NCCC meeting in 1885. At that time the conference adopted W. L. Bull's resolution to refer the whole question of tramping and vagrancy to its standing committee on pauperism for thorough study.[67] The following year the committee made its report to the conference. The committee had sent questionnaires to various societies, organizations, public officials, and prominent philanthropists. Of the 130 returned, approximately half came from the Northeast. While the sample was small, some of the tabulations were nonetheless interesting. Fifty percent of the replies reported that at least half of all tramps were native-born Americans. The committee chairman, W. L. Bull, found this fact "alarming as it is certainly most unlooked for." Sixteen percent of the respondents listed "lack of employment" as one of the causes of tramps, an increase over the number of those who had suggested this reason at the 1877 conference. However, 70 percent noted that personal deficiencies played an important part in the creation of tramps. Among other factors listed were laziness, war, drink, dime novels, tobacco, discontent, shiftlessness, vice, love of roving, heredity, depravity, socialistic ideas, the Chinese, and the devil. To the key question on what percentage of tramps were apparently actually in search of employment, about 50 percent felt that fewer than one in ten was a genuine workman. Ninety percent felt that at least one out of every two unemployed was by nature a tramp.[68]

Chairman Bull synthesized the remedies proposed in the replies to his questionnaire. In regard to the lack of employment, he considered Carroll Wright's report of 1886 on the industrial depression as indicating a need for industrial reform, but then passed it over as being too confusing even to consider. He considered moral causes, but since no clear rules could be drawn, no positive suggestions were reported. Chairman Bull did make three specific proposals to curb tramps. He proposed a twenty-five dollar headright fee to retard immigration. A second proposal was to introduce manual training into public schools and to secure compulsory education. The third proposed to open wayfarers' lodges where work on public roads could be provided.[69] These specific proposals still considered immigration, heredity, indiscriminate charity, and personal failure as the primary reasons for tramping.

Between 1882 and 1894, the policies and actions of the NYCOS and other reform groups were in agreement with the committee's suggestions. The New York reformers had long opposed police station lodging. The SCAA looked with favor upon Boston's Wayfarer's Lodge and felt that New York should have something similar. The COS agreed, and both groups combined to put pressure on the New

York legislature, which passed the Municipal Lodging House Act in 1886.[70] The principal purpose of the lodging house was to provide work in return for shelter. However, reduced numbers seeking shelter after 1886 made the proposed institution seem less important, and the city had taken no action to organize it in spite of the campaigns of reformers who pointed out the great success of cities like Boston, Philadelphia, and Indianapolis in reducing tramps after the establishment of municipal lodging houses.[71]

To strengthen individuals against personal failure, the NYCOS attempted to reinforce the idea of thrift among those most susceptible to economic failure. Under the leadership of Otto T. Bannard, a wealthy banker, the society opened New York's first Penny Provident Fund in 1889. In New York City only one bank accepted deposits of less than one dollar and the poorer classes were rarely able to save a dollar at one time. The Penny Provident Fund accepted funds of less than one dollar for stamps, but paid no interest. When a patron had saved enough, he could withdraw his money and deposit it in a savings bank. The purpose of the fund was "to inculcate habits of providence and thrift" and it did so until the passage of the Postal Savings Law rendered it unnecessary.[72]

In 1894, the NYCOS established the first important Provident Loan Society in the United States to loan money at low rates of interest upon pledges of personal property. It also opened a laundry where women could gain experience while earning money. Not all these methods applied directly to the homeless unemployed, but they are evidence of the general line of thinking of the reformers in strengthening the individual against financial disaster. All these actions also follow the proposals published in the proceedings of the National Conference of Charities and Correction in 1886.[73]

The COS continued to support the Tramp Act of 1880 which had to be reenacted by the state legislature after being inadvertently dropped. It took one further step toward repression of tramps by establishing a special officer whose job was to aid in arresting and securing the conviction of tramps and beggars.[74] Many of those convicted were sent to the workhouse at Blackwell's Island. Superintendent Robert Stocking of the workhouse advised Mayor Abram Hewitt that a problem was arising with increasing frequency. Stocking was convinced that most of the men convicted of vagrancy were destitute only for a short time. He argued that the "indiscriminate and unjust sentencing of men" only created criminals and paupers, instead of saving them from that fate.[75]

One can only surmise the frustration of the "honestly unemployed" at being arrested for vagrancy. For the most part, the homeless unemployed of the nineteenth century are faceless and voiceless. A humorous exception was Daniel Pratt who died in 1887. The only tramp or vagrant listed in the index of the *Dictionary of American Biography*, Pratt garnered his fame by giving guest lectures in New England colleges on such topics as "The Vocabulaboratory of the World's History" and his own problems. In recognition of his talents, Dartmouth College impressively and unofficially awarded him the degree of C.O.D. To be considered in a more serious vein is Hamlin Garland. In his autobiographical *A Son of the Middle Border*, drawn from his experiences in the 1880s, Garland explains how he was occasionally forced by circumstances to assume the posture of tramplike begging on his travels. On one such occasion, Garland and his brother Franklin were making a trip to the big cities in the East. Since they were genuinely willing to work in return for food and lodging along the way, Garland felt that the inhospitality of the farmers was "bitter and uncalled for." On another occasion Garland was returning from his search for a teaching job, and, when night fell, he was twenty miles from relatives. Caught without money or food, he sought assistance from farmers along the road. The piercing bark of a dog and the sharp words, "We don't feed tramps!" made Garland feel, on one hand, great loneliness while on the other hand he felt "bitter, furtive, and ferocious."[76] Unpublished until 1917, Garland's stories show the frustration of men sincerely looking for work at being confused with vagrants in the 1880s.

The New York reformers gradually were becoming aware themselves that the tramps were not a monolithic body composed of voluntary outcasts from society. The reformers had always believed that an extremely small percentage of tramps were unemployed through no fault of their own, but they made only sporadic and ineffective efforts to identify and separate them. In an address at Syracuse in 1886, Louis Seamen pointed out the difficulties of working on Blackwell's Island where tramps, harlots, and the poor were confined together. The good were exposed to the bad who, in turn, associated with new varieties of evil. In a report in 1888, Louisa Schuyler and others of the SCAA said that charities and correction should be separated because "ideas and practices peculiar to one" become mingled with the other.[77]

In 1889, the general agent of the largest relief agency in the city, the AICP admitted that even he was "at a loss to perceive distinctly the difference between destitution and mendicity." The dictionary definitions that he knew did not apply precisely to those seeking aid from his organization.[78] When unemployment levels were low and economic conditions good, the problem of separating the voluntary tramp from the involuntary one was only a problem of academic interest. However, the panics of 1893 and 1907, with their attendant violence and widespread vagrancy, forced the reformers to look again in depth at the relationship of tramps to American society. The new intensive studies resulted in new methods of identifying the genuine work seeker and pointed to the reasons that impelled him to tramp.

NOTES

1. *New York Times*, August 2, 1876. In later discussions of the tramp, popular literature recalled the fable of the lazy grasshopper and the industrious ants or compared tramps to locusts. "The Grasshopper and the Ant," Hamlin Garland, *A Son of the Middle Border* (New York, 1917), 251; "Tramps and the Farmers," *American Agriculturist* 57 (January 1884): 20.

2. Victor Hoffman, "The American Tramp, 1870-1900" (Master's thesis, University of Chicago, 1953) sketches briefly the homeless unemployed in pre-Civil War America; *New York Times*, February 6, 1875.

3. Irving G. Wyllie, *The Self-Made Man in America* (New Brunswick, 1954); Chap. 7, "Preach the Gospel," is a survey of the important books by and about "self-made" men. This theme was also developed in popular magazines, dime novels, and children's stories. The name of the most popular author of this type of story, Horatio Alger, has become synonymous in America with the doctrine of success.

4. George R. Hewitt, "The Blight of Idleness," in *Portraits and Principals of the World's Great Men and Women with Practical Lessons on Successful Life*, ed. William C. King (Springfield, Massachusetts, 1895), 205; Rev. James W. Cole, "The Secret of Saving," in *Portraits and Principals*, ed. King; Brown, *The Development of Thrift* (New York, 1899), chap. 1. Although from a slightly later time period, see the connection drawn between thrift and homeowning in Myron T. Pritchard and Grace A. Turkington, *Stories of Thrift For Young Americans* (New York, 1915), chap. 20, and Brown, *Development of Thrift*, 12.

5. John Fraser, *Youth's Golden Cycle or Round the Globe in Sixty Chapters* (Philadelphia and Chicago, 1885), 269; Theodore L. Cuyler, *Golden Thoughts on Mother, Home, and Heaven* (New York and St. Louis, 1878), 10.

6. For example, see G. S. Weaver, *The Heart of the World or Home and Its Wide Work* (Chicago, 1882), and Charles E. Sargent et al., *Our Home or Influences Emanating From the Hearthstone* (Springfield, Massachusetts, 1899): In Frank L. Mott, *A History of American Magazines, 1885-1905* (Cambridge, 1957), IV :791-858, more magazine titles carry the word "home" than any other word with the exception of "American." Edward Bok, *The Americanization of Edward Bok* (New York, 1920), 168.

7. "The Tramp Evil," *Nation* 26 (January 24, 1878): 50. In addition to the fact that the contemporary news magazines and newspapers document this fully, the popular magazines and novels of the day frequently used the tramp to create an atmosphere of fear. See William W. Nichols, "A Changing Attitude Toward Poverty in the *Ladies' Home Journal*: 1895-1919," *Midcontinent American Studies Journal* 5 (Spring 1964): 9, and J. D. Seelye, "The American Tramp: A Version of the Picaresque," *American Quarterly* 15 (Winter 1963): 540-541. Although W. D. Howells's novel, *The Vacation of the Kelwyns: An Idyl of the 1870's* (New York, 1920), was written in a later period, I believe Howells faithfully reflects the feelings of the people in the countryside in the 1870s toward tramps.

8. *New York Times*, June 6, October 24, 1879.

9. Ibid., August 2, 1876.

10. Jack London, *The Road* (New York, 1907), 24-25.

11. *Railroad Gazette*, July 14, 1876, 309, April 27, 1877, 197, May 18, 1877, 224, October 12, 1877, 460, December 28, 1877, 578; *New York Times*, November 16, 1873.

12. Bread and Beef House, *Second Annual Report to the Executive Committee, 1874-1875* (n.p., n.d.), 4.

13. Richard H. Derby, "Final Report of the Committee on Outdoor Relief Upon Night Refuges," State Charities Aid Association, *Annual Report* (1876), 67; *New York Times*, February 5, 1875.

14. Sinclair Tousey, "The Police Station of the City of New York: Station Lock-ups Described," Executive Committee of the Prison Association of the State of New York, *Annual Report* (1874), 64; Night Refuge Association of New York City, "Report to the State Board of Charities," May 15, 1877; Derby, "Final Report," 76-77.

15. Otto C. Lightner, *The History of Business Depressions* (New York, 1922), 169, 290; H. M. Hyndman, *Commercial Crises of the Nineteenth Century* (London, 1892; reprint, New York, 1967), 117; Robert V. Bruce, *1877: Year of Violence* (Indianapolis, 1959), 19, estimates the actual figure of nationwide unemployment was 1 million, but acknowledges that the cities bore the brunt of hard times. A good critique and explanation of the background of the 3 million estimate is contained in Arthur G. Auble, "The Depressions of 1873 and 1882 in the United States" (Ph.D. diss., Harvard University, 1949), 28-33.

16. NYAICP, *Annual Report* (1875), 35-41. Outdoor relief referred to assistance

administered outside the confines of institutions. Indoor relief referred to relief administered inside institutions such as almshouses.

17. Hyndman, *Commercial Crises*, 117, Bruce, *1877*, 19. Conference of Boards of Public Charities, *Proceedings* (1877), 105, 132. The Conference of Boards of Public Charities became the National Conference of Charities and Correction.

18. Allan Nevins, *The Emergence of Modern America* (New York, 1927), 302; *New York Times*, January 11, August 2, 1876.

19. George L. Cherry, "American Metropolitan Press Reaction to the Paris Commune of 1871," *Mid-America* 32 (January 1950): 3-12; Bruce, *1877*, 226-227; Allan Nevins and Milton H. Thomas, eds., *The Diary of George Templeton Strong: Post War Years, 1865-1875* (New York, 1952), IV:357; Allan Pinkerton, *Strikers, Communists, Tramps, and Detectives* (New York, 1878), 67. The term "communist" was freely applied after the Paris Commune of 1871 to anyone who seemed to support the ideas of Karl Marx.

20. Bruce, *1877*, 227-228; *New York Times*, January 14, 1874. H. G. Gutman, "Tompkins Square Riot in New York City on January 13, 1874: A Re-examination of Its Courses and Aftermath," *Labor History* 6 (Winter 1965): 44-70, is the most recent discussion of the riot. "The Disease of Mendicancy," *Scribner's Monthly* 13 (January 1877): 417.

21. The most descriptive contemporary account is Pinkerton's *Strikers,* while the best secondary account is Bruce's *1877*. David T. Burbank's *Reign of the Rabble: The St. Louis General Strike of 1877* (New York, 1966), claims the St. Louis strike was the first socialistic general strike in the United States; he is supported in this regard by Wilfrid H. Crook's *Communism and the General Strike* (Hamden, Connecticut, 1960), 19-22. *New York Times*, August 24, 1877.

22. New York *World*, July 23, 26, 1877; New York *Evening Mail*, July 23, 1877; William H. Vanderbilt to Mayor Smith Ely, Jr., July 26, 1877, Mayoralty Papers of Smith Ely, Jr., Municipal Archives, New York City; New York *Tribune*, July 26, 1877.

23. "Once More The Tramp," *Scribner's Monthly*, 15 (April 1878): 883; W. H. Brewer, "What Shall We Do With Our Tramps," *New Englander* 37 (July 1878): 532; "From Another Point of View," *Rural New Yorker* 37 (July 13, 1878): 444; *New York Times*, June 18, 1878.

24. Lee O. Harris, *The Man Who Tramps: A Story of Today* (Indianapolis, 1878).

25. Francis Wayland, *A Paper on Tramps Read at the Saratoga Meeting of the American Social Science Association Before the Conference of State Charities: September 6, 1877* (New Haven, 1877), 10, 15.

26. Frank D. Watson, *The Charity Organization Movement in the United States* (New York, 1922), 214, 177; Amos G. Warner, *American Charities* (3d rev. ed., New York, 1919), 455; John Hall, "Discussion on Pauperism in the City of New York," *Journal of Social Science* 7 (1885): 31; Leah H. Feder, *Unemployment Relief in Periods of Depression; A Study of Relief Measures Adopted in Certain American Cities, 1857 Through 1932* (New York, 1936), 46.

27. David M. Schneider and Albert Deutsch, *The History of Public Welfare in New York State, 1867-1940* (Chicago, 1941), 20-21.

28. SCAA, *Annual Report* (1873), 23; *Constitution and By-Laws of the State Charities Aid Association Adopted May 11, 1872* (n.p., n.d.) located in the library of the SCAA in New York City; SCAA, *Annual Report* (1876). The only secondary account of Lowell's career is William R. Stewart's *The Philanthropic Work of Josephine Shaw Lowell* (New York, 1910), which is highly laudatory, and contains a useful collection of published and unpublished writings of Lowell.

29. Frank J. Bruno, *Trends in Social Work as Reflected in the Proceedings of the National Council of Social Work, 1874-1946* (New York, 1948), 4.

30. Josephine Shaw Lowell, "Annual Report of the Committee on Adult Able-Bodied Paupers," SCAA, *Annual Report* (1876), 23-42.

31. Bruno, *Trends in Social Work*, 4.

32. Ibid., chap. 1.

33. NYCOS, *Annual Report* (1884), 34.

34. Edward E. Hale, "Report on Tramps," Conference of Boards of Public Charities, *Proceedings* (1877), 103, 110. According to Schneider and Deutsch, *History of Public Welfare*, 28, in a paper presented to the State Board of Charities in 1875, "Causes of Pauperism," no connection was noted between relief and the depression. *American Rural Home* 8 (August 3: 1878), 246, saw a connection between the development of new machinery and the unemployment of some men, but was quite optimistic that the problem would be solved. Conference of Boards of Public Charities, *Proceedings* (1877), 106.

35. Wayland, *Paper on Tramps*, 16.

36. Conference of Boards of Public Charities, *Proceedings* (1874), 29.

37. Charles Loring Brace, "Mendicity," *Johnson's New Illustrated Universal Cyclopedia* (New York, 1877), III: 410; "Once More the Tramp," 882; *New York Times*, August 24, 1877.

38. Conference of Boards of Public Charities, *Proceedings* (1877), 103; Pinkerton, *Strikers*, 47; *Newburyport* (Massachusetts) *Daily Herald*, June 14, 1878; Harris, *Man Who Tramps*, 18; Joaquin Miller, "The Tramp of Shiloh," *Frank Leslie's Illustrated Newspaper* (January 3, 1880): 324.

39. Conference of Boards of Public Charities, *Proceedings* (1877), 104, 126-128; R. T. Davis, "Pauperism in the City of New York," in Conference of Public Charities, *Proceedings* (1874), 19-23; NYAICP, *Annual Report* (1874), 74; Wayland, *Paper on Tramps*, 17; *New York Times*, July 24, 1874, June 3, 1875.

40. Wayland, *Paper on Tramps*, 5; Pinkerton, *Strikers*, 48; Brace, "Mendicity," III:410.

41. *New York Times*, June 17, 1875.

42. Wayland, *Paper on Tramps*, 16; Conference of Boards of Public Charities, *Proceedings* (1874), 23.

43. R. T. Dugdale, "Hereditary Pauperism," Conference of Boards of Public Charities, *Proceedings* (1877), 81 *passim*; Mark H. Haller, *Eugenics: Hereditarian Attitudes in American Thought* (New Brunswick, 1963), 22-23; R. T. Dugdale, *"The Jukes": A Study in Crime, Pauperism, Disease and Heredity* (New York, 1877); Dugdale's study became a Bible for those who believed moral and social behavior were

hereditary, and his study served as a model for similar later studies, e.g., Henry Herbert Goddard's *The Kallikak Family* (New York, 1912) and Oscar C. McCulloch, "The Tribe of Ishmael: A Study in Social Degradation," NCCC, *Proceedings* (1888), 154 passim.

44. R. T. Dugdale, *The Jukes* (New York, 1910), 65, 66; Haller, *Eugenics*, 24.

45. Brewer, "What Shall We Do With Our Tramps," 530.

46. Robert H. Bremner, *From the Depths: The Discovery of Poverty in the United States* (New York, 1956), 71.

47. Wayland, *Paper on Tramps*, 18; Conference of Boards of Public Charities, *Proceedings* (1877), 106, 130; *New York Times*, November 14, 1875, March 14, 1878.

48. State Charities Aid Association of New York, *Handbook for Visitors to the Poorhouse* (New York, 1877), 49; Brace, "Mendicity," III: 411; Conference of Boards of Public Charities, *Proceedings* (1877), XXIII, 106; Wayland, *Paper on Tramps*, 18.

49. Wayland, *Paper on Tramps*, 18; "Debate on Tramps," Conference of Boards of Public Charities, *Proceedings* (1877), 131; Haller's *Eugenics*, 40-50, has an interesting section on the struggle by a vocal minority to prevent further degeneracy by asexualization.

50. Conference of Boards of Public Charities, *Proceedings* (1877), 107-109, 127.

51. *New York Times*, November 17, 1875; Earl W. Hayter, *The Troubled Farmer, 1850-1900: Rural Adjustment to Industrialism* (Dekalb, Illinois, 1968), 299; Bruce, *1877*, 6; NCCC, *Proceedings* (1886), 197; C. S. Denny, "The Whipping Post for Tramps," *Century Magazine* (N.S.) 27 (April 1895): 794: "Switching Off Tramps," *American Rural Home* 15 (June 6, 1885): 201.

52. SCAA, *Annual Report* (1876), 53; SCAA, *Handbook for Visitors to the Poorhouse*, 52.

53. Conference of Boards of Public Charities, *Proceedings* (1877), 132, 108, 128, 129.

54. Wayland, *Paper on Tramps*, 20-22; Edward T. Devine, "Mrs. Lowell's Services to the State," *In Memoriam Josephine Shaw Lowell* (New York, 1905), 45.

55. Stewart, *Philanthropic Work*, 89; Devine, "Mrs. Lowell's Services," 46.

56. SCAA, *Annual Report* (1880), 84-85; Proceedings of the Third Conference of the State Charities Aid Association held in New York City, December 8 and 9, 1880, November 1881, located in the SCAA files in New York City.

57. John J. McCook, "Tramp Census and Its Revelations," *Forum* 15 (August 1893): 156, 765; Harry A. Millis, "The Law Affecting Immigrants and Tramps," *Charities Review* 7 (September 1897): 587-594, is an analysis of tramp legislation.

58. "Debate on Tramps," Conference of Boards of Public Charities, *Proceedings* (1877), 130.

59. SCAA, *Annual Report* (1881), 8.

60. Ibid. (1883), 36.

61. The *New York Times* index lists no entries under "tramps" from February 1880 until May 1883. See also *Poole's Index to Periodical Literature* for the same period.

62. Robert Sobel, *Panic on Wall Street: A History of America's Financial Disasters* (New York and London, 1968), 222; Samuel Rezneck, "Patterns of Thought and Action

in an American Depression, 1882-1886,'' *American Historical Review* 61 (January 1956): 286-288; New York, State Bureau for Labor Statistics, *Annual Report* (1886), 24, 36; Auble, ''Depressions of 1873 and 1882,'' 143.

63. Bruno, *Trends in Social Work*, 101, 102; Schneider and Deutsch, *History of Public Welfare*, 20-22. New York State created the NYSBC in May 1867. It was composed of eight unsalaried members who had the responsibility of visiting and inspecting all charitable and correctional institutions once each year and all almshouses every two years. The members were to investigate, call witnesses, and submit annual reports to the legislature. From 1873 to 1880 the SCAA served as an inspecting arm for the NYSBC, but in 1880 the SCAA evolved into a fully independent status. See Schneider and Deutsch, *History of Public Welfare*, 15-16, 30-33. Lilian Brandt, ''The Charity Organization of New York 1882-1907,'' NYCOS, *Annual Report* (1907), 17. The Rev. Gurteen published *A Handbook of Charity Organization* (Buffalo, 1882), to aid new societies in forming.

64. Warner, *American Charities*, 457, 459. The best volume on the COS is Watson, *Charity Organization Movement*. In addition to the works in the preceding footnote, see also Charles D. Kellogg, ''Charity Organization in the United States,'' in NCCC, *Proceedings* (1893), 52-93, and Ruth Scannell, ''A History of the Charity Organization Society of the City of New York from 1882-1935'' (Master's thesis, New York School of Social Work, 1938).

65. Warner, *American Charities*, 468.

66. Watson, *Charity Organization Movement*, 218.

67. NCCC, *Proceedings* (1885), 469.

68. Ibid. (1886), 192-195.

69. Ibid., 200-201.

70. SCAA, *Annual Report* (1883), 35-40; Brandt, ''History,'' 22; John McKim to S. B. French, March 12, 1886, Mayoralty Papers prior to 1896, Municipal Archives, New York City.

71. *State Charities Record* 1 (January 1890): 26; ''Report of the General Agent (NYAICP) for December, 1890,'' January 12, 1891, 227, Papers of NYAICP, Archives of the Community Service Society of New York City.

72. NYCOS, Penny Provident Fund Broadsheet, ''Save Your Pennies,'' n.d., Papers of Mary Richmond, Columbia University School of Social Work; Provident Loan Society of New York, *Annual Report* (1908) (n.p., n.d.), 8; Brandt, ''History,'' 126-129; Brown, *Development of Thrift*, 45-48; Community Service Society of New York, *Frontiers in Human Welfare* (New York, 1948), 38.

73. Brown, *Development of Thrift*, 140-141; NCCC, *Proceedings* (1886), 200-201. Senator Stanford's proposals for eliminating poverty were almost exactly the same as those published by the NCCC in 1886. ''Senator Stanford's Cure for Poverty,'' NYCOS, *Monthly Bulletin* (April 20, 1888): 8.

74. Brandt, ''History,'' 21, 22.

75. Supt. R. Stocking to Mayor Abram Hewitt, January 27, 1888, Mayoralty Papers prior to 1896.

76. Donald Pizer, *Hamlin Garland's Early Work and Career* (Berkeley and Los

Angeles, 1960), 170, 171, 175; Jean Holloway, *Hamlin Garland: A Biography* (Austin, Texas, 1960), chap. 13; Garland, *A Son of the Middle Border*, 252, 288.

77. Louis L. Seamen, "The Social Waste of a Great City: A Paper Read Before the American Association of the Advancement of Science," August 20, 1886, Papers of Jacob A. Riis, City College of the City University of New York; "A Report on the Administration of Charities and Correction in the City of New York," State Charities Aid Association, February 1888, Papers of SCAA.

78. Report of the General Agent to the Board of Managers (NYAICP) for September 1889 (October 14, 1889), Papers of NYAICP, Archives of the Community Service Society of New York City.

2

"Unmasking the Tramp":

Discovering the Unemployed

AS THE IMPACT of the depression of 1882-1886 lessened, unemployment figures dropped, and public interest in tramps declined as well. Popular magazines and newspapers carried only a few articles on tramps and these were principally human interest stories. For example, the *Railroad Gazette*, which showed a considerable interest in tramps from 1873 to 1880 and again from 1882 to 1885, carried no articles on tramps between 1889 and 1893. Interest declined even among reform groups. After the discussion on tramps at the NCCC in 1886, the reformers did not again raise the problem at a national forum until after the panic of 1893. Between 1889 and 1893, the tramp was little discussed; apparently he was not considered a problem.

During the panic of 1893 the appearance of countless job seekers on the city streets again revived concern over the tramp problem. Regarding many of the jobless tramps, the reformers concluded that the pre-1893 vagrancy laws, repressive measures, and charity organization had failed to end the problem. Thus they sought new explanations of the reasons why men tramped and new ways to end tramping. Studies initiated by reformers during the next two decades demonstrated that most men assumed to be voluntary tramps were on the road because of involuntary unemployment.[1]

Sometime New Yorker Henry George anticipated much of the reformers' "discoveries." Brought up in Philadelphia, George went to New York City in 1855 at the age of sixteen to go to sea. After a voyage as a foremast boy and a short career in California as a prospector and poverty-stricken journalist, he returned to`New York for a visit in 1869. On this trip he was struck by the "shocking contrast between monstrous wealth and debasing want" and made a vow to do what he could to remedy the situation.[2] In *Progress and Poverty* (1879), George first wrote of the connection between unemployment and tramps. He pointed out that society was responsible for producing tramps because of its failure to provide men with adequate means of securing a livelihood. Moving to New York City in1880, he published *Social Problems* (1883), a collection of his articles explaining how tramps evolved in much the same way the New York reformers viewed them after 1900. He wrote:

> What is a tramp? In the beginning he is a man able to work and willing to work . . . but who, not finding opportunity to work where he is, starts out in quest of it; who failing in this search, as in a later stage, driven by those imperative needs to beg or to steal, and so losing self-respect, loses all that animates and elevates a man to struggle and to labor; becomes a vagabond and an outcast.[3]

Henry George's views on unemployment remained consistent through the years, and, in the panics of the 1880s and 1890s, he continued to insist on the single tax as a means of eliminating it. However, George's single tax concept had only a limited influence on society as a whole; the dedicated following that espoused his views in fiction and action was small.[4]

The radical labor press and the Populists also had discovered a relationship between unemployment and the tramps. The *National Labor Tribune* in 1875 reported that "the tramp is a man, an unfortunate man, who can find no work." He was a "product of the times." The *Weekly Worker* reminded society that Christ himself was a tramping vagabond.[5] A significant number of Populists also correctly assessed the connection. Although urbanites tended to lump all farmers and Populists together, a sharp distinction in attitudes toward tramps existed between many farmers and the Populist press. Farmers feared and hated the tramp as an individual, because of the violent encounters they had with him in isolated areas. However, the Populist press, look-ing at the tramps as a group, pronounced them victims of an unjust economic system. The first formal statement by the Populist party to this effect was in its national platform of 1892, which blamed unjust government policy for breeding "the two great classes—tramps and millionaires." Other prophets who asserted American capitalism was responsible for producing unemployed included the Greenback Labor party and most Christian Socialists and economists like John R. Com-mons.[6]

The "Industrial Black Friday" on May 5, 1893, combined with other economic problems and set against a background of labor vio-lence and fear of socialism, raised again the spectre of the tramp in America. The United States quickly plunged into the major depression of the nineteenth century with more men out of work involuntarily than ever before. Governor Roswell P. Flower of New York pointed out in September that the army of the unemployed was huge, but that no one could really give an accurate estimate. *Bradstreet's* estimated eight to nine hundred thousand; Richard Ely gave a "safe estimate" of 2 million; Samuel Gompers suggested a minimum of 3 million; and Jacob Coxey gave the top guess of 4 million.[7]

While the number of unemployed in the nation was of academic interest, local relief agencies and public departments were vitally interested in the numbers of unemployed in their own cities. In a study of the unemployment situation in principal American cities, economist Carlos Closson sent questionnaires to many different public and private agencies in major cities asking not only how many persons were unemployed, but also what action each city was taking with regard to them. In New York City, Closson found that the estimate of unemployed varied from 80,000 in a health board census to the police department's estimate of 90,000 to the New York *World*'s estimate of about 100,000. The New York *Post* suggested that in addi-tion to those unemployed one should consider those working half time or less. It estimated that this figure was at least equal to those fully employed.[8]

Individuals and agencies working directly with the unemployed did not agree on the depth of unemployment either. In a survey of opinions taken late in 1893 in New York City, religious leaders felt that newspapers exaggerated the numbers involved. But the secretary of the Bowery branch of the YMCA and Robert Hebberd, financier and philanthropist of the COS believed that the press accounts were essentially accurate. All, however, agreed that the situation was the worst in memory, that the extent of destitution was unparalleled, and that accurate information was needed on the real number of the unemployed.[9]

As in previous depressions the public image of the individual unemployed man was blurred—little or no distinction was made between the tramp and the involuntarily unemployed. From some contemporary accounts, one could conclude that if a man were unemployed, he was a tramp, especially if he moved in search of a job. For example, newspapers and periodicals reported a sharp increase in tramps in New Haven, Connecticut. The *Yale Review* viewed this development as perhaps due to indiscriminate charity, but also pointed out that the increase indicated "that an unusually large number of persons who are on the dividing line between the steadily employed and the tramp may have been obliged to take to the road during the winter."[10] While the journal correctly saw a connection between the panic and the increased number of tramps, it recognized no middle ground between the steadily employed and the tramp. In Birmingham, Alabama, a newspaper commented on the unemployed much as the *Yale Review* did about those in New Haven. It talked of "a vast horde of tramps, more or less deserving" which "the closing down of great industries of the country has turned loose upon us."[11] Indeed, society readily confused the man genuinely seeking work with the tramp who would not work.

An increasing public interest in the tramp problem after the panic began resulted in many published articles by tramps or men who posed as tramps. Of these authors, Josiah Flynt and Walter A. Wyckoff were the most widely read. While the articles principally discuss the life of the homeless, both authors differentiate between men voluntarily and involuntarily unemployed.

Writing from the view of the man who tramped by choice, Josiah Flynt made clear that there was a difference between the professional tramp and the man who tramped looking for employment, and he looked upon the latter with disdain.[12] After a restless boyhood in

Illinois at the home of his uncle, Francis Willard, Flynt ran away
from home, living off the land, begging, riding freights, and serving
time in prison. Flynt did most of his tramping during an eight-month
period in 1889 and published his first article two years later. Other
articles by him followed in such periodicals as *Contemporary Review*,
Atlantic Monthly, Harper's Weekly, and *Century*. Each was a graphic
description of some phase of the life of the tramp, and the articles
eventually won him the accolade of the founder of "realistic
sociology." *Tramping With Tramps*, a collection of his articles,
became a classic in sociology.[13]

Flynt was at his best when describing the day-to-day existence
of the tramp. Some of his accounts of tramp life, such as homosexuality between young and old, were undoubtedly new to the general public, as were many of his descriptions. When based on personal observations, his accounts were plausible and substantiated by other
sources. For example, he said that a majority of tramps were native
Americans and not immigrants. When talking about the causes of
tramps, he only reflected what most Americans and New York reformers believed. He doubted that fluctuations in the labor market
created tramps, and, instead, cited such conventional explanations as
love of liquor, wanderlust, county jail policies, indiscriminate charity,
and reform school practices. He also tended to believe that such
characteristics as laziness could be passed from generation to
generation.[14]

Flynt's work, published in popular magazines, had two principal
effects. First and most important was that he had opened up a whole
new way of looking at a problem—by looking from the inside. As
Flynt put it, he felt his work among tramps was "scientific insofar
as it deals with the subject on its own ground and in its own peculiar
conditions and environment."[15] By moving among tramps and other
groups in society, reformers and would-be reformers were better able
to understand the problems faced by them. This new empirical observation approach was followed by dozens of others trying to fathom
the tramps. That New York reformers were familiar with Flynt's work
and recognized him as an expert is seen in his later appointment to
participate in the Pittsburgh Survey of 1907-1908.[16] Secondly, Flynt
raised the point that the so-called tramps were not all so voluntarily,

but were composed primarily of men who *would* work, much to his disgust.

Another author who wrote about tramping "from the inside" was Walter A. Wyckoff. However, unlike Flynt, Wyckoff wrote from the point of view of the man genuinely seeking work, rather than that of the man who tramped by choice. In the summer of 1891 young Wyckoff decided to make "an experiment into reality" by traveling as an itinerant unskilled laborer to supplement his "slender, book-learned lore." While moving through rural areas, questions about where he was raised and sights of happy farmers' sons brought on great feelings of homelessness and isolation. Like Garland, Wyckoff was also confused and dismayed at being the unfailing object of distrust. He had thought he would find the poverty-stricken more understanding, but they were as unfriendly as the rich. A common answer to his request for work was a slammed door and a key turned in its lock.[17]

In the city, Wyckoff received more of the same treatment. He quickly learned what it meant to look for work, and not to find it, and to be reduced by hunger and self-preservation until any job would be desirable. After a violent rejection by a prospective employer, Wyckoff mused that he had the uncomfortable feeling of not having been taken "for an unemployed laborer in honest search of work, but for one of the professionally idle." On another occasion another prospective employer, incensed that Wyckoff had even approached him, shrieked to one of his employees: "I've told you to keep these bums out of here!"[18] Resentment grew easily under these circumstances.

Wyckoff found that such hostile rejections by employers could eventually transform one into a tramp. Continual refusals left a man with no money to clean himself, service his clothes, or secure a good rest. As time continued, the outward physical signs of tramping grew and the barriers to real employment became greater. While waiting outside a factory gate with other job seekers, he saw many "in face . . . who, if not already of that class, are approximating to professional tramps." The struggle for acceptance only served to delay the plunge into the abyss, and one soon became a veteran in the army of the unemployed. Wyckoff said that eventually the police looked less repressive and more like the arm of society designed to bring the nonsocial being "into the body politic once more and to set you to fulfilling a functional activity as part of the social organism." He felt that sometimes the feeling became so strong to become part of that organism that tramps committed crimes to restore a relationship with the rest of society, if only in a criminal sense.[19]

Populist Governor Lorenzo D. Lewelling of Kansas thought the debate over voluntary and involuntary tramps was academic, and he disputed the contention that being unemployed was a crime. In an executive decree of December 1893, Lewelling attacked the Kansas vagrancy statute of 1889, which had assumed there was always work for all able-bodied men. He termed men convicted of being "without some visible means of support" no better than municipal slaves and, therefore, he set aside the 1889 statute. The New York reformers were dismayed about the "Tramp Circular," and they read dire predictions in *Charities Review* about the huge number of tramps that were bound to engulf Kansas.[20] But these reports, along with articles published by Wyckoff, Flynt, and others, signalled the beginning of a widespread recognition that a connection existed between hard times and tramps. Once this was recognized as a possibility, agencies dealing with charity and unemployment found it desirable to differentiate between voluntary and the involuntary tramps. And the increasing social violence during the panic seemed to make the differentiation not only desirable but necessary if society were to survive.

New Yorkers, like most other Americans, were confused, dismayed, and frightened by labor violence intensifying in 1893. The Haymarket affair was within memory of most adults, and news of the Homestead Strike in 1892 had filled long columns in New York City newspapers. In addition to these nationally known strikes, numerous small ones kept alive the labor problem in the consciousness of all concerned adults. One author in the YMCA's *Young Men's Era*, for instance, expressed concern over the growing antagonism between capital and labor, and recalled to his readers the French Revolution. If his readers were tempted to dismiss this concern as alarmist talk, they were advised to recall Homestead, Buffalo, and Pittsburgh.[21]

In August 1893, New York newspapers published many accounts of socialist and anarchist meetings and demonstrations in the city, which reflected the fear of radicalism. At one meeting, unemployed Hebrew workmen were advised by an anarchist leader to stop paying rent, and a riot of about 5,000 unemployed developed. At another meeting of the unemployed at Walhalla Hall, Emma Goldman, the famed anarchist leader, urged the men that if they were hungry and needed bread, to "go and get it."[22] If they encountered trouble, they were advised by Goldman and others to use dynamite as the yeast to raise the bread. The *New York Times* accused socialists and anarchists of trying to speak for the poor and unemployed, although they did not actually represent them. The superintendent of the New York City police force, Thomas Byrnes, asserted that he was going to move against the demonstrators. He warned the agitators that he would not allow a lot of incendiary speeches to be made "to influence the minds of an ignorant lot of people and turn them into a lawless mob." Although the anarchists made little headway in New York City because the police quickly suppressed them, the *New York Times* insisted that Emma Goldman and other Russian Jews of the same class as Louis Lingg of Haymarket fame should not be allowed to exploit the unemployed. While the *New York Times* felt that the situation was dangerous, it stated that the anarchists would ultimately fail because so many Americans held a "stake" in society. One person in thirteen had a savings account and when added to those with land and life insurance, the number was gratifying.[23]

Unfortunately from this point of view, the tramp held no such stake and this point was made frequently in discussions of Coxey's Army.[24] On Easter Sunday, 1894, "General" Jacob Coxey and his "industrial army" began their "petition in boots" to Washington to secure help from Congress for the unemployed through the enactment of Coxey's Good Roads Bill and Non-Interest Bearing Bonds Bill. Eventually no fewer than seventeen different industrial armies formed in different areas of the country and headed for Washington. Three of the more famous of the armies were Frye's 600 men from Los Angeles, Kelly's 700 from San Francisco, and Fitzgerald's New England Army, which left Boston toward the end of April. Although most were completely independent of Coxey's orders, the general public referred to the overall movement as "Coxeyism."

Most contemporary newspapers and magazines viewed Coxey's Army as composed almost entirely of tramps. A parody of an old English verse on beggars published in the Pittsburgh *Press* put the feeling in poetic form. It observed:

Hark, Hark! Hear the dogs bark!
Coxey is coming to town.
In his ranks are scamps
And growler fed tramps
On all of whom working men frown.[25]

As the industrial armies tramped toward their destination, metropolitan dailies gave the movement increasing coverage. Not surprisingly, the socialist and populist press favored the movement, while the conservative press found it repulsive though not to be feared. The armies received much criticism because they moved from one area to another in the West on stolen trains, and the battles that ensued kept the nation in a constant state of excitement. Once an army seized a train, the Coxeyites usually reached at least the next town because the police rarely tried to stop the trains between towns. However, police acted to stop the thefts. On one occasion "Jumbo" Cantwell's division stole an empty cattle train and ran it into Milwaukee. When the train arrived, the police sealed all the doors, ran the train outside of town, and left the army caged and without food on a siding while they decided what action to take with the men. In addition to this police suppression, the railroads increasingly used the courts to prevent interference with the trains, and set precedents, which later were applied to Eugene Debs.[26] Many considered this illegal use of trains by the industrial armies a threat to private property, and this argument was often made in the press. When the general manager of the Chicago, Rock Island and Pacific Railway lines observed that the members of Kelly's Army were not tramps, but sober and intelligent men, he was accused of lying so that the tramps would not damage his railroad. The *Nation* said the movements were a national disgrace and only encouraged the "Henrys" who wanted not labor, but only the fruits of labor.[27]

Most of the eastern press did not consider the Coxeyites a threat as long as the armies were in distant states. City newspapers actually considered the whole movement as a joke, and they looked at Coxey as some kind of national freak; at least three dime museums asked him to go on exhibit. But as he neared Washington, the patronizing attitude of the East came to an end. One Hoboken, New Jersey, preacher said that America owed the tramps nothing more than a funeral, and the New York *Herald* suggested lead (bullets) to satisfy their craving appetites. The Washington *News* announced it was time for "Washingtonians to consider what can be done to arrest the threatened invasion of the district by this swarm of human locusts."[28]

On April 7,1894, Captain George Primrose and his division from Texas arrived in Washington as the vanguard of the industrial armies. They were promptly arrested for vagrancy and at their hearing the magistrate judged them all to be tramps. Things did not bode well for Coxey's arrival. Attempting to preclude further legal action against the industrials, one Populist senator offered a resolution that would have permitted Coxey to present his petition without harassment, but the Senate did not pass it. On May 1, Coxey's valiant five hundred led by two "Goddesses of Peace" marched toward Pennsylvania Avenue. The whole march ended, with no petition presented, when the Capitol guards arrested Coxey for walking on the grass. After Coxey's arrest, when the movement began to disintegrate, the *Nation* observed smugly that a few thousand ragamuffins could not put the United States government or social order into peril. However, it warned that to allow this disorder to continue without retribution would endanger America in the same way that France had been threatened prior to the French Revolution. W. T. Stead expressed a similar fear, but was more sympathetic to the unemployed on the march.[29]

Reinforcing the atmosphere of anxiety that Coxey's Army created was the continued labor unrest in the spring of 1894. Morrison Swift, a New England socialist leader, was agitating "foreigners" in Boston, and two hundred Hungarians murdered the chief engineer of the H. C. Frick Coke Company at Uniontown, Pennsylvania. After the engineer was downed by a volley of assorted missiles, each member of the mob hurled one more stone at the helpless victim. The mob then threw the body into an oven. A *New York Times* correspondent wrote that the region was "fairly trembling on the brink of revolution." Never before were the dangerous foreigners so thoroughly aroused.[30] Groups of industrials continued to roam the countryside, and strikes were increasing in frequency and size. The Pullman Strike was the largest and most famous. Class conflict seemed almost inevitable to many.[31] That anarchist and socialistic ideas and actions were on the minds of the New York City populace in 1894 can be inferred from a *New York Times* advertisement on April 6: "BOMB THROWING—is mighty dangerous but not a bit more fatal in its results than filling the system with Mercury Iodide of Potassium and other deadly drugs under the name of Spring Medicine. Buy only Riker's Sarsaparilla." The use of the phrase "bomb throwing" was certain to catch the reader's eye at a time when the New York press was headlining labor violence.

That the city was concerned about a possible outbreak of violence during the panic years can also be seen in articles published about the National Guard armories in New York City. Benjamin O. Flower, editor of the *Arena*, referred to them as "Plutocracy's Bastilles" and asserted that if work were provided to the unemployed, patriotism would flourish and armories would become unnecessary.[32] In this regard, one Salvationist went to Madison Square and recruited 450 homeless unemployed to bring them to the Fourteenth Street headquarters of the Salvation Army. As they marched along, the Salvationist compared the superiority of the Army's method of dealing with the unemployed to that of the Ninth Regiment Armory of the New York National Guard, which stood opposite the mission on Fourteenth Street. He referred to the armory "with its black, slit-like windows and sharp slanting stone sills, constructed for the use of rifles and especially to make it easy to direct fire on the street beneath." The officer warned that "the simplicity and promptness with which these idle men had been organized into a force" made him think of the armory as if it were asleep. However, the promise of it waking up sometime "made a picture to think about."[33] The National Guard and the city officials ignored proposals to use armories to shelter the homeless unemployed, lending support to Flower's inference that the armories were ready to deal with the homeless unemployed in other ways should the need arise. As the winter came to a close, however, the NYAICP breathed an editorial sigh of relief that no serious conflict had come to pass.[34]

Of all the radical activity, that of Jacob Coxey was perhaps the most influential because his combining of theory with nationwide militant protest caught the public imagination. Thorstein Veblen in 1894 stated that Coxey represented the change of attitude toward the unemployed between the "civil republic of the nineteenth century and the industrial republic of the socialists.''[35] This new attitude evolved rapidly as reformers developed new methods and encouraged studies of the unemployed in reaction to the fear and unrest brought about by the movement of masses of men seeking work.

As the numbers of homeless men seeking work steadily increased in New York City in the 1890s, the reformers first sought ways to discourage men from tramping in the city. They tried to limit or regulate the number of places in which a man could live free or inexpensively, cooperated with the police to reduce street begging, and encouraged institutions and relief agencies to require work before providing charity to the homeless.

Tramps moving into the city sought the cheapest and safest shelter possible, and, for those with limited funds, lodging houses were the choice. These unregulated houses were, as a rule, unsanitary, unventilated and demoralizing for the occupant. In New York City alone, in 1894, 105 such lodging houses existed, with space for sixteen thousand homeless at a nightly rental ranging from three to thirty-five cents.[36]

In 1897 Josephine Shaw Lowell summarized most reformers' arguments against lodging houses. The houses, she said, were at the level of the degraded homeless and therefore failed to uplift him. And if the homeless person was not corrupt before entering, he was sure to be so before his departure. Worse, the houses enabled inefficient persons to live so cheaply that they had no desire to become more efficient. If a man could secure a room for ten cents, why should he work for a dollar? Jacob A. Riis, journalist and reformer, stated that the only worse place for a man to stay would be a ''stale-beer dive.'' Usually a back-alley cellar, the dive sold unlicensed beer collected from the bottoms of kegs, which stood on the street in front of saloons awaiting the brewer's cart. Purchasing a round of this flat brew gave the tramps the right to spend the night on a chair, a table, or over a barrel.[37]

One activity in the lodging houses seemed to indicate to the reformers that tramps had no grasp of the significance of democratic institutions—their votes went for sale to the highest bidder. Politicians canvassed cheap lodging houses, as well as workhouses, for votes. After providing the participants in democracy with food and drink, politicians like big Tim Sullivan shepherded their charges from one

In Darkest New York—Midnight

Helen Campbell, *Darkness at Daylight* (Hartford, 1897), 653

polling place to another. In the face of restrictive laws and aggressive poll-watching by civic organizations, vote brokers and lodging house owners continued their mutually advantageous cooperation.[38] Even arresting the tramps seemed useless. One official at Blackwell's Island pointed out to Riis that the 275 tramps sentenced to serve six months that very week would not serve their full sentences because it was within a month of an important election. Frustrated by such machine politics, reformers despaired of their ability to stop politicians from vote buying and instead suggested that perhaps tramps should be forbidden to vote at all.[39]

New York reformers urged organizations not to open more lodging houses and at the same time worked for revision of New York laws with respect to cheap lodging houses. Robert Hebberd of the COS said the lodging houses and beggars fed on each other. The lodging houses constituted "a serious menace" to the "peace, comfort, and order of the city" and should be suppressed.[40] However, other than attempting to clean up the lodging houses and to discourage the institution of new ones, the reformers could do little in this area.

The homeless with cash could stay in the cheap lodging houses, but those with no money most often sought shelter at a police station. Since the 1870s, the reformers had fought against the use of police stations for the same reasons that they were opposed to cheap lodging houses. They felt that the houses were a form of indiscriminate charity, attracted lower classes to the city, and exposed the morally upright to the company of the bad.

The most influential reformer working on this problem was Jacob Riis, who had stayed in a police station as a youth. Riis' one night in the station was a memorable one—he was terribly uncomfortable, his watch was stolen, and his dog's brains were beaten out on the steps of the station house. One can still detect the bitterness in Riis' autobiography written some thirty years after the event.[41] In 1891 Riis wrote to police and charity officials in many cities and inquired about their policies and recommendations in regard to police station lodging. Most answers stated that station lodging still existed. But if existing wayfarer's lodges required work, police sent as many applicants as possible to them. Zilpha Smith of the Associated Charities of Boston told Riis that the police had originally requested the establishment of a wayfarer's lodge in Boston. On the margin of her letter, Riis wrote that he would have to look into the attitude of the New York City police on this issue.[42]

A typhus outbreak in New York City in January 1893, which apparently began in a police station lodging room, gave Riis the occasion to inspect the stations and to find out the police attitude toward housing tramps. At the Park Street station, he noted that the air was "so bad that even the camera revolted," and at another he wrote that the only real weapon against typhus—fresh air—was not to be had. The police, he found, did indeed want to keep out the tramps because of the diseases and filth carried by them into the station houses. Thus they supported Riis in his effort to end station lodging. His findings were discussed at various meetings of experts in the fields of medicine, public service, and philanthropy.[43]

Although the reformers agreed that cheap lodging houses and police stations were not acceptable for housing tramps, they did recognize the need for a place to house the worthy on a temporary basis. Since they had no intention of lodging voluntary tramps, they tried to establish an institution to reduce this likelihood. One possible solution was to have the COS operate a wayfarer's lodge where the homeless could receive food and lodging in return for work. The police could refer all applicants for lodging to it. Only those really willing to work would go to the lodge and receive assistance. Those unwilling to work would not go to the lodge at all, and thus those really deserving of help would be identified.

The COS sent Robert Hebberd on a tour of wayfarer's lodges in other cities to find ideas for developing a similar institution in New York. While Hebberd became convinced that the concept of a lodge operated by organized charity was valid, he was disappointed at the actual operations of the lodges. Boston's Wayfarer's Lodge had the best reputation, but its sleeping accommodations led Hebberd to comment "that most of the lodgers got under the covers in a manner which indicated that while hopeful for the best, they were fearful of the worst."[44] Based on his report and also on the number of homeless unemployed anticipated in New York City during the forthcoming winter, the NYCOS opened its Wayfarer's Lodge in November 1893.[45]

Soon, however, the facilities of the lodge became inadequate for the huge numbers of unemployed in New York City. The society lacked resources to investigate each applicant and to provide work for all applicants; therefore, it began actively to urge establishment of a Municipal Lodging House already authorized by the state legislature in 1886. The proposed institution would serve a function similar to that of the Wayfarer's Lodge, but would be run by the city government rather than by a private charity. All homeless unemployed would be referred to it, and employment would be provided for those wishing shelter in order to identify those willing to work.

Josephine Shaw Lowell was one of the dissenting voices with regard to a municipal lodging house prior to the panic of 1893, opposing the plan on the grounds that a "rotten" city government could not set up any decent institution. The municipal lodging houses, she warned, would eventually be no different from the station house lodging, and she instead recommended that each morning the police turn over all station lodgers to the commissioner of charities who would determine their final disposition. Riis, however, preferred that the process be taken out of the hands of the police completely.[46]

In the process of working out a solution for temporary lodging, the reformers' goal shifted from discouraging all homeless from entering the city to one of separating voluntary tramps from involuntary ones (the worthy unemployed). The worthy could be helped to rejoin society, and the voluntary tramps could be confined and taught how to work. For example, although Riis and Lowell did not agree on methods of separating the tramps, they did agree that a "humane sifting" of all those "helpable" had to be instituted.[47] The key to the sifting process in the 1890s was still based on worthiness and willingness, or, in other words, on the character of the individual. Initially, reformers believed that a separation could be made by a "labor test"[i] such as the one used by the Wayfarer's Lodge. This test consisted of tasks like "oakum picking" (separating strands from a rope soaked in tar) or, more often in New York, by cutting wood. The COS had originally opened the woodyard used by the lodge "not with any ideas of providing work at a fair price to the unemployed but purely as a means by which to test the good faith of those asking relief under the pleas of inability to procure work."[48]

But after the winter of 1893-1894, a small group of NYCOS members raised serious questions as to the efficacy of wood cutting as a test. James B. Reynolds, Lawrence Veiller, and others inspected the woodyard and concluded that the work, which took four to five hours for the most experienced to finish, was too severe. The inspection team saw that "experienced-looking" men had worked more than seven hours. The labor test, they reported, "is a test of a man's willingness to work, not of his ability to work. It is this willingness that determines worthiness."[49] The labor test was inadequate for the very young, old, infirm, or inexperienced manual laborers. And when the test was completed, what really had been proved?

One writer in *Charities Review* pointed out that the notion of a test implied that something would happen to those passing it successfully. What, he pondered, can the COS do for a man "after it has put him to a proper test by labor, and thus has proved to its satisfaction that he is able to work and willing to work, and therefore is worthy?"[50] Clearly it could do nothing when large numbers of men were involved. The reformers turned to the hope that a public institution could accomplish this task. A municipal lodging house was a place where physical and moral reformation could be accomplished and where the unemployed could be forced to work in payment for food and shelter. Of course even a public lodging house would not answer the critic in *Charities Review*. In reality, the municipal lodging house was only a more efficient and effective way of forcing men to work.

But the NYCOS considered with jubilation the opening of a barge for use as a temporary municipal lodging house in March 1896, followed the next year by a rented building, since, at the same time, police station housing also ended. Desk sergeants were to send applicants for lodging to either the COS Wayfarer's Lodge or the City Lodging House where each applicant would be investigated. Individuals no longer were to stay in the police stations of their own volition. The chief of police supported the new system, certain that it would aid the deserving and get rid of tramps. Theodore Roosevelt, president of the New York City Police Board, who had many friends among New York reformers, considered the city's action an important piece of reform, especially in the detection of those habitual tramps who refused to help themselves. Josephine Shaw Lowell, in a letter to Jacob Riis, congratulated Riis on his part in securing the Municipal Lodging House and also asked what she could do "directly" for Roosevelt because he was her "best good citizen."[51]

While habitual tramps could be detected at the Municipal Lodging

A City Tramp at Work
Century Magazine 47 (March 1894), 712

House, as Roosevelt pointed out, mendicants who did not apply were also presumably not worthy. Since its inception, the COS had concerned itself with eliminating the problem of street begging, which it regarded as indiscriminate charity. By reducing the possibility of a tramp's begging free food after the panic of 1893, the reformers thereby hoped to encourage them to leave the city. As early as 1890, the society had established special mendicancy officers, deputized by the police, who were to arrest and prosecute street beggars.[52] Eventually, however, the officers stopped arresting beggars except in cases of fraud, because ugly crowds collected and generally supported the beggar suspect against the officer. To aid the police in stopping fraudulent begging, the society attempted to get an antifreak bill enacted in New York. It patterned the proposed bill after a similar law passed by the Pennsylvania legislature that made a misdemeanor of exhibiting "any physical deformity to which he or she shall be subject or which is produced by artificial means for hire or for the purpose of soliciting alms." In addition, the COS saw its mission as one of educating the public to see that money given to beggars was wasted. It investigated beggars and publicized names of those who would not work and had not done so for years. Not only was begging harmful for the morals of the beggar, but also for those of innocent bystanders. Police official Addison Jerome observed that, for women in a "delicate condition," passing the crippled and maimed beggars "must be offensive and in some cases harmful."[53]

Even if an officer desired to arrest a particular beggar, it was difficult because many beggars worked under a cloak of legality by obtaining licenses from the city to peddle articles and to play hand organs. Edward Devine of the COS wrote to Mayor Strong, requesting that no further licenses of this type be issued, because most recipients were vagrants anyway. To preclude the possibility that some persons might be deprived of earning a legitimate living, Devine offered the voluntary service of the society to investigate all cases, but at first the city took no action.[54]

To identify the professional vagrants, the COS employed exhaustive techniques. As early as 1882, it had begun to compile a list of known "rounders," "repeaters," and "deadbeats." The list was expanded into files, including complete identification and aliases. For identification it used the French Bertillon method, based on standardiz-

Turning Misfortune to Account
Scribner's Magazine 6 (December 1889), 741

ing head and body measurements with a maximum of precision by use of mechanical and photographic means.[55] Also included in the files were case studies with resumés of the mendicant's career. For example, the files identified James Grady, who was born in a small town in New York, and characterized him as a common loafer. While tramping, he lost his right leg below the knee and afterward, in New York City, became a beggar-cripple. He eventually left New York City with a fellow cripple. A notation on the four-page record raised the question of society's responsibility in allowing an environment to exist which could corrupt a man like Grady. Another case study described Owen O'Malley, who was unable to do heavy work because of a hernia sustained in a fight and a limp which developed from an ill-judged leap off a moving train. He was characterized as a "tramp, loafer, general outlaw, and enemy of society."[56]

Based on its files, the COS circulated confidential bulletins to members and businessmen. It included some pictures and listed individuals under their distinguishing physical characteristics. For example, one section was headed "Cripples; Migratory and Semi-Migratory" and a key specified physical characteristics such as "amputation of the right leg above (+) or below (*) knee for each man."[57]

At the same time that the society was working with the police to end station housing, discussions were apparently underway on mendicancy as well. In the same letter of February 1896, which closed police station houses, Police Chief Conlin urged his men to arrest all street beggars and to contact the COS for assistance in securing "a full pedigree" on all professional beggars. The following year, the chief of police spelled out in a special order what he expected his officers to do. With the aid of the COS, they were to differentiate on the street between "the unfortunate person who is perhaps driven to beg by stress of circumstance" and the professional tramps who "cannot be made to work, who resort to all sorts of tricks and devices to create sympathy for their apparently pitiable condition."[58] While Chief Conlin felt the former should receive sympathy and be directed toward helping themselves, he argued that the latter should be prosecuted.

Conlin's order was another form of public recognition that even seemingly worthless persons such as street beggars must be investigated to identify those who were simply unfortunates out of work involuntarily and to separate them from their evil environment. In doing so, Chief Conlin asked for a social awareness and sophistication not previously demanded of city police. He realized that time and experience were needed "to discriminate between this class of the unfortunate and the professional," but he expected the distinction to be made. After a policeman identified the professional tramp, Conlin said, the problem was not ended. Officers had to be "so careful, so discreet, and so intelligent in their work as to make the Magistrates feel that when a case is presented to them it is a good case, a good arrest, an arrest that is justified by the facts and the conditions of the case."[59] In spite of Chief Conlin's warning, obtaining enough evidence to secure convictions continued to be a problem.

Some judges had already shown sympathy for the men brought up under vagrancy charges. One judge, in refusing to "commit a tramp for the mere offense of being what he is," jailed only about 20 percent of those brought before him on vagrancy charges. Mrs. Lowell argued with Crane in court, but to no avail. The judge told her he had been homeless himself and could not be too strict with "decent men who were merely unfortunate," even though she asserted that the workhouse was better than the street for professional tramps.[60]

The president of the COS, Robert DeForest, a wealthy New York lawyer, applauded the police order in a letter to Theodore Roosevelt. He especially praised the instructions for discriminating between the unfortunates and the professionals and hoped that assigned officers would "measure their zeal not only by the number of professional beggars and vagrants they arrest, but by the number of unfortunates for whom they are instrumental in securing needed relief."[61] He and others considered social awareness by the police to be of great importance. John A. Kingsbury pointed out that the "billy club" was "no longer the most essential equipment of a policeman. His mental equipment and his attitude toward society" were more important.[62]

The collaboration between the COS and the police did not run smoothly. Police who were assigned to work with the mendicancy problem frequently had to handle other duties. Also, as economic conditions improved and as street begging lessened, police interest in the problem declined. Finally, in March 1906, police support for the operation was discontinued, and the COS decided not to continue without their cooperation.[63]

Even when street mendicancy increased again during the depression winter of 1907-1908, the police were not willing to cooperate with the society. James Forbes, mendicancy specialist of the society, felt that the public unfortunately interpreted the program of the society's mendicancy committee as "the suppression of street begging." The work obviously needed publicity to show the opportunities for "constructive social work in the rehabilitation of unfortunates" and the prosecution of the rest.[64] But neither the public nor the police were to be convinced. For a short period, the police continued to give the society Bertillon photos and descriptions, but with the adoption of fingerprinting they ceased to send photographs or to use its records. In commenting later on this chapter in COS activity, Edward Devine wrote to John D. Rockefeller that investigation and prosecution of men for mendicancy was really outside the province of voluntary groups and should be handled by public agencies. Men within the police department, specially trained, would be more effective. Henceforth, the COS restricted itself to publishing occasional bulletins on imposters and to supporting publications such as the *Directory of Cripples*, which listed all the true unfortunates.[65]

Official responsibility for dealing with beggars, impoverished persons, tramps, and criminals in New York City rested with the Department of Charities and Correction prior to the panic of 1893. Reformers had long urged the division of this department into two separate ones because of the practices of putting all types of individuals (tramps, the poor, the ill) subject to the control of the agency into the same institutions, such as poorhouses.

In 1893 one author in the *Charities Review* thought that the tramp was the biggest obstacle to the separation of charities work from the correction department. How was this "living link" between charity and correction to be handled?[66] This question was answered in the law establishing two new departments and assigning the responsibility for the tramp to the Charities Department. After January 1, 1896, the commissioner of public charities had the direction and general charge of all institutions devoted to the destitute, while the commissioner of corrections had "no authority" and was "subject to no obligation in respect of any destitute person not charged with or convicted of any crime or misdemeanor."[67] The passage of the law did not completely

separate the two departments because a century of common administration made the unwinding difficult. But for the resolution of the
problem of the homeless unemployed, it was another step toward public recognition that the tramp's condition in itself was not a crime.[68]

Laws in themselves, however, were not sufficient to solve the
tramp.problem. Education was badly needed for reformers, and for
the public as well, if science were to be successfully applied to social
problems. Richard Ely, well-known American economist and Christian
Socialist, pointed out in 1893 that evils in the social body could be
attacked only after a sufficient amount of scientific skill had been
acquired by long and patient study. Ely said that "when we have
schools of social science as well equipped as the best medical schools
are now, we shall be on the road to prevent crises such as have produced so much suffering in the present century."[69]

Edward Devine of the COS agreed with Ely and advocated and
planned formal training for social workers in order to qualify them
for their duties. The result of this was a six-week training class in
applied philanthropy which began in New York City in 1898. The
Central Council of the NYCOS hoped that the program would grow
into an endowed school attracting the best minds and setting an example for the rest of the nation.[70] After a few years of operation, the
school was endowed with $250,000 by New York philanthropist John
S. Kennedy, and the New York School of Philanthropy became a reality. It became the best known school of professional social work in
the United States. More important, it was an immense step in developing the concept of the professionally trained social worker or as one
recent historian noted, "the professional altruist."[71]

To supplement the formal schooling, the reformers supported
city, state, and national meetings of reform groups to provide forums
for the free interchange of ideas. For example, Robert Hebberd proposed a state conference of charities and correction "to enable those
who are sincere and disinterested to come to a common ground of
understanding." At the first meeting of the New York State Conference of Charities and Correction in 1901, John Glenn stressed the
importance of the organization for the education of the reformers by
constantly keeping them in touch "with the best thought and experience of the rest of the world." In 1902 William R. Stewart lauded

the efforts of the reformers in moving toward greater cooperation. The School of Philanthropy and the conferences were "all education movements" of the greatest importance.[72]

The printed word was also an important educational device. All the various reform conferences published their proceedings, and the organizations liberally distributed their annual reports. Reform journals, moreover, contained articles by reformers and public officials from all over the country. The most important of these were the publications that merged piecemeal to form *Survey* in 1909: *Charities, Charities Review, The Commons, Jewish Charity,* and *Charities and The Commons.*

Education and science, when applied to solve the problem of the tramp, provided reformers and the general public with some interesting information and explanations of the development of tramps. The first attempt to survey the tramps systematically in the United States was by Josiah Flynt in 1891. Flynt wrote that more than half of the tramps were native Americans; many of the remainder were Irish- and German-born. Tramps, said Flynt, took to the road because of laziness or drink, that is to say, because of individual failure.[73]

While Flynt's ideas were drawn from observation, Professor J. J. McCook applied "science" to the problem and took a "tramp census" of 1,349 individuals. He found, as Flynt did, that most tramps were native Americans. Almost 60 percent were intemperate; about 60 percent had a skill; 75 percent were under forty years of age; and over 80 percent reported their health as good. McCook concluded that neither health nor age precluded the average tramp from working, although over 80 percent claimed to have taken to the road to look for a job. Less than 1 percent of the tramps were Negroes. McCook concluded that moral causes, chiefly drunkenness, were responsible for the average tramp. "If this be not the chief cause," he said, "I confess to have been unable to find any other."[74]

The massive unemployment of 1893-1894 helped McCook find a cause other than drunkenness, for two years after his first "census" was published, he refuted his own conclusions. After the first bad winter of the panic of 1893, he saw a listing of the number of tramps located in Massachusetts each year for the previous twenty years and noticed substantial increases of tramps listed for the years 1874 and 1894. What, he asked, was the reason? Of course, financial depres-

Tramps and Boys
Century Magazine 47 (November 1893), 102

sions! With this observation in mind, he revised his original study, now stressing that the average tramp was originally a skilled laborer and minimizing other conclusions of his earlier study. But still he was not completely convinced. He hoped that the use of alcohol would end, and he warned parents to keep their children away from tramps who might lure them to the road. Published in the National Conference of Charities and Corrections *Proceedings* in 1895, McCook's analysis of the connection between tramps and depressions received an airing before the reformers. By 1902 McCook in the *Independent* stated definitively that most tramps were not professionals but men involuntarily out of work.[75] But even though McCook was convinced, most reformers were not.

Thus early in 1907 Robert Hebberd asked Orlando Lewis, sociologist and prison reformer, to present a paper on vagrancy at the NCCC. To gather information, Lewis submitted questionnaires to one hundred charitable societies and fifty railroads. His conclusions appear to have been overly influenced by the railroads' position that vagrancy was not due to "any inherit defect in the industrial system but to unenforced or inadequate laws."[76] He concluded that deterrence should be increased and that the vagrants should be kept away from the railroad. In addition to repressive tactics as a preventive, Lewis also stressed improved home conditions to keep children more satisfied with domestic life. While Lewis' paper showed the growing importance of environmentalism, his stress was still on personal rather than societal failure.

The railroad theme proved to be popular. The national press gave wide coverage to Lewis' discussion on the railroad and the tramp, particularly his figures from the Interstate Commerce Commission reports for 1901-1905, which stated that five thousand trespassers were killed on railroads annually. At least half of them were purportedly tramps.[77] At the annual meeting of the New York SCCC in 1907, Lewis and others discussed the subject again. Arthur Towne acknowledged that industrial conditions, as well as other reasons, produced tramps, but the thrust of his article was to warn that riding trains made boys into tramps; therefore, boys had to be kept away from moving trains.[78] The discussion following his talk produced one general conclusion: vagrancy must be headed off early in life. Educa-

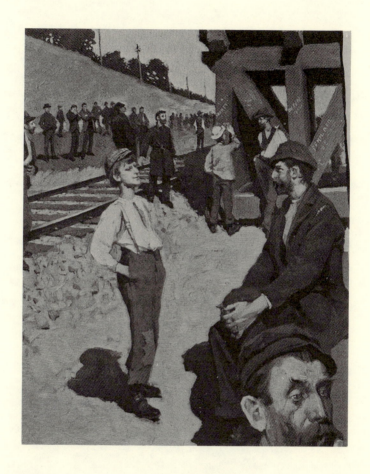

The Tramp Depot
Century Magazine 48 (June 1899), 264

Riding on the Bumpers
Century Magazine 47 (February 1894), 524

tion, training, and reformatories had to guard children against the dangers of trampdom.

That railroads were responsible for youth becoming tramps was the theme of a whole series of "true life adventures" by Leon R. Livingston, who wrote under the pen name of A-No. 1. He described his life as a tramp and depicted the worst aspects of tramp life in lurid detail. On the inside cover of the *Curse of the Tramp Life* appeared a warning to able young men and boys: "Do not jump on moving trains or streetcars, even if only to ride to the next street crossing, because this might arouse 'the Wanderlust' besides endangering your life and limbs." He warned that 95 out of 100 would have a miserable fate, "an accident, and almshouse, but surely an unmarked pauper's grave." Of the thrilling adventure of "riding the rods," he wrote that the least slip of his grip "meant a horrible death underneath those ghostly wheels behind me which now, like arch fiends with wide slobbering maws were only waiting to grind and crush me into a scattered mass of quivering pulp." Stay at home, he advised. Do not be like the young man who was shot and thrown off a speeding boxcar by outlaw hoboes and whose last word was "Mother."[79]

In addition to keeping unattended children away from the railroads, others felt "a proper kind of education" would substantially reduce the number of tramps. In fact, to end the problem completely, compulsory education was regarded as a "social imperative."[80] Many articles stressed industrial and manual training in the schools in order to provide each youth with a vocational skill. William E. Dodge of Phelps, Dodge and Company and wealthy patron of the Young Men's Christian Association, pointed out that in the "next" generation "the value of all our institutions and all our properties will depend on the character of the young who are now preparing for active life." In 1909, Jacob Riis wrote from Denver that he had heard a demand for more schools and a municipal lodging house in the same breath. He noted they were not without connection although it might not be apparent at first, and the demands reminded him of those in New York City after the panic of 1893. With more schools, children would not become idlers and tramps; with a municipal lodging house, the homeless need not necessarily become tramps. The municipal lodging house would also serve as "a logical step toward parting the goats from the sheep, so that the tramp may be dealt with as such and the honestly homeless on his merit.''[81]

After the panic of 1893 subsided, reformers continued to be concerned with unemployment and its relationship with social unrest. Their entry into tenement house reform and their support of Seth Low, a fusion candidate nominated by both the Republican party and the independent Citizens Union against the Tammany nominee, reflected their overall concern with urban problems. Low won the election, and reform-minded New Yorkers were jubilant. At a victory dinner commemorating the campaign participation of NYAICP members Robert Fulton Cutting, New York City financier, and E. R. L. Gould, president of City and Suburban Homes Company, the common theme of the speeches was optimism—optimism based not only on hopes for the new administration but also on the fact that the working classes had followed the reformers' lead. Gould asserted that he was a "conservative" and urged the "men of means" attending the banquet, "rather than your radical fellow citizens," to continue to lead the way for civic improvement. Cutting also applauded the reform efforts and hoped for a "true democracy, based on the fundamental value of the individual and that will never succumb to the fatal flight of socialism." Homer Folks, newly appointed commissioner of civil service reform in the new administration, warned of the dangers of law breaking, which he called "the parent of the spirit of anarchy which is today the most dangerous foe of our republic."[82] While none of these speeches indicated a great sense of foreboding, there was, nevertheless, an awareness that social conditions were not as stable as the speakers would have desired and that it was their responsibility to help alleviate conditions.

Popular literature also reflected the awareness of a fear of growing class tensions. *Cosmopolitan Magazine*, *Outlook*, *North American Review*, and *American Magazine* contained frequent articles on this theme. For example, one character in the novel, *Cash Intrigue*, published in *Cosmopolitan Magazine*, organized an army from the urban unemployed to help him overthrow the existing government. In a 1906 nonfiction article, Morris Hillquit, Robert Hunter, and Ambrose Bierce participated in a round table discussion on social unrest. In Bierce's view, a "bloody revolution" was coming to America.[83]

As long as economic conditions were good, however, the reformers were not unduly concerned. Jacob H. Schiff, wealthy Jewish banker and philanthropist, wrote to Lillian Wald about a prophecy of Lord Macaulay, which stated that American institutions would be put to the test when land was no longer available. But Schiff cautioned Wald not to be concerned: "Conditions now in this country are by no means such as he [Macaulay] foresees, for his views were based on a supposition of want of work for the masses and low wages, but just the contrary is and has been the fact for a considerable time."[84] Implicit in Schiff's letters was a concern over instability resulting from adverse economic conditions.

When the panic of 1907-1908 occurred, reformers were intensely aware of the seemingly direct connections between unemployment and acts of violence and unrest. In Chicago, a nineteen-year old boy attempted to assassinate the chief of police; in Telluride, Colorado, a bomb was placed under the bed of General Bulkley Wells; and police were called in Philadelphia to disperse a mob of unemployed marching on the city hall. President Roosevelt called for the suppression of an anarchist paper in Paterson, New Jersey, and sent a special message to Congress on the subject of legislation against anarchists.[85] Mass demonstrations of the unemployed were appearing like desert wildflowers after the spring rains. In Cleveland and other Ohio cities, mass meetings of the unemployed in public squares made profound impressions on city officials. In Chicago, Ben L. Reitman and J. Eads Howe attempted to organize a march of unemployed along the lines of Coxey's in 1894. Unemployed in St. Louis marched and demanded work from dismayed officials. In Boston, Morrison Swift, former Coxey lieutenant and Socialist, began recruiting an army of the unemployed and gained wide notoriety by disturbing a Sunday service in Trinity Church and demanding the day's collection for the unemployed.[86]

In New York City, the atmosphere was tense. When the Central Federated Union planned a mass demonstration in February 1908 to protest the suspension of public works contracts, the COS intervened with city officials to have projects continued. Then on March 28, a Saturday afternoon, a huge crowd assembled in Union Square in response to a handbill distributed by New York Socialists calling for a mass meeting of the unemployed. Unknown to the crowd, however, the city fathers had refused to issue a permit, and the police were

ordered to clear the square. Freely swinging nightsticks, the mounted
police rode into the mob driving them into side streets and doorways,
while the mob hoarsely sang "The Marseillaise." After clearing the
square of all but about a thousand people, the police regrouped and
awaited orders.[87]

Meanwhile, a nineteen-year old Russian immigrant, Seelig Silverstein, saw the regrouping police as his opportunity. In his hand
was a bomb that he had fashioned in his home—a ball from the post
of a brass bedstead, which he had filled with broken nails, nitroglyc-
erin, and gun powder. Suddenly the police noticed Silverstein's
upraised arm holding the bomb with a sputtering fuse, and then a
tremendous explosion echoed throughout the square. The prematurely
detonated bomb blew a bystander to pieces and frightfully maimed
the youthful immigrant. Even with his hand and eyes blown away
and his body filled with bits of metal, Silverstein sneered, expressing
sorrow that no police had been killed and saying also that he had
no accomplices. Police investigators found that Silverstein held a
membership card number in the Anarchist Federation of America,
signed by Alexander Berkman, a well-known anarchist whom the public connected with the shooting of Henry C. Frick. Newspapers compared the recent anarchist activity to the Haymarket incident. Although
police claimed no "Red Plot" existed, nevertheless they swarmed
over the immigrant-dominated East Side, forcibly breaking up gather-
ings and arresting suspected anarchists. The March 31 edition of the
New York Times blazed a front page story, asserting that all New York
reds were in federation with other reds across the nation. There was
little doubt that a conspiracy was afoot.[88]

An editorial in *World To-Day* pointed out what it considered to
be the problem in an article entitled "The Emergence of Class Consciousness." Discussing the election of 1908, the editorial expressed
concern over the Socialist vote and asserted that the days of "unmod-
ified individualism" had passed. It concluded that "what was needed
was for the government to find a way for fraternal cooperation of
economic classes."[89]

The activities of the Industrial Workers of the World (IWW) in
fomenting strikes and disorder sustained the apprehension over class
tensions. Founded in 1905 on the principles of revolutionary industrial
unionism, the IWW represented the unskilled and frequently the job-

less unskilled after the withdrawal of the politically minded and more moderate elements in 1908. The popular press saw the IWW as a horde of hoboes whose negative philosophy was dedicated to the over-throw of capitalism.[90] The IWW never denied its tie with hoboes and even its own songs reflected such kinship. One of the most popular was "Hallelujah on the Bum," which asked:

> O why don't you work
> Like other men do?
> How in the hell can I work
> When there's no work to do?
>
> Hallelujah, I'm a bum,
> Hallelujah, bum again,
> Hallelujah, give us a handout—
> To revive us again.[91]

The IWW insisted its members were hoboes rather than tramps. "Tramp" connoted a man who would not work even if work were offered. "Hobo" was a compromise, describing a man who moved and did not have a job but who would work if a job were offered. Chicago millionaire "tramp" Ben L. Reitman wrote the most widely quoted definition. The tramp he said, "dreams and wanders," while the hobo "works and wanders." E. L. Baily wrote in *Forum* that tramps were so by choice, but that hoboes were products of the indus-trial revolution. Jefferson Davis, "king of the hoboes" and founder of the International Itinerant Worker's Union, agreed; the hobo would work.[92]

When the panic of 1907-1908 again forced thousands of unem-ployed into the streets, reformers realized that the Municipal Lodging House was not really distinguishing the tramps as they had hoped. Moreover, they still had little information on the tramps, so they began a number of sophisticated studies to determine who the tramp really was and why he was in New York City.

To aid in the investigation of the lodgers at the Municipal Lodg-ing House, the United Hebrew Charities, the COS, and the AICP employed a joint social secretary at the center in 1908 to interview applicants and to help them obtain proper care or find the right place after leaving the house.[93] An advisory committee for the lodging house was set up, which included Paul U. Kellogg, then editor of *Survey*, and Walter Lippmann.[94]

Working closely with the unemployed, the social secretaries were able to throw new light on these amorphous masses. One, H. F. Cook, pointed out that on first becoming social secretary he was anxious to find out how many of the homeless were really tramps. Each applicant at the Municipal Lodging House was required to give as a reference the name of a former employer. The secretary then wrote to the references. To his amazement, Cook found that the deserving were not the exception, but the majority. The main problem for those who held the position of social secretary, as he saw it, was providing work for the needy. He said that many people felt the vagrants were all criminals and should be imprisoned, but Cook said that "we are the guilty ones, we are the criminals." Men came with good references and the house could not even provide work in the charity woodyard because of the overproduction of wood.[95]

The first major published study of the homeless unemployed, *One Thousand Homeless Men* by Alice W. Solenberger, was issued by the Russell Sage Foundation of New York City in 1911. This study was conducted in Chicago and became a classic model in the field of sociology. Its purpose was to try to fathom "inductively" who the homeless men were and why they were in that condition.[96] Of the 1,000 men the author interviewed, the average homeless man was white, less than forty years of age, single, physically defected, and native born. Five percent of her sample were mentally ill, almost 5 percent were blind, and about 33 percent were crippled, paralyzed, or deformed. Nearly 4 percent were too senile to work.

Throughout her study Mrs. Solenberger noted connections between industry and tramps. She found that seasonal work seemed to be particularly debilitating. She also criticized the organization of modern industry for massing thousands of homeless in urban areas. In order to be continually employed, these men had to move fairly often. While these traveling workmen were not tramps, the differences, she found, soon disappeared between them. Yet she concluded that the men she studied were tramps because of personal weaknesses. Obviously influenced by Orlando Lewis, she stated that keeping the unlawful away from the railroads would eliminate "the largest single contributory cause of vagrancy'' and the problem of the tramp would be solved.[97]

The publication of this study led to others in New York City. Mortimer M. Singer told the chairman of the COS Woodyard Committee that he felt that no permanent good was being achieved at the woodyard. So that results might be made permanent, he offered a thousand dollars enabling the committee to hire a social secretary for the woodyard.[98] The Rev. Frank C. Laubach who was hired produced a series of one hundred case studies of men applying at the woodyard, and the COS subsequently sponsored the publication of Laubach's findings, but at the secretary's own expense.[99] His statistics confirmed the general outline of Solenberger's study. Twenty of the one hundred men were crippled, and sixteen were senile. Although many should have been placed in specialized institutions, most were willing to work, and forty possessed industrial skills.[100]

The most detailed study of homeless men in New York City was made by Charles Barnes. The study was never published, but a general profile of the homeless men drawn from this study is in substantial agreement with the others. Most homeless were white, Roman Catholic, and either mentally or physically disabled. Barnes pointed out that approximately 40 percent of the city's population was foreign born and that this figure had a close correlation to the percentage of homeless aliens. In his survey, Barnes pointed out that every social ill created the homeless. Unemployment, an important cause, was "inherent in the industrial system" and should be taken care of by industry. He proposed a special court to try all cases of the homeless. The court would act as a clearinghouse with skilled officers and mendicancy officers present, who would be qualified to send each of the homeless to the proper institution.[101]

Two prominent groups appeared only in very small numbers in the profile sketches. The Jewish tramp was referred to by one worker with the Volunteers of America as a "rara avis." Jewish beggars were rarely seen because they were cared for by their "co-religionists" or fellow Jews. Not until after 1909 was a voice raised concerning the increasing numbers of Jewish tramps.[102] The other large group of Americans not to appear was the Negro. Apparently one reason why the Negro did not tramp is because he was not "socially acceptable." It apparently was difficult for a Negro to beg successfully, and in

New York City the majority of lodging houses did not admit Negroes. One lodging house owner explained to Charles Barnes that white men "would not stand for it."[103] James Forbes, formerly head of the COS mendicancy squad, wrote in 1911 that "a marked feature of trampdom is the caste or color line, which is drawn against the 'shine' or Negro." And there are frequent enough references to this theme in books and articles written by pseudotramps or tramps to indicate that it was true.[104]

Another study, which received wide publicity, was made during March 1914 at the Municipal Lodging House.[105] Fifteen hundred men were interviewed for twenty to thirty minutes each. The results were similar to previous tramp profiles, but the data was presented differently. Six categories of causes were established. Three related to physical and mental incapacity for work, and the three others were moral, moral and industrial, and industrial. Some of the data were broken down into age groups. For example, one fifth of the young, one half of the median group (between thirty-five and thirty-nine years of age), and three-quarters of those over forty years of age drank excessively. The study concluded that "a great many men who have become unemployable will not work or cannot hold a steady job, started on their downward course because of low wages, enforced unemployment, or other industrial conditions for which they were blameless." Thus a large percentage of those in the study classed as being at the Municipal Lodging House for "moral" causes (e.g., alcoholism) "would have been classed for industrial causes (involuntary unemployment) earlier in life."[106]

All these studies gave a new dimension to the tramp. In the first place, he probably was not a voluntary tramp, but a man looking for work or a one-time steady worker who had fallen on hard times. Very possibly he was physically or mentally unable to do sustained labor. The traditional explanations of the origins of tramps accounted for few.

The problem, then, was not merely that of separating the worthy from the unworthy. It was, moreover, complicated by the recognition that worthy men became tramps for many reasons and had to be treated individually. From almost the beginning of the planning for the Municipal Lodging House, many hoped that it would act as a social sieve to sort the homeless according to their problems. Required in this scheme was a man with a sociological background who could decide intelligently between the employable and the unemployable, find work for the employable, and permanent institutional care for the unemployable.[107] The hope that a social secretary could make the Municipal Lodging House operate as a sorting agency was proving illusory. The secretary could not handle the great numbers of applicants, and he did not have proper institutions to which he could refer the homeless.

Journalist Edwin A. Brown toured the country from 1908 to 1910 looking into public accommodations for the homeless unemployed. He would check into a hotel (in New York City, the Waldorf Astoria), dress like a tramp, and then seek a place to stay without money. The following day, he would write an exposé about his poor treatment at the hands of the city authorities. New York's Municipal Lodging House he found the best in the nation because it was the only one that approximated a true clearinghouse, although the concept of one was over a decade old.[108]

For the clearinghouse concept to function effectively, specialized institutions to treat and shelter those unfit for work were required. Reformers had worked hard to get these institutions established. During the panic of 1893, the state had taken responsibility of New York City's insane; Craig Colony for Epileptics was established, and New York had erected a custodial asylum for mental defectives. In 1903, the name of the almshouse on Blackwell's Island was changed to the Home for the Aged and Infirm, and a hospital was set up on the island to receive the physically ill sent from the Municipal Lodging House. Tuberculosis patients were sent to asylums, and reformers hoped to assist them to find work upon release. For those who would not work, the reformers proposed an inebriate colony and a farm colony to force hardened tramps into working. Neither of these institutions was to be in operation by 1916.[109]

To the man without a home in a strange city, New York's Municipal Lodging House was not a clearinghouse nor was it scientific. It provided a bath, a clean bed, fresh clothes, and a shelter from the natural elements and other men. In short, it was relief he badly needed. If he received the relief, he could tolerate the lecturing of men like Theodore Roosevelt: "Help him if he stumbles; Help him up. Help him to walk . . . you can help him only if you try to help him help himself.''[110] This help was the function of relief agencies in New York City. And along with the changing view of involuntary unemployment came changing views on relief and charity as well.

NOTES

1. Many authors today imply that the position was widely acknowledged and accepted as early as the 1870s. The writers often fall into this trap because of their source material. For example, Kenneth Allsop in his popular account, *Hard Travellin':* *The Hobo and His History* (New York, 1967), used socialist newspapers in the Tamiment Library in New York City to get society's view of the tramp. He succeeded, of course, in getting principally a minority view.

2. Charles Albro Barker, *Henry George* (New York, 1955), 121.

3. Henry George, *Progress and Poverty* (New York, 1955), 545, 546, 552, and *Social Problems* (New York, 1934), 129.

4. Henry George, ''The Crime of Poverty,'' April 1, 1885, Russell Sage Collection, and ''How to Help the Unemployed,'' *North American Review* 158 (February 1894): 183-184; Robert H. Cowdrey, *A Tramp in Society* (Chicago, 1891), 168, 235-241. See also H. F. Ring, *The Problem of the Unemployed* (Houston, 1905).

5. Quoted in Allsop, *Hard Travellin'* , 118. See also Herbert Gutman, ''Protestantism and the American Labor Movement: The Christian Spirit in the Gilded Age,'' *American Historical Review* 62 (October 1966): 86-87.

6. Norman Pollack, The *Populist Response to Industrial America: Midwestern Political Thought* (Cambridge, Massachusetts, 1962), chap. 2; Kirk H. Porter and Donald Bruce Johnson, comps., *National Party Platforms, 1840-1960* (2d ed., Urbana, 1961), 90; Sidney Fine, *Laissez Faire and the General Welfare State: A Study of Conflict in American Thought, 1865-1901* (Ann Arbor, 1956), 192, 322-323, 327-328; Frederick C. Mills, *Contemporary Theories of Unemployment and Unemployment Relief* (New York, 1917), chap. 3, Mills's study is much stronger on England than the United States.

7. Causes, theories, and background of the panic are surveyed by Charles Hoffmann, ''The Depression of the Nineties,'' *Journal of Economic History* 16 (June 1956): 137-164; Samuel Rezneck, ''Unemployment, Unrest and Relief in the United States During the Depression of 1893-1897,'' *Journal of Political Economy* 61 (August 1953): 324-345, quotes the phrase ''Industrial Black Friday'' on p. 324; Douglas W. Steeples, ''The Panic of 1893: Contemporary Reflections and Reactions,'' *Mid-America* 47 (July 1965): 155-175; and Rendig Fels, *American Business Cycles, 1865-1897* (Chapel Hill, 1959), 179-228; Richard T. Ely, ''Unemployed,'' *Harper's Weekly 37* (September 2, 1893): 845; *New York Times,* April 22, 1894. Charles Hoffmann, *The Depression of the Nineties: An Economic History* (Westport, Connecticut, 1970), 109, estimates a total unemployment figure of from 2.452 to 2.714 million.

8. Carlos C. Closson, ''Unemployed in American Cities,'' *Quarterly Journal of Economics* 8 (January 1894): 175.

9. "The Unemployed: What Shall Be Done with the Worthy Poor?" *Outlook* 48 (December 30, 1893): 1229-1230.

10. "Comment—Some Notes on the Winter's Distress," *Yale Review* 2 (February 1894): 343.

11. Closson, "Unemployed in American Cities," 201.

12. Josiah Flynt, "The American Tramp," *Contemporary Review* 60 (August 1891): 254; C. W. Noble, "Border Land of Trampdom," *Popular Science Monthly* 50 (December 1896): 253.

13. Robert H. Bremner, *From The Depths: The Discovery of Poverty in the United States* (New York, 1956), 142. Most of the background material in this paragraph is taken from Bremner. Josiah Flynt, *Tramping With Tramps* (New York, 1899).

14. Flynt, "The American Tramp," 254, his *Tramping With Tramps*, 30, 336-354, his "How Men Become Tramps," *Century* (N.S.) 28 (October 1895): 941-945, and his "Homosexuality Among Tramps," in *Studies in the Psychology of Sex*, ed. Havelock Ellis (New York, 1936), II: 359-367. See also NCCC, *Proceedings* (1886), 193.

15. Flynt, *Tramping With Tramps*, ix.

16. Paul U. Kellogg, "Memo," to Edward Devine, February 13, 1907, Papers of NYCOS, Archives of the Community Service Society of New York City. See also NYSCCC, *Proceedings* (1911), 42.

17. Walter A. Wyckoff, *The Workers, An Experiment in Reality: The East* (New York, 1897), vii, viii, 3, 7, 11, 16, 19.

18. Walter Wyckoff, *The Workers, An Experiment in Reality: The West* (New York, 1897), 11, 50. Many of Wyckoff's experiences were published in *Scribner's Magazine*.

19. Ibid., 71, 61, 78, 127, 133.

20. Norman Pollack, ed., The *Populist Mind* (Indianapolis and New York, 1967), 330-332; S. O. Preston, "Treatment of the Unemployed," *Charities Review 3* (March 1894): 222.

21. C.M. Hobbs, "Association Work on the Railways," *Young Men's Era* 19 (October 12, 1893): 1186.

22. *New York Times*, August 18, 19, 1893.

23. Ibid., August 19-26, 1893 (Byrnes's quotation is in the August 26 issue). Louis Lingg was convicted for his alleged participation at the Haymarket Riot and committed suicide by biting on a fulminite cartridge.

24. "Protection and the Proletariat," *Review of Reviews* 10 (July 1894): 67.

25. Donald L. McMurry, *Coxey's Army: A Study of the Industrial Army Movement of 1894* (Boston, 1929), 49. McMurry's is the best study of the industrial army movement. His general view is that the army was composed not of voluntary tramps, but of workmen looking for jobs. Henry E. Roos, "The Tramp Problem: A Remedy," *Forum* 25 (March 1898): 91; *New York Times*, April 7, 22, 1894. Jack London, "Two Thousand Stiffs," in *The Road* (New York, 1907), judged the members of Kelly's Army to be hoboes. Thomas Byrnes (superintendent of the New York Police Department), "Character and Methods of the Men," *North American Review* 451 (June 1894): 697.

26. McMurry, *Coxey's Army*, 220, 222.

27. "Vagabond's Disease," *Nation* 58 (April 12, 1894): 266; *New York Times*, April 8, 22, 1894; *Railroad Gazette*, April 20, 27, May 18, 1894; "Organized Tramp: Coxey's Army," *Nation* 58 (April 26, 1894): 306. "Henrys" referred to the Parisian anarchist and dynamiter, Emile Henry.

28. Louis Adamic, *Dynamite: The Story of Class Violence in America* (reprint, Gloucester, Massachusetts, 1960), 113; Washington *News* quoted in McMurry, *Coxey's Army*, 105.

29. McMurry, *Coxey's Army*, 106, 110-111, 115, 119; *New York Times*, April 27, 1894; "The New Lawlessness," *Nation* 58 (May 10, 1894), 340; "The Coxey Problem," *Nation* (May 17, 1894), 358; W. T. Stead, "Coxeyism: A Character Sketch," *Review of Reviews* 10 (July 1894): 56.

30. "The Unemployed in Boston," *Harper's Weekly* 38 (March 10, 1894): 233-234; *New York Times*, April 5, 1894.

31. Joseph V. Tracy, "A Mission to Coxey's Army," *Catholic World* 59 (August 1894): 66; Stanley Buder, *Pullman: An Experiment in Industrial Order and Community Planning* (New York, 1967), 178.

32. B. O. Flower, "Plutocracies' Bastilles; or Why the Republic is Becoming an Armed Camp," *Arena* 10 (October 1894): 601-621 and "Emergency Measures Which Would Have Maintained Self-Respecting Manhood—The Mississippi Levees," *Arena* 9 (May 1894): 826.

33. "Icy Hand of the Blizzard Brings Untold Suffering," *War Cry*, February 13, 1897, 4-5.

34. For an example see W. J. Gill (editor of the New York *Mail and Express*) to Mayor T. F. Gilroy, February 10, 1895, Mayoralty Papers of Thomas F. Gilroy, Municipal Archives, New York City. For an example of reformer relief, see NYAICP, *Semi-Centennial Annual Reports* (1893-1894), 52.

35. T. B. Veblen, "The Army of the Commonwealth," *Journal of Political Economy* 2 (June 1894): 458.

36. Civic League of St. Louis, *Unregulated Cheap Lodging Houses* (St. Louis, 1913); Josephine Shaw Lowell, "Cheap Lodging Houses: Their Influence on City Pauperism," reprint from the New York *Evening Post*, February 20, 1897 (New York, n.d.), Papers of NYCOS, Archives of the Community Service Society, New York City.

37. Lowell, "Cheap Lodging Houses"; Jacob A. Riis, *The Peril and the Preservation of the Home* (Philadelphia, 1903), 17-21, points out the importance of the home and its influences in preserving the nation and also discusses the danger of homeless men to the nation. Jacob A. Riis, *How the Other Half Lives* (New York, 1957), 55.

38. Alvan F. Sanborn, "Study of Beggars and Their Lodgings," *Forum* 19 (April 1895), 212; City Club of New York, *A Plain Statement of the Election Law as in Force in New York City for the Use of Voters, Watchers, and Election Officers* (New York, 1894); Jefferson M. Levy, comp. *The Elector's Hand Book or Digest of the Laws of the State of New York Applicable to the City of New York* (New York, 1895). New York City Police Department, *Annual Report* (1897), 37; Charles E. Russell, "At the Throat of the Republic," *Cosmopolitan Magazine* 44 (December 1907): 141-157 and (January, 1908), 259-271; John J. McCook, "Some New Phases of the Tramp Problem," *Charities Review* 1 (June 1892): 364.

39. John J. McCook, "The Alarming Proportion of Venal Voters," *Forum* 14 (September 1892): 2; Edward T. Devine, "The Shifting and Floating Population," *Annals* 10 (September 1897): 153; John Glenn, "Cooperation Against Beggary," *Charities Review* 1 (December 1891): 68; Riis, *How the Other Half Lives*, 55.

40. Josephine Shaw Lowell to Commander Booth Tucker, September 30, 1896, reprinted in William Rhinelander Stewart, comp., *The Philanthropic Work of Josephine Shaw Lowell* (New York, 1910), 449; F. W. Motley, "Report on Lodging Houses," October 5, 1912, Robert Hebberd to D. B. Anderson, March 27, 1892, Papers of NYCOS.

41. Jacob Riis, *The Making of an American* (New York, 1947), 44-45.

42. John Lamon (superintendent of Bureau of Police of Philadelphia) to Jacob A. Riis, June 18, 1891; Josiah Kinsey (secretary of Board of Police Commissioners of Baltimore) to Jacob Riis, June 24, 1891; Zilpha D. Smith (General Secretary of the Associated Charities of Boston) to Jacob Riis, June 15, 1891: Papers of Jacob A. Riis, The City College of the City University of New York.

43. Notes written in Riis's hand while on his inspections of the police station in 1893, Papers of Jacob A. Riis; New York City Police Department, *Annual Report* (1894), 12, and *Annual Report* (1895), 12-14; SCAA, *Annual Report* (December 1893), 24.

44. NYCOS, *Annual Report* (1893), 37; Robert Hebberd, "Inspection Report on the Boston's Wayfarer's Lodge," June 2, 1893, Papers of NYCOS.

45. Robert DeForest and C. D. Kellogg, "Plan for Society's Wayfarer's Lodge" to Otto Bannard, August 15, 1893, Papers of NYCOS; "Report of the Committee on the Wayfarer's Lodge," NYCOS, *Annual Report* (1893), 37-41.

46. Josephine Shaw Lowell to Jacob A. Riis, December 4, 1893, February 27, 1897, Papers of Jacob A. Riis. The plan was the subject of discussion in the NYCOS Executive Committee "Minutes," December 5, 1893, Papers of NYCOS.

47. Josephine Shaw Lowell to Jacob A. Riis, December 16, 1893, Papers of Jacob A. Riis; "Report of Committee on Vagrancy submitted to the Conference on Charities,. May 13, 1896," Papers of NYCOS.

48. "A Documentary History of the Wood Yard Compiled by the Secretary of the Wayfarer's Lodge Committee," n.d., 1, Papers of NYCOS; NYCOS, *Monthly Bulletin* (October 25, 1887): 2; Bremner, *From the Depths*, 52.

49. S. S. Bogert, H. J. Rode, James B. Reynolds, and Lawrence Veiller to Secretary of the Woodyard Committee, NYCOS, July 20, 1894, Papers of NYCOS.

50. Ansley Wilcox, "Concerning Labor Tests," *Charities Review* 4 (January 1895): 122.

51. Robert Hebberd to George L. Cheney (general secretary, NYCOS), April 7, 1896, Papers of NYCOS; New York City Police Department, *Special Order 261B* February 11, 1896, Papers of Jacob A. Riis; Peter Conlin (chief of police) to All Commanding Officers, New York City Police Department, February 12, 1896, Papers of NYCOS; New York City Police Department, *Annual Report* (1896), 5, 12; Theodore Roosevelt, "Municipal Administration: New York Police Force," *Atlantic Monthly* 80 (September 1897): 229; "Tramps Lodging House," *Outlook* 71 (July 12, 1902): 670; Josephine Shaw Lowell to Jacob A. Riis, January 30, 1896, Papers of Jacob A. Riis.

52. NYCOS Committee on Mendicancy, "Proposed Rules for the Government of Special Officers Under Its Direction," April 1890, Papers of NYCOS.

53. Notes on Charles D. Kellogg and the Pennsylvania Anti-Freak Bill (Act No. 208, June 5, 1895), Addison Jerome to Charles D. Kellogg, October 2, 1895, Papers of NYCOS.

54. Jerome to Kellogg, October 2, 1895, Papers of NYCOS; Edward T. Devine to Mayor William L. Strong, December 30, 1895, Papers of NYCOS.

55. Charles D. Kellogg to Cornelius Vanderbilt, June 23, 1882, Papers of NYCOS. For a discussion of the man and his method, see Henry T. F. Rhodes, *Alphonse Bertillon: Father of Scientific Detection* (New York, 1956).

56. NYCOS, Case Record, "James Grady, Jr., Mendicancy No. 1295," NYCOS, Case Record, "Owen O'Malley alias Clint," Papers of NYCOS.

57. NYCOS, *Confidential Bulletin No. 126* (October 15, 1903): Section V.

58. Conlin to All Commanding Officers, February 12, 1896, Papers of NYCOS; New York City Police Department, *Special Order No. 2639*, February 2, 1897, Papers of Jacob A. Riis.

59. New York City Police Department, *Special Order No. 2639*, 2, 3.

60. New York *Evening Sun*, January 20, 1896; Josephine Shaw Lowell to Jacob Riis, January 29, 1896, Papers of Jacob A. Riis.

61. Robert W. DeForest to Theodore Roosevelt, February 3, 1897, Papers of NYCOS.

62. John A. Kingsbury, "The Social Usefulness of the Police Force," Conference of Mayors and Other City Officials of the Cities of New York State for the Discussion of Mutual Problems, *Proceedings* (May 1911), 97.

63. Frederic Jennings, "An Open Letter from the New York Charity Organization Society to the Police Commissioner in Regard to Abolition of the Mendicancy Detail; March 28, 1906," *Charities and The Commons* 16 (April 14, 1906): 113, 114; NYCOS, Executive Committee, "Minutes" (March 20, 1906), Papers of NYCOS.

64. James Forbes to Frederic Jennings (chairman of NYCOS Mendicancy Committee), September 23, 1908, Papers of NYCOS.

65. Edward T. Devine to Robert DeForest, September 24, 1908, to Robert Woods (New York City police superintendent), December 12, 1908; NYCOS Executive Committee, "Minutes" (February 24, 1909); Robert Woods to Frank Persons, February 20, 1909; Edward T. Devine to John D. Rockefeller, May 23, 1910: Papers of NYCOS. "Directory of Cripples," *Survey* 32 (April 11, 1914): 66.

66. Rosalie Butler, "Separation of Charities and Correction," *Charities Review* 2 (June 1893): 169.

67. *An Act to Abolish the Department of Public Charities and Correction in the City of New York* . . . (New York, 1895), paragraphs 4 and 5, Papers of NYCOS.

68. SCAA, *Annual Report* (November 1, 1896), 10-12.

69. Ely, "Unemployed," 845.

70. Edward T. Devine, "The Value and Dangers of Investigation," NCCC, *Proceedings* (1897), 199; NYCOS, Executive Committee, "Minutes," January 25, 1898.

71. Elizabeth G. Meier, *A History of the New York School of Philanthropy* (New York, 1954); Lilian Brandt, "History of the Society: 1882-1907," NYCOS, *Annual*

Report (1907), 44-45; Roy Lubove, *The Professional Altruist* (Cambridge, 1965), 140. Today, the New York School of Philanthropy exists as the Columbia University School of Social Work.

72. Robert W. Hebberd, "Charity and Civil Government," *St. Vincent de Paul Quarterly* 3 (November 1898): 270; John M. Glenn, "Address," New York State Conference of Charities and Correction, *Proceedings* (1901), 15; William R. Stewart, "The Progress of Twenty Years," State Board of Charities of the State of New York, *Annual Report* (1902), 178.

73. Flynt, "The American Tramp," 254-255.

74. J. J. McCook, "The Tramp Census and Its Revelations," *Forum* 15 (August 1893): 758, 759.

75. J. J. McCook, "The Tramp Problem: What It Is and What to Do With It," NCCC, *Proceedings* (1895), 288-302, and his "Increase of Tramping: Cause and Cure," *Independent* 54 (March 13, 1902): 620.

76. Orlando Lewis, *Vagrancy in the United States* (New York, 1907), 1.

77. Orlando F. Lewis, "Report of the Committee on Vagrancy and Homelessness," NYSCCC, *Proceedings* (1907), 237, *Vagrancy*, 7; and "A National Committee on Vagrants," *Charities and The Commons* 18 (June 29,1907): 342-344. Frank V. Whiting, "Trespassers Killed on Railways, Who Are They?" *Scientific American* 73, Supplement No. 1897 (May 11, 1912), 303, 304, refutes Lewis's contention that most trespassers were tramps.

78. NYSCCC, *Proceedings* (1907), 252-259.

79. Leon Ray Livingston, *The Curse of Tramp Life* (Erie, 1912), 25, 100.

80. Orlando F. Lewis, "The Tramp Problem," *Annals* 40 (March 1912): 226; C. E. Adams, "Real Hobo: What He Is and How He Lives," *Forum* 33 (June 1902): 449.

81. Walter S. Beach, "The Danger of Unskill," *Popular Science Monthly* 77 (August 1910): 185; "Manual Training—Its Destiny," *Young Men's Era* (October 26, 1893): 1219; Frederick Almy, "The End of Poverty in Cities," Annual Conference of Mayors and Other Officials of the Cities of New York State, *Proceedings* (1912), 181; C. R. Henderson, "The Relation of Philanthropy to Social Order and Progress," NCCC, *Proceedings (1899)*, 11; NYSCCC, *Proceedings* (1911), 50; William E. Dodge, "The Value of Property Depends on the Character of Young Men," *Association Men* 26 (March 1901): 189. Jacob A. Riis, "Wearing Our Way," *Survey* 22 (May 1, 1909): 171.

82. Richard A. Skolnik, "The Crystallization of Reform in New York City, 1890-1917" (Ph.D. diss., Yale University, 1965) explores in depth the participation of reformers in municipal politics. *Banquet to R. F. Cutting and E. R. L. Gould* (n.p., 1902), 33, 42, 66.

83. See chapter 3. "Menace From Below: Labor in America, 1900-1914," in Maxwell H. Bloomfield, *Alarms and Diversions: The American Mind Through American Magazines, 1900-1914* (The Hague and Paris, 1967); "The Social Unrest," *Cosmopolitan Magazine* 41 (July 1906): 301.

84. Jacob H. Schiff to Lillian Wald, June 10, 12, 1907, Papers of Lillian Wald, Columbia University.

85. "A Review of the World," *Current Literature* 44 (May 1908): 461; *New York Times*, March 29, 1908, 5.

86. James F. Jackson to Mary Richmond, March 21, 1908, Papers of Mary Richmond, Columbia University School of Social Work; "Meetings of the Unemployed," *Association Men* 33 (March 1908): 267; Alice L. Higgins (Associated Charities of Boston) to Frances MacLean, January 18, 1908, Papers of Mary Richmond; "The Unemployed," *Outlook* 88 (February 1, 1908): 241-242; Leah Hannah Feder, *Unemployment Relief in Periods of Depression: A Study of Relief Measures Adopted in Certain American Cities, 1857 Through 1922* (New York, 1936), 197.

87. NYCOS Executive Committee, "Minutes," January 15, 1908, Papers of NYCOS; "A Review of the World," 461-468; Arthur P. Kellogg, "Traffic Squad at Union Square," *Charities and The Commons* 20 (April 4, 1908): 9-12.

88. "A Review of the World," 461, 463; *New York Times*, March 29, 1908, 1, 2, 5, March 30, 1908, 1-3, March 31, 1908, 1.

89. "The Emergence of Class Consciousness," *World To-Day* 15 (December 1908): 1195-1196.

90. Paul Frederick Brissenden, *The I.W.W.: A Study of American Syndicalism* (New York, 1919), 8-9 passim; Bloomfield, *Alarms and Diversions*, 93.

91. Joyce L. Kornbluh, ed., *Rebel Voices: An I.W.W. Anthology* (Ann Arbor, 1964), 71.

92. Edmund Kelly, *The Elimination of the Tramp* (New York and London, 1908), 104; E. L. Bailey, "Tramps and Hoboes," *Forum* 26 (October 1898): 220; *New York Times*, April 6, 1968, 40.

93. NYAICP, Board of Managers, "Minutes," January 20, 1908, Papers of NYAICP.

94. John B. Andrews to the Advisory Committee for the Municipal Lodging House, January 11, 1910, Papers of NYCOS.

95. H. F. Cook, "Report of the Social Secretary at the Municipal Lodging House for October, 1910," Papers of NYCOS; see also his report for January 1911, 5, 7.

96. Alice W. Solenberger, *One Thousand Homeless Men: A Study of Original Records* (New York, 1911), 3, 13.

97. Ibid., 232 passim. Solenberger's familiarity with Lewis's work can be seen in her footnotes on pp. 215, 232. The Russell Sage Foundation's Charity Organization Department in New York City advertised the book as a classic that all social workers should read. *Charity Organization Bulletin* 2 (June 1911): 1.

98. Mortimer M. Singer to Charles Merrill (chairman of the COS Woodyard), November 19, 1912; Charles Merrill to Mortimer M. Singer, December 2, 1912; Mortimer M. Singer to Johnston DeForest, February 10, 1913: Papers of NYCOS.

99. Rev. Frank C. Laubach to Charles Merrill, "Case Histories at the Woodyard," February 28, 1914, Papers of NYCOS; NYCOS, Executive Committee, "Minutes," September 30, 1914, Papers of NYCOS; Rev. Frank C. Laubach, *Why There Are Vagrants: A Study Based on an Examination of One Hundred Men* (New York, 1916).

100. Laubach, *Why There Are Vagrants*, 48, 60-64, 72, 81.

101. Charles B. Barnes, "The Homeless Man: A Study in New York City," 1914, 2 vols., I:382, 387, ms. located at Columbia University School of Social Work. Hutch-

ins Hapgood, "Organized Charity—The Radicals' Viewpoint," (New York) *Globe and Commercial Advertiser*, March 6, 1913, perhaps sheds some light on why the study was never published. Hapgood accused the Russell Sage Foundation, which secretly sponsored Barnes's study, of suppressing (or at least not publishing) a study on tanneries. He said that there were four or five similar reports also not made public because "in the opinion of the radicals they revealed too strikingly the industrial causes of poverty."

102. "A Trip to the Bowery with the Police Patrol Wagon," *Volunteer's Gazette* (June 5, 1897): 15; I. L. Nascher, *The Wretches of Povertyville: A Sociological Study of the Bowery* (Chicago, 1909), 128-130; Boris D. Bogen, "The Jewish Tramp," *Jewish Charities* 1 (November 1910): 3-5; Barnes, "The Homeless Man," I: 14.

103. Barnes, "The Homeless Man," I: 41.

104. Flynt, "The American Tramp, Geographically," 109; James Forbes, "The Tramp; or Caste on the Jungle," *Outlook* 98 (August 19, 1911): 874; G. Mullin, *Adventures of a Scholar Tramp* (New York, 1925), 189.

105. Stuart Rice, "Report on Investigation of Homeless Men Made at the MLH March, 1914," n.d., Papers of NYCOS; New York *Evening World*, May 14, 1914, clipping, Papers of NYCOS; New York *Press*, January 25, 1915; John A. Kingsbury, "Rehabilitation of the Homeless Man," NYSCCC, *Proceedings* (1914), 33.

106. Rice, "Report," 15, 13. This theme was treated earlier by others. For example, see Robert Hunter, *Poverty* (New York, 1965), 131; Scott Nearing, *Social Adjustment* (New York, 1911), 276; and Samuel Rabinowitch, "Transients," *Jewish Charities* 2 (June 1912): 17.

107. "Summary of the Report of William Albert Whiting on the Investigation of the Homeless Unemployed which was Held at the Municipal Lodging House in March, 1914," n.d., typed copy, Papers of Mary Richmond; "Diagnosing the Workless," *Literary Digest* 48 (May 16, 1914): 1200-1205; Alice L. Higgins, "Comparative Advantages of Municipal and COS Lodging Houses," NCCC, *Proceedings* (1904), 152; "Tramps—Cost Prevention," *Christian Science Monitor*, May 27, 1913; NCCC, *Proceedings* (1914), 459; Solenberger, *One Thousand Homeless Men*, 23; John A. Kingsbury, "Humanity and Economy in the Care of the City's Poor," to Mayor John Purroy Mitchel, December 31, 1915, letter of transmittal for the New York City Department of Public Charities, *Annual Report* (1915).

108. Edwin A. Brown, *"Broke," The Man Without A Dime* (Chicago, 1913), 340, Appendix.

109. SCAA, *Annual Report* (1896), 10-12; Schneider and Deutsch, *History of Public Welfare*, 101, 78; New York City Department of Charities, *Quarterly Report* (January-March, 1903), 3; and *Annual Report* (1909), 68; NYSCCC, *Proceedings* (1913), 120; NYSCC, *Proceedings* (1907), 243; Kingsbury, "The Rehabilitation of the Homeless Man," 37.

110. Theodore Roosevelt, "An Address," *Association Men* 28 (June 1903): 392.

3

"Soup, Soap, and Salvation":

Relief and the Unemployed

AFTER THE 1870s, the city became the delta of rivers of depression and economic displacement. The stream that swept up the human debris dislocated by its force and deposited it in the city was almost irresistible to the unemployed; at the end of the journey was the hope of work and relief. Although few homeless found jobs in depression years, relief in some form was almost always available to them—in good times or bad—even though it was only on a subsistence level. But no law guaranteed such relief. The State Pauper Act of 1873 directed the secretary of the State Board of Charities to return any homeless individual who had not lived sixty consecutive days in any New York county to his place of origin or official residence in the United States. In actual practice, however, few of the homeless unemployed were forced to appear before the board and fewer were deported involuntarily.[1]

The Pauper Act certainly did not discourage the thousands of homeless unemployed who entered New York City to find work after the panic of 1873. When those who found no work ran out of money, they applied for relief along with thousands of unemployed residents. Newspaper accounts of destitution alarmed the public, and emergency relief committees sprang up all over the city. Some five thousand to seven thousand hungry ate daily at thirty-four free soup kitchens, and free lunches were made available at many other locations in the city.

The homeless slept wherever they could find shelter: in hallways, boats, sheds, missions, and police stations.

This outpouring of relief was far from gratifying to those who feared that indiscriminate charity (relief based on apparent need) destroyed character or even created paupers. Whether relief should be offered on the basis of apparent or actual need was to be debated over the next forty years. The traditional approach of the reformers was clearly stated by the New York Association for Improving the Condition of the Poor in 1874: "morbid sympathy" generated more needy persons, and demoralized and pauperized those touched by it.[2]

In 1842, Robert Hartley had founded the New York Association for Improving the Condition of the Poor to combat the "questionable" relief methods employed in New York City during the panic of 1837. Formed in a climate of American individualism and laissez-faire economics, and also affected by the debates over the English Poor Laws, its attitude toward relief in 1873 was predictable.[3] From its inception, the organization had not "blindly" dispensed its favors but "detected the imposter and arrested the vagrant." According to the AICP, those seeking aid should not "suffer unrelieved," but should receive relief in accordance with principles that best suited the community, as well as the individual. If able-bodied, males "should be compelled to work or left to suffer the consequences of their misconduct."[4]

To keep relief from ruining character, the AICP membership and the reformers who joined the COS agreed that "indiscriminate" relief should be stopped. While the two organizations could not restrict churches from extending such relief, they did work to end all public relief outside of public institutions. At their insistence, and also since a shortage of public money existed, such relief was temporarily halted in the summer of 1874. When it was resumed, the only direct relief made available was coal for needy families and cash for blind adults. In 1879, even these forms of public relief ended. Josephine Shaw Lowell, who was instrumental in ending all public relief outside of institutions, noted with satisfaction that the event did not precipitate the suffering that many had anticipated.[5]

The desire of the social welfare reformers to end indiscriminate charity in New York had led to the formation in 1873 of the Bureau of Charities, comprised of many relief agencies. The AICP joined the bureau because it shared common policies with other relief agencies. Once the bureau began operating, however, the AICP came to fear the loss of its own identity among so many constituted agencies and withdrew.[6] But the AICP retained its relief policy. Applicants seeking aid were all investigated for worthiness. To an organization that believed in self-help and individualism, the large number of claimants for relief was frustrating and the huge percentage of fraudulent claims disgusting. One AICP official suggested that perhaps "each applicant must be considered as unworthy, until the contrary is proven," rather than the reverse.[7] Although the AICP official was perhaps only talking tongue-in-cheek, the homeless unemployed often believed that agencies staffed by social welfare reformers felt precisely that the destitute were unworthy.

On the other hand, churches and organizations with religious affiliation generally considered the homeless persons "worthy" of aid, and thus provided relief in a manner designed to provoke gratitude rather than anger or shame. The concept of relief in religious thinking was closely intertwined, if not identical with, the virtue of charity, and assistance could not easily be denied to those who asserted need for it. Churchgoers were continually admonished with the Beatitudes. Nevertheless, church philosophy concerning the homeless unemployed meshed smoothly with individualistic notions in the nineteenth century. Many clergy felt that the man who now sought help had fallen in the eyes of his Creator. And his fall, caused by sin, was a personal failure rather than one of society.

Thus the churches felt justified, if not impelled, to provide relief to the bodies while they tried to reclaim the souls for God. The fallen men were told to accept their earthly plight as a blessing from God. Indeed, they were fortunate that God had imposed misery upon them so that by patience and resignation they might attain the "Crown of Life Eternal." However, the unemployed should regard their condition not "as a command to, or permission for idleness, but rather as a direct incentive to effort." In spite of such admonitions to work harder while accepting their lot, the churches did not threaten to withhold relief if the unemployed did not apply themselves, because it was "un-Christian" to do so. Thomas Mulry of the St. Vincent de Paul Society expressed precisely the relationship of the homeless unemployed to the churches in repeating the Benedictine admonition: "Let all strangers be received and welcomed as Christ himself."[8]

The tramps were the "strangers" in the nineteenth century for whom the rescue mission was developed. Like the older religious institutions, the Protestant missions saw the problem of the homeless wanderer as one of individual failure brought on by sin—usually alcoholism.[9] While supporting antisaloon activities to end the temptation of drink, the missions believed that the only effective way to reclaim the spiritual derelicts was to teach them to accept Christ as their savior. The tramps then would be strengthened internally and spiritually and might more easily triumph over external adversity.

With this goal in mind, missions opened on the most notorious streets and alleys in all the large cities. On New York's Water Street in the 1870s and the Bowery in later years, sin and salvation stood side by side. Water Street was a particularly apt example. Dark dens filled with drink, song, sex, and mysterious disappearances were inhabited by the most improbable of characters. At Kit Burns' Rat Pit, where dogs fought dozens of rats in the fabled arena, Burns' son-in-law on special occasions would enter the arena against the rats armed only with his teeth. Another resident, Gallus Mag, a six-foot English-woman, who held up her skirt with suspenders, wore a pistol on her belt, and carried a club. She fought at the least provocation and treasured in a jar of alcohol the ears that she bit off her opponents in combat. The holy missionary who opened the Water Street Mission, Jerry McAuley, was no less colorful.[10]

McAuley spoke with a slum accent and was a powerfully built, rough-hewn man with long arms and huge hands. Based on his physical appearance, contemporary physiognomists pronounced him a bully and a criminal on sight; his forehead retreated from deep-set eyes, which peered over a nose and mouth too large for his face. He had served seven years in Sing Sing Prison and was widely known as a former alcoholic and thief. McAuley's wife Maria, a motherly, gentle woman, assisted him on the platform. She publicly testified often about her former career as a prostitute. All of their experiences helped make Jerry McAuley and his wife be accepted by those whom they wished to serve.

What usually made the missions initially attractive to the home-

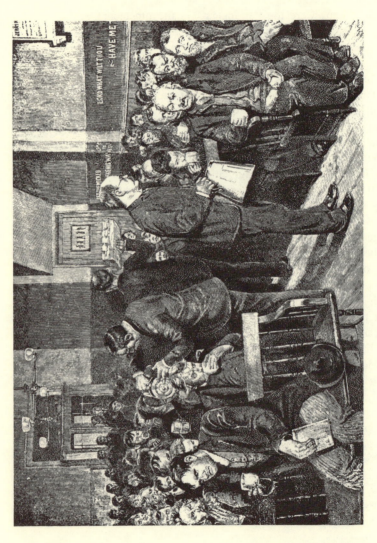

Coffee Night at the Water Street Mission

Helen Campbell, *Darkness at Daylight* (Hartford, 1897), 85

less, however, was not the men like McAuley who ran them, but rather shelter from the elements, if only for an hour. The missions looked much alike. Each evening, hard wooden benches facing a raised platform slowly filled with myriads of wanderers who had entered with no questions asked. The men, and occasionally women, slumped heavily onto the benches and relaxed under the influence of the warmth of the room and the tones of the organ. Looking around, the homeless saw a room whose drabness reflected their own existence and which was only slightly altered by religious verses inscribed in frames or painted on the walls themselves.

At the appointed hour, a missionary mounted the platform and began the services with a prayer. Hymns followed, and then the missionary gave a brief sermon as the services evolved slowly toward the climax—the testimonials. Generally the missionary, or some guest on the visitors' bench facing the congregation, began the testimonies by reciting the degradations of his past and the beauty of his life once he had committed himself to Jesus. Eventually testimony was heard from regular members of the congregation who had found salvation and then, hopefully, one or more of those yet unregenerate would be sufficiently moved to publicly confess past sins and to accept Christ.

This confessional, of course, was looked upon by the missions as the key to returning men to society. Outsiders called the witnesses who later received food and lodging "mission stiffs." Many, perhaps even most, who attended services were never affected by testimonies. For example, Walter Wyckoff who entered one mission out of a freezing rain dreaded the intonation of the benediction, which signalled his return to the street. However, some men's lives apparently did change for the better after their religious experience in a mission.[11] William James described the conversion of Samuel Hopkins Hadley at McAuley's second mission, The Cremorne. Hadley was an alcoholic who, in the midst of others' testimonies, became overwhelmed with guilt and remorse for his own sins. Falling to his knees in front of all, he shook with fear and became confused. Then his face measurably relaxed and he regained composure as the feeling of rebirth swept over and through him.[12] Hadley never drank again and went on to become the director of the Water Street Mission, later opening a mission of his own.

For the missionaries and some of the congregation, the crucial point of the services was the testimonies, but, for the needy, the climax came after the services, when the mission passed out food and arranged shelter. The Bowery Mission, which opened in 1879 with the aid and encouragement of McAuley, provided such relief. In the 1890s, after its incorporation and affiliation with the *Christian Herald*, the mission was financially able to provide more relief than ever before. It offered sleeping accommodations for two hundred each night, and Mrs. Sarah J. Bird, "The Mother of the Bowery," gave out coffee and sandwiches after services twice each week. Funds were not unlimited, but the missions gave as much as possible to the men who attended services.

In addition to the relief provided in conjunction with services, missions offered relief in other ways. Some operated employment offices, and almost all had bathing and shaving facilities to make their guests more acceptable to all the senses. Some ran bread lines, especially during cold spells. For example, the Bowery Mission provided a "promenade breakfast" of coffee and rolls to a "bread line" of over one thousand men nightly. It served the breakfast at one o'clock in the morning in order to make certain that the men seeking the food were really without lodging for the night.[13] Owen Kildare, a contemporary social critic, watching the trembling line inch forward one blustery evening, felt that it was worth "offending sociology by offering the warming cup of coffee to the poor famished creatures."[14] The observers from the COS did not agree, invariably judging that few of the men on the line were actually "hopelessly homeless" or deserving.[15] They criticized the practice of some missions that either let too many men sleep in the same room or use rooms not designed for sleeping.[16] The criticisms had no effect on the missions—they would not send a hungry man out into the night when food, room, and possible salvation were at hand.

In spite of public criticism by the NYCOS and NYAICP, the missions at the lower end of Manhattan were able to enlist active administrative and financial assistance from wealthy members of those organizations. This was particularly true in the 1870s and 1880s when the rescue missions seemed to offer one of the few paths to the regeneration of the tramps. William E. Dodge, a member of Congress and a founder of the YMCA in New York City, was a generous and constant contributor to McAuley's missions. Dodge's wife obtained for McAuley a deputy sheriff's badge so that he might operate more freely around the lower reaches of New York City. A trustee of McAuley's Water Street Mission, Robert Fulton Cutting, represented one of New York's most prestigious families, known for its activities in business, banking, and philanthropy. Cutting eventually became president of the NYAICP. Both men later became life members of the COS.[17]

Among the major contributors to the Bowery Mission in 1883 were Cornelius Vanderbilt, who also handsomely supported the Railroad Branch of the YMCA, and James Talcott, later president of the New York Stock Exchange. The *Annual Report* of the Bowery Mission in 1883 acknowledged the support of such people: "It is gratifying to note that from year to year the importance and value of this work [of] the Mission has commended itself more and more to businessmen. Its reformatory influence upon the lawless and dangerous classes is a matter of record."[18]

General William Booth, the founder of the Salvation Army in England, was also particularly interested in working with these "dangerous" classes, which he included in that part of society he called "the submerged tenth."[19] Booth sent the Salvation Army's first official mission to the United States in 1880 to work among the urban poor. Its purpose was to redeem "fallen souls" for Christianity through a mixture of social and religious services. The fallen might be converted to the Army's faith, but the Salvationists were satisfied when the poor returned to the churches of their choice. Its workers went to the slums, alleys, bars, and brothels to urge "the fallen" to attend services much like those at the rescue missions; but men who gave testimony and accepted Christ often joined the Army as Salvationists. Because of this, public opinion ordinarily excluded the Salvationist ministers from the reverence granted most clergy, holding the Salvationists to be only a step above the drunkards whom they saved.[20]

Booth spelled out the social schemes of the Army in his book, *In Darkest England and the Way Out* (1891). Upon its publication, Booth's daughter-in-law Maud and his son Ballington began immediately to expand the social work of the Salvation Army in the United States. One of their first actions was to provide shelter for the "weary head of the homeless tramp." To answer the question

of what should be done with the "out of works," the Booths proposed
to open shelter houses where the tramps could receive plain, good,
substantial food. After supplying their bodily needs, the tramps were
to be brought "within the influence of that grace which supplies their
spiritual needs."[21] In 1891 the first low-cost Salvation Army lodging
house opened in Greenwich Village for 64 men, and by 1900 the
Army had six shelters in New York City with accommodations for
over 700. In addition the Army provided day nurseries, food depots,
and other social services.

The churches did not accept the Salvation Army at first. The
Army's methods, military dress and customs, and, in the beginning,
British accents, marked them as being different. When a church north
of New York City in Hartford, Connecticut, refused to let a Salvationist preach in its pulpit, the Reverend John S. Kimball lectured his
congregation on the virtues of tolerance. Certainly, he pointed out,
if God "wants to reach down amid the muck and filth and coarseness
and brutality of the lowest strata of society . . . he does not send
an Emerson or a Channing, but a redeemed rum-seller or a converted
pugilist to do it."[22]

Gradually the hard work of the "redeemed" and the "converted"
in the field of social service, along with enlightened leadership,
improved the Army's public image. The New York *Tribune* reported
that public reaction had evolved from violent persecution through
"contemptuous toleration" to acceptance and the acknowledgment
that the Army was doing "good." Even though the social work was
what caught the public imagination, and the Army emphasized this
aspect of its services publicly, the Salvationists were not permitted
to forget that it was only an aid to the primary work of the
Army—saving souls.[23]

In the 1890s, the Salvation Army expected all those who planned
to sleep in its facilities to attend services first in an effort to save
their souls. Yet the bodies had to be saved as well. To do this without
destroying the needy's character, the Army charged the homeless a
small fee for food and lodging. If unable to pay, a man was generally
required to do chores in return for food and lodging.[24] The Army
believed in helping men to help themselves. Yet the New York reformers considered the Army's system to be indiscriminate charity
because of the low fees. Thus, the reformers said, the Salvationists

were actually contributing to the problem of tramps. General Booth himself was ambivalent about the reasons for the tramps, and his ambivalence was reflected in the ideas of American Salvationists. For example, Richard Holz said that most tramps were victims of their environment and circumstances, but he added that if there were to be "a permanent improvement in the circumstances of these people, there first must be a renewal of character and a change of the inner man, which can be brought only by the grace and power of our Lord Jesus Christ."[25]

Another organization that provided relief to the homeless unemployed was the Young Men's Christian Association (YMCA). In 1872, the YMCA began its work in New York City when it opened the Bowery Branch for destitute men. Although oriented toward religious principles, the YMCA did not attempt conversion to Christianity as did the evangelical missions. Along with the institutional churches, it preached self-help to attain its goal of "uplifting the whole man instead of a fraction of him and to the salvation of the society as well as that of the individual."[26]

Its Bowery Branch taught that "in order to be an acceptable Christian and good citizen, one must exercise his brain and hands in self-supporting works" because God only respected those who respected themselves. The branch worked to change men who were downhearted and discouraged, "either through their own indiscretions or the power of bad habits," into hard working, self-respecting, and law-abiding citizens.[27] To do this, the YMCA provided men with food, clothing, baths, shaves, industrial training, transportation, and employment services. It preferred to provide most of these services to the men at low cost to teach them self-respect and independence. If men had no money, however, it provided the services anyway as a "loan," which it hoped the men would repay once they became self-sufficient. One annual report noted that about half of the men had repaid the YMCA for the assistance received free as a "loan."[28]

The YMCA's apparently successful method of helping men to help themselves by providing a multitude of services encouraged other agencies to follow its lead. The Industrial Christian Alliance, incorporated in 1891, had as its motto, "Helping men to help themselves." Its objective was to provide a home for the homeless, give them food, clothing, a bath, and generally to put them under "Christian influences'' until they were physically able to work in existing positions in the labor market.[29]

Thus the missions, the Salvation Army, and the YMCA blamed individual shortcomings when a man became a tramp, but all recognized the environmental importance of home and parents in helping the individual become an integral part of organized society. The organizations tried to keep their buildings as clean and as homelike as possible, not only to make their homeless feel more comfortable, but to remind them of the homes left behind.[30] Signs like ''There's No Place Like Home'' and ''How Long Since You've Written Mother?'' adorned the walls of hallways and lounges as reminders and also as suggestions to reestablish contact. At the religious services, one of the most popular hymns was ''Oh Where Is My Wandering Boy Tonight?'' which told each man he was ''the joy of his mother's pride.'' These various appeals to the wanderers were made in the hope that the young men might end their tramping. But this was rarely the outcome.

As the winter of 1893-1894 approached, New York newspapers predicted great hardships among the poor because of unemployment. But the reformers believed that the popular press was greatly exaggerating conditions and would make the public more willing to donate to emergency relief schemes if any were proposed.[31] In an attempt to forestall any indiscriminate outpouring, the COS in September 1893 sponsored a petition presented to the citizens of New York City. The petition acknowledged the existence of bad conditions, but, using the traditional arguments, it urged citizens not to give relief without investigation because such action would only pauperize the recipients and attract vagrants. Seventeen agencies providing relief in one form or another signed the petition, which was published in New York newspapers.[32]

But the thousands of unemployed coming into New York City, in addition to the unemployed residents, made it difficult for those who signed the petition to maintain their principles. Existing relief agencies proved hopelessly inadequate to deal with all the needy. The emergency conditions convinced some that due to the special conditions, the doors of relief should be opened as widely as possible until the crisis was over.[33] One of the trustees of the Bowery Mission stated that, while the methods of the charity organization societies were excellent "in ordinary circumstances," they were too slow in a crisis.[34]

Prominent New York newspapers rapidly established special funds and advertised them widely in spite of reformer protests. The *World* had a bread fund, the *Herald* a clothing fund, and the *Tribune* a coal fund. Wealthy individuals, such as Nathan Straus, set up special funds with their own money. Churches did what they could, and the American Red Cross provided relief. The reformers, like everyone else, were simply overwhelmed by the numbers of needy. Even if they had been given the opportunity to investigate all the applicants applying to relief societies, the task could not have been accomplished. For example, the *Herald* decided to cooperate with its critics and referred applicants for its clothing fund to COS. In ten days, four thousand applicants appeared at the COS. Needless to say, the society was frustrated. It was not staffed to take care of such a large number of applicants, and, in addition, it doubted the value of the fund in the first place. The COS feared, however, that to turn down the *Herald* would have been a rejection of the principle that investigation was necessary before any relief was given. Even more important was the fear of incurring the possible future wrath of a powerful adversary. Thus the COS accepted the work, but the investigations of the applicants were perfunctorily performed for pragmatic reasons rather than fulfillment of principle.[35]

In addition to the special funds established by private sources, the New York City administration tried to provide relief for its beleaguered citizens. In a meeting of representatives from all city departments in January 1894, Mayor Thomas F. Gilroy urged them to hire all possible additional help within existing budgets. The commissioners of street cleaning, public works, and parks all reported doing so, but the extra hiring affected less than a thousand men. The mayor then proposed unprecedented programs to aid the unemployed. First, he recommended a special public works program to improve Central Park, which would be financed by a special bond issue of a million dollars. Second, he requested that all city employees donate not less than 1 percent of their salaries to provide additional relief funds.[36] He also formed a Citizen's Relief Fund Committee and urged city residents to donate money, which the committee would then distribute to existing relief agencies. The committee was a thoroughly blue-blooded one, composed of such famous New Yorkers as Cornelius Vanderbilt, Jacob Ruppert, Eldridge T. Gerry, William E. Dodge, and J. P. Morgan. The funds collected by this committee went to the AICP, the Society of St. Vincent de Paul, and the United Hebrew Charities. The employees' donations went principally to these three agencies and the Relief Association of the 23d and 24th Wards.[37]

The consensus in the winter of 1893-1894 was that an emergency situation existed in New York and that unprecedented relief activity was essential. Humanitarianism was, of course, involved, but a fear persisted that if sufficient relief were not made available, dire consequences might follow. For example, the AICP anticipated "riot and discord" because of the unemployment. An editorial in the YMCA's *Young Men's Era* in September 1893 defended the unemployed as willing to work and said that they were not all anarchists and loafers. The editorial writer feared that too many citizens were growing increasingly distrustful and suspicious of those who had only labor to sell. Social classes had to work together to provide a livelihood or relief for all men. If the unemployed could find no work, "they must starve or adopt the only other alternative, rebel." What might follow would only be the "logical sequence," that is, "the suicide of a nation."[38]

Edward T. Devine of the COS noted that charity was considered "a palliative, modifying in some degree the hardships of the industrial process and so reconciling the elements which would otherwise be in revolt." While he agreed that there was some truth in this position, he asserted that the desire to reclaim and efficiently help the homeless "should inspire the community rather than a desire merely for self-protection." Nonetheless, fear partly inspired relief giving. An article in *Harper's Weekly* in the middle of the winter of 1893-1894 praised the enormous relief activity as inspiring, because "such generous assistance as is extending now to the unemployed tends to weld class with class," and thereby strengthens the republic.[39]

Even New York reformers became convinced of the emergency needs and supported the Citizen's Relief Fund Committee, although it violated their principles of voluntarism and investigation. In 1894 at the NCCC, Charles D. Kellogg, organizing secretary of the NYCOS, in describing the events did not roundly criticize the mayor's proposal for public works as one might have expected.[40] And even more surprisingly, the reformers organized special work relief committees of their own. Josephine Shaw Lowell, who had vociferously opposed outdoor relief, helped organize the East Side Relief Committee, explaining that New York was suffering from an "acute disease" and, therefore, had to be aided. But care was needed in giving this aid lest the condition of unemployment become "chronic" as, for example, in London. Thus the East Side Relief Committee tried to follow charity organization principles as best it could.[41]

Josephine Shaw Lowell, like the founders of the NYAICP, was deeply influenced by the English experience in formulating her ideas about relief. In a report furnished to the State Board of Charities in 1884 and in her book, *Public Relief and Private Charity* (1884), she quoted at length from the British Poor Law Commission of 1834, summarizing its arguments against outdoor relief. The law sapped habits of industry, discouraged frugality, encouraged improvident marriages, and produced discontent. In her view, the situation was the same in the United States. She insisted that "every man in this country *at least* should be able to earn enough to support himself [emphasis added]" and that public relief should be given only when men driven to desperation threaten violence, or whenever it is to the benefit of the entire community.[42]

Mrs. Lowell felt churches and others misconstrued the real meaning of charity. By her definition, charity was "a voluntary, free, beneficent action performed toward those who are in more destitute circumstances and inferior world position"; in other words, public relief was eliminated because it was not voluntary. Also since indiscriminate charity and systematic doles were harmful in her view, they did not fall under her definition of true charity. She labeled as "indiscriminate" any relief given without investigating the applicant. Such thinking led the COS to oppose any establishment subsidized by donations, which sold meals below cost because such actions tended to pauperize the recipient.[43]

In 1890, Mrs. Lowell stated that many mistakes in relief-giving were occurring due to the abuse of the word "charity." She also asserted that relief-giving would always fail because it sought "material ends by material means" while true relief aided the character as well. She used a biblical quotation to put her point across: "What shall it profit a man if he gain the whole world and lose his own soul?"[44]

The East Side Relief Committee was typical of similar special relief agencies, organized by volunteers in many cities, which provided relief by developing work projects for the unemployed. Begun in New York with a contribution of a thousand dollars by Seth Low, and with other financial and administrative aid from wealthy New Yorkers, the committee began its work. Since complete investigation of all clients was impossible, the committee tried to control and limit grants of relief by giving ticket entitlements for work to churches, philanthropic societies, and trade unions. They hoped these organizations would give the tickets to those known to be deserving. When the employment seeker presented a ticket, the East Side Relief Committee set the applicant to work on jobs that it hoped would not compete with the existing labor market, such as street sweeping, tailoring, and tenement renovation. Sewing and quilting work were sometimes given to women in their homes. Although the reformers designed this program to help families, many of the homeless unemployed were aided by the funds given by this committee to the missions. All in all, the committee provided work for about five thousand applicants.[45]

The emergency situation forced the reformers to reconsider their philosophy of relief and charity, or at least to justify their actions in terms of their principles. In the case of the East Side Relief Committee, Josephine Shaw Lowell and its other members adopted a resolution in 1894 condemning their own work, which all had formerly found effective. Their resolution was designed to discourage other groups from establishing similar programs. And in one of its final actions, the East Side Relief Committee suggested that the mayor's Relief Committee use any excess funds to study the problem of overcrowding in relation to unemployment, rather than to use any more funds for relief-giving.[46]

To promote character, reformers insisted that the needy should work for any relief received. The homeless unemployed were usually prepared to ask for work in return for food or money and most people were prepared to give relief, but only if the unemployed performed chores first. The reformers anticipated that only "real" tramps would avoid work, so that offering work to an unemployed man could serve as a condition of relief, as well as a test of worthiness. Joseph Lee expressed the point in poetry of sorts on the cover of an antitramp leaflet:

> Dirt without work
> Delights the shirk
> The tramp or hobo flagrant;
> Work without dirt
> Rewards desert
> And terrifies the vagrant.[47]

The reformers opposed on principle the provision of special "make work" relief projects, such as the East Side Relief Committee had made available. After the challenge to order presented by the huge numbers of tramps and other unemployed during the panic of 1893, however, the reformers qualified their position. If an emergency situation did exist, such relief might be risked if the work was underpaid, unadvertised, and hard.[48] However, during good economic times such work relief was never excusable. It led men to indolence, weakened independence, and undermined the existing labor market. One lecturer in England viewed American charity as perhaps too generous overall, but he was pleased that the charity was at least "qualified by the obligation of self-help" such as this kind of work provided.[49]

Charles D. Kellogg referred to the tramps in 1894 as "that great army of city locusts which annually glean the fields of disorganized and municipal charity." For these unworthies, the tramps who avoided work, the only cure was work. And if they would not do so voluntarily, they had to be forced.[50] In most cases this meant labor under confinement by order of the public authorities. The reformers thus supported workhouses, instead of county jails, which demanded no work of their denizens, and indeterminate sentences, which allowed a jailer some leverage to insure that the work rehabilitation of his tramps was successful.[51]

Some methods proposed by public officials to accomplish this task were quite violent. One Westchester County official proposed a "hydropathic hospital" for curing tramps. Each person convicted of vagrancy would be placed in a tank in which the level of water would slowly rise. The tramp could keep his head above the water only by vigorous bailing or pumping. If he stopped or slowed down, he would drown. The idea probably originated in Holland which purportedly used a similar system. The plan was highly criticized in New York and was never put into operation. Another method, rarely used, of forcing the tramps to work was to hire them out involuntarily as contract labor to farmers, which would have resulted in virtual slavery.[52] Excluding support for such grotesque ideas, the general public and reformers favored forced labor as useful in reducing vagrancy, and it was put into effect almost everywhere. In New York City a State Farm Colony for tramps to achieve this purpose gained wide support.[53]

In the reformer view, along with the investigation of applicants and the provision of work, relief given had to be "adequate." While the reformers were never clear on the exact meaning of "adequacy," relief was less broadly conceived of than it is today. It was almost never given in cash, but rather as food and lodging to single people and occasionally coal to families. Thus, it was impossible to get money for special schooling to learn a trade or for travel to seek work. In addition, voluntarist agencies and even public agencies lacked sufficient funds to support all individual applicants adequately. The relief agencies had to be selective, and, in depression years, funds were limited even for worthy applicants. The men regarded as tramps were never eligible for more than bare subsistence relief.

The Jews were much closer to modern ideas on relief than any other group or the community in general. Before 1910, they had sufficient relief funds to aid their own homeless, and so few Jewish tramps were reported. As the number of Jewish immigrants continued to increase, however, their relief system broke down in the depression years just before World War I. That Jews made money available can be traced simply to the Jewish concept of charity and relief. Amos Warner, author of *American Charities* and leader in the charity organization movement in Maryland, was considered by New York reformers to be an expert in the field of philanthropy. He pointed out the irony that the church practicing "Christian charity" most kindly and wisely was not the Christian, but Jewish.[54]

"Charity," in fact, does not exist as a word in Hebrew. Instead, Jews use "Zedakah," which implies "righteousness, signifying that whoever possesses more than a sufficiency for his own needs is in justice bound to assist those who do not have sufficient.'' The Jewish sages drew on a base of holy scriptures (Isaiah and Deuteronomy, for example) to charge individuals with the duty of taking care of the less fortunate and also the community to care for the material and moral welfare of the dependent.[55]

Although slow to reach the point where the Jews began, the New York reformers themselves eventually dropped the word ''charity'' from their official language. In the 1880s the formation of the COS itself was a rejection of charity as traditionally defined. However, although this was a step toward the rationalization of social work, the emphasis was still on charity.[56] For example, the cable address for the NYCOS was ''Charity, New York.'' At first, rather than rejecting the word ''charity'' itself, the reformers began differentiating between ''old'' and ''new'' charity. In an address to the NYCOS in 1886, the Reverend H. L. Wayland called this quibbling; the real charity was the new type, which thought more of the needy than the self-indulgence of the giver. It was also the only charity that was ''scientific'' enough and flexible enough to restore the wretched to society.[57]

While some of the reformers defended their policies after the panic of 1893 by distinguishing the ''new'' from the ''old'' type of charity, others said that this distinction was no longer adequate.[58] In 1896 the president of the NCCC, Albert D. Wright, noted that many social welfare and philanthropic groups refused to join his organization because of objections to its name. Such groups believed that use of the words ''charities'' or ''correction'' misrepresented their aims. Among the objecting groups were social settlements and institutions for the deaf and blind.[59]

Dropping ''charity,'' however, from the vocabulary of the reformers proved to be a difficult process. The evolution of the name of the magazine associated with the NYCOS from *Charities* to *Charities and The Commons* to *Survey* took nine years and considerable arguments among the reformers themselves. The president of the COS, Robert W. De Forest, argued that dropping the word ''charities'' from the title would create an impression of change in scope and would affect ''support and interest in the venture.'' Paul U. Kellogg, Devine's youthful assistant editor and apparently prime mover for dropping ''charity'' out of the title, agreed that this was possible. In a letter, Kellogg told De Forest that he appreciated his efforts in "interpreting charity organization work to men who of themselves have come to view with something like alarm many movements which call themselves progressive." Kellogg, nonetheless, insisted the change had to be made, and he gained the support of many involved for his position. Finally the Charities Publication Committee agreed to change the name of *Charities and The Commons* to *Survey* effective April 1, 1909.[60]

De Forest's and Kellogg's concern about what the public thought about *Charities* and, in turn, the charity organization movement was absolutely crucial. Above all things the COS needed the fullest cooperation from the citizenry and all philanthropic organizations if it were to be successful. Obtaining cooperation from others was always a problem for society because it was never really able to explain what it was trying to do. In the public image, the COS was cool and aloof from human compassion, as this couplet illustrates:

Organized charity scrimped and iced
In the name of a cautious statistical Christ.[61]

Unfortunately for the COS the public derived most of its information about it from the popular press. In the beginning the society received the support of influential New York papers. Later, however, the popular press began its own special relief funds, and the COS was continually in the position of attacking the very instrument needed to secure public support. In the view of the reformers, the newspapers were being "indiscriminate" with bread and soup lines at best; at worst they were interested only in "advertisement," not "charity."[62] And the reformers believed this indiscriminate charity helped attract tramps into the city.

The COS attacked the bread line concept in its own publications and in public and personal letters to editors of the various newspapers, but to no avail.[63] In return, the newspapers attacked the COS at its weakest point by publishing unfriendly letters to the editor or articles that noted the disparity between funds collected by the COS and its distribution to the poor. For example, the editor of the New York *Morning Telegraph* charged that in 1910 the society received $250,000 but gave only $80,000 to the poor. He suggested that the COS be renamed "The Society for the Paying of Salaries to Philanthropists Who Need Money." The COS, of course, was not a relief agency and little of its funds went directly to the needy. Although Frank Persons of the COS objected to the article, the editor refused to print a retraction.[64] The reformers attempted often to have newspapers publish stories as well as favorable editorials about the COS, but they were not always successful.[65]

In addition to seeking support from the public, the COS needed cooperation from all relief agencies in New York if it was to perform its function as a clearinghouse to prevent frauds. Beginning in 1893, the COS had moved closer in its relations with the AICP as both occupied quarters in the new United Charities Building. In November 1893, they opened a Joint Application Bureau, which took applications of the homeless to both agencies, the costs of relief being borne equally by the COS and AICP.[66]

The COS did not have as close a relationship with settlement houses as it hoped. As far as the tramps were concerned, the settlements did not deal with them at all, but stressed work with neighborhood families. The COS worried that organized charity's ideas of relief were being undermined in the settlements whose workers stressed that social and economic conditions caused poverty while the society looked toward individual causes.[67] Thus the settlement workers, especially the younger ones, were rarely concerned with the problem of indiscriminate charity. Robert Hunter, author, socialist, and settlement worker, confirmed this view in his jocular description of the charity worker as the Hamlet type—always pondering whether "to do or not to do." Yet Hunter hoped that the two groups would grow increasingly closer and cited COS interest in tenement reform and tuberculosis as examples of the COS moving toward the settlement views. This did, in fact, occur under pressure of repeated economic crises. The COS reformers slowly moved toward the settlement worker's position.[68]

Churches moved slowly to cooperate with the COS. Catholics realized that, with the increasing complexity of modern industrial conditions, more cooperation was necessary to administer charity properly. But one principle prohibited full cooperation with the COS. Catholics refused to expose the misfortunes of their poor, or in other words, did not want to provide names to the COS for use by its clearinghouse.[69] In fact, this was a major stumbling block for other churches as well, but nevertheless cooperation was increasingly preached, although not practiced as a proper way to handle relief matters. Critics of the Salvation Army found that it was also noncooperative with the COS.[70]

The institutional churches, which worked to improve the total environment of their members, were the most willing to cooperate. The Rev. Edward Judson of the Memorial Baptist Church in New York City said that he kept the "closest relations" with the COS and AICP and cordial relations with most other churches and church affiliated groups. The churches had to supply "social pabulum" to the people to improve environment and strengthen character.[71] Generally speaking, though, churches still refused to cooperate. Mrs. Simon Borg, in an address before the New York section of the National Council of Jewish Women, sounded a clarion call for unity of relief societies benefiting the "entire community." If all worked together, she foresaw a future in which "anarchism and socialism have taken flight. Good will prevails throughout the earth. . . . The millennium has come, and we have been the means of establishing the Brotherhood of man."[72]

Unfortunately for New York City, Mrs. Borg's millennium failed to arrive before the panic of 1907-1908. Tens of thousands of tramps entered the city to the consternation of relief workers, but no notable innovations in expanding relief giving took place in New York in an effort to aid the unemployed.[73] But, a distinctive innovation appeared in an effort to stem the tide of relief usually forthcoming in a depression.

In January 1908, Mary Richmond of the Field Department of *Charities and The Commons* wrote to the charity organization societies in sixteen cities, asking each to send her a confidential report every week on its efforts to insure that relief activity was not overdone. Then she would forward the letters to all participating societies so each could borrow useful techniques and avoid errors.[74] At the end of the winter of 1907-1908, the correspondents met and discussed their overall experiences. In their judgment, the exchange of letters had provided useful information for everyone. Frank Persons of the COS stated that the "great lesson to be learned from the unemployment crisis was that no charity organization society could hope to deal with it adequately and that they must use every method to make others feel their responsibility."[75] Since the COS had no authority over other relief agencies, it was necessary to stress the need for cooperation.

The COS, by continually stressing the need for centralization of relief activity, was unwittingly pointing up the need for public action in the relief field.[76]

The masses of tramps entering the city in the aftermath of the panics of 1893 and 1907-1908 forced the reformers to break with their principles regarding the distribution of relief. Ideally the reformers believed the COS should thoroughly investigate each applicant for relief by interview and letters of inquiry to his references, his home town, his family, and public authorities. Sheer numbers of applicants rendered this impossible during the height of the panics, but relief was necessary for humanitarian reasons and because the wretched unemployed posed a threat to society. After the panics receded, the investigation of the homeless unemployed revealed that a high percentage of applicants were genuinely looking for work. Long-term relief for these individuals by voluntarist agencies was neither possible because of cost nor desirable because of principle. The reformers then tried to answer the question of what could be done to return the men to work without endangering unfettered capitalism or individualism. The answer seemed deceptively simple to many in the 1890s and the first decade of the twentieth century. Since the wellspring of capitalism and individualism was in the rural areas, and since society believed jobs were always available there, why not just return the workless to the soil?

NOTES

1. David Moses Schneider and Albert Deutsch, *The History of Public Welfare in New York State* (Chicago, 1941), 109-122; NYAICP, *Semi-Centennial Annual Reports* (1893-1894), 70.

2. NYAICP, *Annual Report* (1874), 33. Although the NYAICP was not in strictest terms part of the charity organization movement, its policies conformed closely. Thus the word "reformers" in this study also applies to its social welfare workers.

3. Leah Hannah Feder, *Unemployment Relief in Periods of Depression: A Study of Relief Methods Adopted in Certain American Cities, 1857 Through 1922* (New York, 1936), 20; Frieda M. Kuhlman, "A Study of Varying Trends in the Treatment of the Poor" (Master's thesis, New York School of Social Work, 1937), 86.

4. NYAICP, *Annual Report* (1842), 22, and its *Annual Report* (1847), 12-13.

5. Josephine Shaw Lowell, *Public Relief and Private Charity* (New York, 1884), 60-62.

6. Feder, *Unemployment Relief,* 46.

7. NYAICP, *Annual Report* (1877), 27-28.

8. Charles M. Hevisler, "The Society and Pauperism," *St. Vincent de Paul Quarterly* 1 (February 1896): 112; Daniel R. Noyes, "The Employment Seeker," *Young Men's Era* 20 (February 15, 1894): 5; Thomas M. Mulry, "Catholic Conception of Poverty," *St. Vincent de Paul Quarterly* 7 (May 1902): 120. Mulry was a banker and an active participant in the St. Vincent de Paul Society (Roman Catholic) and in the COS in New York.

9. Bowery Mission and Young Men's Home, *Annual Report* (1881) (n.p., n.d.), 9; McAuley's Water Street Mission, *Annual Report* (1889) (n.p., n.d.), 6.

10. Arthur Bonner, *Jerry McAuley and His Mission* (Neptune, New Jersey, 1967). Whether this was the first rescue mission (1872) as Bonner claims is largely a problem of definition. The New York City Mission and Tract Society opened a mission in New York a little earlier than McAuley, but it did not seek out the very lowest type of "tramps" as did McAuley. McAuley's mission was possibly the first to encourage all men to attend services and was by far the most influential mission in New York during his lifetime.

11. Walter Augustus Wyckoff, *The Workers: An Experiment in Reality: The West* (New York, 1898), 17. For examples of testimonies at a New York City mission see ibid., 14-21, and Helen Campbell, *Darkness and Daylight; or Lights and Shadows of New York Life* (Hartford, 1896), 53-67.

12. William James, *The Varieties of Religious Experience* (New York, 1908), 198-199.

13. Charles M. Pepper, *The Life-Work of Louis Klopsch* (New York, 1910), 261.

14. Owen Kildare, *My Old Bailiwick* (New York, 1906), 191, 192.

15. For examples see Frank E. Wings, "Observations on Free Coffee and Sandwich Distribution in a New York Mission," *Annals* (December 1904): 174; Albert W. VanNess, "A Night With the Bread Lines," *Charities* 13 (March 1905): 555-557; C. C. Carstens, "The Bread Line," *Charities* 13 (October 1, 1904): 51.

16. Mary E. Richmond to Edward T. Devine, October 7, 1898, Edward T. Devine to Mary E. Richmond, October 10, 1898: Papers of NYCOS, Archives of the Community Service Society, New York City.

17. Bonner, *Jerry McAuley's* 48, 58, 81, 67; NYCOS, *Annual Report* (1893), 79-80.

18. Bowery Mission and Young Men's Home, *Annual Report* (1883) (n.p., n.d.), 12.

19. General William Booth, *In Darkest England and the Way Out* (New York, 1891), chapter ii.

20. Ballington Booth and Maud Booth, *New York's Inferno Explored* (New York, 1891), vii.

21. Ibid., 42. Oscar Handlin's "Poverty from the Civil War to World War II" in *Poverty Amid Affluence*, ed. Leo Fishman (New Haven, 1966), 6, views "soup kitchen philanthropy" as being motivated by humanitarianism mitigating the severity of the position which refused to recognize the able-bodied homeless unemployed. Actually in New York City many of the soup kitchens were run by evangelical religious groups,

which regarded the homeless unemployed as a sinner against God and accepted him as such. The kitchen sponsors did not blame society, but rather the individual.

22. John C. Kimball, *The Salvation Army, Its Significance in our Day and Its Claim to Fair Treatment—A Sermon for Unity Church, January 24, 1886* (Hartford, 1886), 6.

23. Herbert A. Wisbey, Jr., *Soldiers Without Swords: A History of the Salvation Army in the United States* (New York, 1955), 93, 95; Richard Holz, Handwritten notes from a Staff Council Meeting held on July 10, 1894, Papers of Richard Holz, Eastern Territorial Headquarters, Salvation Army.

24. *Second Annual Meeting of the Amity Missionary Conference held at Amity Baptist Church*, (New York, 1895), 15.

25. Lt. Col. Richard Holz, "Social Summary for 1898," *Harbor Lights* 2 (February 1899): 54-56; Booth, *In Darkest England,* 85-86.

26. Graham Taylor, "An Address," *Young Men's Era* 21 (May 16, 1895): 331. Charles Stelzle, *The Workingman and Social Problems* (Chicago, 1903); Josiah Strong, "The Times and Their Appeal to Men," *Empire State* 12 (April 1900): 48-49, and *Religious Movements for Social Betterment* (New York, 1900), 13. The scope and services of an institutional church can best be seen in George Hodges and John Reichert, *The Administration of an Institutional Church* (New York, 1906).

27. NYC YMCA, *Annual Report* (1897), 43, and *Annual Report* (1892), 108. An excellent overview of the missions, the Salvation Army, and the YMCA is included in Aaron Abell, *The Urban Impact on American Protestantism* (Cambridge, Massachusetts, 1943).

28. Cleveland E. Dodge, *YMCA: A Century at New York (1852-1952), An Address Delivered to the Newcomen Society* (New York, 1952); NYC YMCA, *Annual Report* (1909), 59.

29. Industrial Christian Alliance, *Helping Men to Help Themselves* (n.p., [1903?]).

30. Bowery Mission and Young Men's Home, *Annual Report* (n.p., n.d. [1882]), 12; "Bowery Shelter Opened," *War Cry*, January 30, 1897, 5; John F. Moore, *The Story of the Railroad "Y"* (New York, 1930), 72.

31. Charles D. Kellogg, "The Situation in New York City During the Winter of 1893-94," NCCC, *Proceedings* (1894), 21.

32. "Concerning Special Relief Funds in Times of Great Industrial and Commercial Depression—A Statement to the Public through the Daily and Weekly Press, September, 1893," NYCOS, *Annual Report* (1893), 25.

33. For an example see F. de L. Booth Tucker's statement printed in *War Cry*, February 25, 1899, 5.

34. Rev. D. Talmage, "A Bread and Beef Charity," *Christian Herald and Signs of the Times* (January 10, 1894), 19.

35. Feder, *Unemployment Relief*, 34.

36. "Minutes of Meeting for the Purpose of Determining a Plan for Offering Employment to Unemployed in the Office of the Mayor," January 3, 1894, Mayoralty Papers of Thomas F. Gilroy, Municipal Archives, New York City.

37. Mayor Thomas F. Gilroy to "The People of the City of New York," February

9, 1894, "Minutes of a Special Committee Appointed by the Mayor to Dispense Funds Donated by City Employees," January 15, 1894, Mayoralty Papers of Thomas F. Gilroy. The COS felt it was inexpedient even to apply for any of the mayor's fund. See NYCOS, Executive Committee, "Minutes," March 13, 1894, Papers of NYCOS.

38. NYAICP, *Semi-Centennial Annual Reports* (1893-1894), 52; "The Problem of Today," *Young Men's Era* 19 (September 7, 1893): 1050.

39. Edward T. Devine, *The Practice of Charity* (New York, 1904), 8, 29. A report published in Indianapolis confirmed his view in that city. It stated that "account was taken of the fact that relief had a motive of police protection as well as humanity." See *Relief for the Unemployed in Indianapolis: Report of the Commercial Club Relief Committee and its Auxiliary the Citizen's Finance Committee, 1893-94* (Indianapolis, 1894), 32. Andrew Carnegie was a life member of the NYCOS. For his view of charity as a palliative, see his "Altruism as an Investment," *Eleventh Annual Meeting of the National Civic Federation* (January 1911), 185-188. Junius H. Browne, "Succor for the Unemployed," *Harper's Weekly* 38 (January 6, 1894): 10.

40. Kellogg, "The Situation in New York City," 25.

41. Josephine Shaw Lowell, "Methods of Relief for the Unemployed," *Forum* 16 (February 1894): 655.

42. Josephine Shaw Lowell, "Report," NYSBC, *Annual Report* (1884), 143-150, 160. Although Mrs. Lowell is quoted at length in this chapter, her views were common with the New York social welfare reformers in the NYCOS and NYAICP. See also Josephine Shaw Lowell, "Criminal Reform," *The Literature of Philanthropy*, ed. Frances A. Goodale (New York, 1893), 9-10.

43. Lowell, *Public Relief and Private Charity*, 89. For examples see "Mrs. Lamadrid's Meal Booths," NYCOS, *Monthly Bulletin* (March 15, 1887): 1; "St. Andrew's Coffee Stands," NYCOS, *Monthly Bulletin* (November 25, 1889): 3.

44. Josephine Shaw Lowell, "The Economics and Moral Effects of Public Outdoor Relief," NCCC, *Proceedings* (1890), 91.

45. "Five Months' Work for the Unemployed in New York City," *Charities Review* 3 (May 1894): 323-399; College Settlements Association, *Annual Report* (September 1, 1893-September 1, 1894), 6.

46. Josephine Shaw Lowell, "Poverty and Its Relief: The Methods Possible in the City of New York," NCCC, *Proceedings* (1895), 44; Davis, "Mrs. Lowell and the Unemployed," 56; "Five Months' Work for the Unemployed," 337-338.

47. Joseph Lee, *The Tramp Problem* (Boston, 1905), cover. This was a leaflet published by the Massachusetts Civic League.

48. Lowell, "Methods of Relief," 660; NCCC, *Proceedings* (1885), 470.

49. W. Grisewood, *The Relief of the Poor in America: A Lecture Delivered in Connection with the School of Training for Social Work, University of Liverpool* (n.p., 1905).

50. Kellogg, "The Situation in New York City," 23. In all cases, work meant physical labor. Men could only prove worthiness by their hands and not their minds. Many willing to do work, but unable to do physical work for one reason or another, had difficulty proving they were not tramps.

51. SCAA, *Annual Report* (1877), 63.

52. "Tramps and Labor," *New York Times,* December 22, 1886; Newburyport (Massachusetts) *Daily Herald,* June 14, 1878; *New York Times,* December 26, 1886; Kenneth Allsop, *Hard Travellin': The Hobo and his History* (New York, 1967), 112-113.

53. "Work-Cure for Tramps," *Nation* 72 (January 24, 1901): 64-65; Samuel Lane Loomis, "The Tramp Problem," *Chautauquan* 19 (June 1894), 309, 312. The farm colony idea originated in Europe's experiments with forced labor colonies.

54. Amos G. Warner, "Our Charities and Our Churches," NCCC, *Proceedings* (1889), 36-37. One Protestant text that acknowledged Jewish leadership in social service was Harlan Paul Douglass, *The New Home Missions: An Account of Their Social Re-Direction* (New York, 1914), 119. Some Jewish tramps refused to visit the Baltimore Friendly Inn because the food served there was not kosher. Some more cynical persons felt that perhaps it was that the work test given there was not "kosher." "Some Jewish Strangers," *Jewish Charities,* 2 (September 1911): 4.

55. United Hebrew Charities of New York, *Annual Report* (1899), 74; Boris D. Bogen, *Jewish Philanthropy: An Exploration of the Principles and Methods of Jewish Social Service in the United States* (New York, 1917), 17-18; Harry S. Lewis, *Liberal Judaism and Social Service* (New York, 1915), 73.

56. Community Service Society of New York, *Frontiers in Human Welfare* (New York, 1948), 10. Milton D. Speizman, "Attitudes Toward Charity in American Thought" (Ph.D. diss., Tulane University, 1962) is a sweeping compendium of what nonsocial welfare reformers thought about charity.

57. H. L. Wayland, *The Old Charity and the New: An Address* (n.p., 1886) (n.p., 1900), Papers of Mary Richmond, Columbia University School of Social Work.

58. Jane Elizabeth Robins, "Charity That Helps and Other Charity," *Forum* 18 (December 1894): 502; Albert O. Wright, "The New Philanthropy," NCCC, *Proceedings* (1896), 11; Josephine Shaw Lowell, "The True Aim of Charity Organization Societies," *Forum* 21 (1896): 494.

59. Wright, "The New Philanthropy," 11.

60. John M. Glenn to Robert W. De Forest, December 10, 1900; Paul U. Kellogg to Robert W. De Forest, July 25, 1908, 8; Charity Publications Committee, "Minutes," December 5, 1908, 3-6, Papers of NYCOS.

61. From John Boyle O'Reilly's "In Bohemia" quoted in Gary A. Lloyd, "Social Work Concepts of the Causes and 'Treatment' of Poverty: 1893-1908" (Ph.D. diss., Tulane University, 1965), 74.

62. Charles D. Kellogg, "Address," *Report of a Conference of Charities* (Baltimore, 1887), 6; Lillian Wald to Jacob Schiff, August 29, 1893, Papers of Lillian Wald, New York Public Library; James B. Reynolds to Jacob Riis, February 27, 1897, Papers of Jacob A. Riss, The City College of The City University of New York.

63. NYCOS, *Charity Organization Bulletin,* no. 11 (March 18, 1914); Bailey Burritt to Editor, New York *Sun,* March 14, 1914, Papers of NYAICP; Frank Persons to Editor, New York *Sun,* March 24, 1914, Papers of NYCOS.

64. "Society For The Congealing of Charity," New York *Morning Telegraph,* January 8, 1911; W. E. Lewis to Frank Persons, January 23, 1911. For other examples see Fred Gray, "Letter to Editor," New York *Morning Sun,* March 27, 1914; "Charity Over-Organized," Letter to Editor, *New York Times,* December 28, 1907; "Indis-

criminate Charity Upheld," New York *Herald*, March 5, 1885. All articles are from a clipping file in Papers of NYCOS. The NYCOS did distribute relief through a Provident Relief Fund and in other ways after 1900, but this relief was a minor part of its function.

65. Karl deSchweinitz to Frank Persons, March 30, 1914, Papers of NYCOS.

66. Robert DeForest, *The Story of the United Charities Building* (New York, 1931), 5, 14; NYAICP Board of Managers, "Minutes," December 11, 1893. The Joint Application Bureau continued in operation until the merging of the COS and AICP into the Community Service Society of New York.

67. Allen F. Davis, *Spearheads for Reform* (New York, 1967), 18-25; Mary Kingsbury Simkhovitch in Greenwich House, *Annual Report* (October, 1904), 9; Lowell, "Poverty and Its Relief," 53.

68. Robert Hunter, "The Relation Between Social Settlements and Charity Organization," NCCC, *Proceedings* (1902), 308, 313.

69. First National Conference of Catholic Charities, *Proceedings* (1910), 10; D. J. McMahon, "United Charities—A Plea for Cooperation in Benevolent Work," *St. Vincent de Paul Quarterly* 6 (November 1901): 255-267; William J. Kerby, "Social Work of the Catholic Church in America," *Annals* 30 (1907): 481.

70. George B. Mangold, "The Church and Philanthropy," *Annals* 30 (1907): 522-538; Henry K. Denlinger, "How Shall Church and Charity Cooperate to Prevent Distress?" NYCCCC, *Proceedings* (1911), 91-92; C. C. Carstens, "The Salvation Army—A Criticism," *Annals* 30 (1907): 553; Edward G. Lamb, *The Social Work of The Salvation Army* (New York, 1909), 132.

71. Edward Johnson, "The Church in its Social Aspect," *Annals* 30 (1907): 435-436.

72. Mrs. Simon Borg, "A Practical View of Philanthropy," *American Hebrew*, (May 1, 1896): 745, 747.

73. Schneider and Deutsch, *History of Public Welfare*, 200.

74. Mary Richmond to Co-operating Societies, January 13, 1908, Papers of Mary Richmond; *Charity Organization Bulletin* 5 (November 1914): 125.

75. Field Department Committee, "Minutes," May 9, 1908, 7, Papers of Mary Richmond.

76. Ibid., 10.

4

"No Nation Was Ever Overthrown

by Its Farmers":

The Back-to-the-Land Movement

and the Unemployed

BOTH THE BELIEF that the yeoman farmer made the ideal citizen and the myth that there was full employment for all Americans who "really wanted to work" were deeply rooted in the rural ethic of nineteenth-century America.[1] When social unrest and massive unemployment appeared in the 1890s, city reformers naturally and logically looked toward the soil for relief. The yeoman farmer of Thomas Jefferson had led a wholesome, happy, and independent existence, which strengthened not only his physical being, but his moral fiber as well. In addition, the yeoman farmer, being a property owner with a stake in society, was the "best and most reliable sort of citizen."[2]

The lack of class tensions in the rural areas was attributed to the availability of land and thus the apparently logical conclusion was made as early as the 1830s that the land was, in effect, a social safety valve, and that when land was no longer available class tensions would arise.[3] George Henry Evans, publisher of the *Working Man's Advocate*, the official organ of the Workingman's party in the 1830s, contended that free land in the West would attract the unemployed from the cities.[4] Horace Greeley's advice, "Go West Young Man," dated from the Panic of 1837, when Greeley encouraged westward movement as relief from poverty and unemployment. Greeley also toasted the Homestead Act in 1862 as a means of reducing idlers and paupers.[5]

In the 1890s historian Frederick Jackson Turner gave intellectual formulation to the safety valve concept and the frontier's effect on America. To Turner, the vacant lands in the West provided an outlet "whenever society gave signs of breaking into classes. Here was a magic fountain of youth in which America continually bathed and rejuvenated." Reformer Walter Weyl agreed with Turner and feared that with the closing of the frontier there would be "no outlet for the unemployed and discontented of our cities."[6]

Affected by the experience of the depression of 1929, historians in the 1930s attempted to demonstrate statistically that Turner's safety valve had not really existed. Few persons, they showed, fled from the city to the country compared to those going from the country to the city; the city was actually the safety valve for rural discontent. That so few urban dwellers actually went "back to the country" did not obviate the belief in the rural ethic as an outlet for urban unrest. Turner's defenders have pointed out, and rightly so, that psychologically the concept did exist.[7] But in the 1890s, reformers and others of influence firmly believed rural America could help solve the ills of the city. Thus many of their early reactions to the problems of the unemployed related to inculcating rural values in the unemployed and to encouraging the unemployed to return to rural America.[8]

The belief in the rural ethic was predicated on the assumption that full employment was possible for everyone in the United States because of vacant western lands. Charles Loring Brace, founder of the Children's Aid Society in New York City, assumed that the United States had practically an unlimited supply of arable land and that the demand for rural labor would always exceed the supply. The best place for the vagrant and homeless child, he asserted, was a farmer's home where he would learn rural values and trades and thereby avoid becoming a vagrant and a member of the "dangerous classes."[9] Brace's basic assumption was never seriously challenged in the last third of the nineteenth century. His only trenchant critic was the

Roman Catholic church, which felt Brace's real purpose in sending
urban youth to the country was to proselyte Catholic children by placing them with rural Protestant families. Other charitable groups also
sought to place homeless boys on farms, because the training they
received would always be required in the United States.[10]

The idea of constant availability of rural work can also be found
in literature dealing specifically with tramps. Walter Wyckoff wrote
three books on tramping, parts of which were published in *Scribner's
Monthly*. In *A Day with a Tramp and Other Days*, Wyckoff wrote
that in the warm months there was always work on farms. He also
denied that rural work was only seasonal. Once on his way to the
city in late fall, he recalled receiving and refusing many farmers'
offers of employment as a general utility man. Later, when he could
not find work in the city, he reflected on the grim irony of his situation. In an earlier work, Wyckoff had recorded his conversation with
a farmer who told him "there's hardly a day in the year when I
haven't a job for any decent man who'll ask for it."[11]

Not only was work available, but writers preserved the fiction
that farmers were content with their life. To those in the cities who
thought that social discontent in the city might ripen into social revolution, one author in *Forum* reminded them that those outside the urban
areas had to be taken into account before any social upheaval could
succeed. He glossed over Populist discontent as limited to areas of
poor climate and little consequence. Farmers as a whole, he pointed
out, could be referred to as "the contented masses."[12] City dwellers
believed in rural contentment and blamed their separation from the
soil as responsible for much of the anxiety and discontent in the city,
and they attempted to make a new alliance with the outdoors in the
1890s, as evidenced in public support for the founding of the Boy
Scout movement, arbor days, and the playground movement.[13]

The reformers supported a multitude of programs designed to reduce
the number of urban unemployed and to encourage rural employment.
One basic approach was to encourage rural residents not to leave the
farm. In 1894, in order to find out the extent of rural migration to
the cities, the AICP appointed a special committee to study the matter.
The committee hired J. W. Kjelgaard, an agricultural expert, to survey
the problem. After interviewing farmers, he reported that 75 percent
of them claimed that the general tendency of farmers was to leave

their farms rather than to remain on them. Fully 30 percent asserted that they would leave their agricultural occupations immediately if they had any assurance of a job. Concerned, the committee recommended that the State Department of Agriculture or the New York legislature take immediate action "to reawaken interest in the farming industry." In a related action, the Board of Charities of New York City hired an agricultural educator, George T. Powell, to initiate a program of experimental nature study. Powell established the courses in Westchester County schools, just north of the city, "as an approach to the improvement of rural life."[14]

Although the New York charity organization reformers supported programs in rural areas to retard migration to the cities, most of their energy was expended in attempting to promote the settlement of urban labor in rural areas. This involved educational programs to inculcate a love of the soil, such as the school gardening movement. The vacant lot gardening movement also provided a form of relief, as well as educational benefits. The reformers were interested, moreover, in voluntary colonization experiments and supported farm colonies for tramps who would not work.

The school garden movement began in 1890 when the Massachusetts Horticultural Society sent a representative to Europe to study gardens there. The idea spread rapidly in the United States, and a children's school farm in New York City was established in DeWitt Clinton Park. The first annual report of the school stated that the school gardens in New York City were not started "simply to grow a few vegetables and flowers. The garden was used . . . to teach children . . . some necessary civic virtues: private care of public property, economy, honesty, application, concentration, self-government, civic pride, justice, the dignity of labor, and a love of nature." In addition, the school garden gave "a much needed and most valuable experience of the sense of ownership and of the institution of private property as seen from the inside." The child would learn that property was something more than a material substance to be transferred by the might of the strongest, "that in essence it is an expression of character, a part of the life of the person who has made or earned, and who values it."[15]

To make programs like school gardens and vacant lot gardening a reality, land was needed in and around cities. At a debate held in

New York City in 1896, Ernest Crosby asserted that preaching thrift and temperance to the unemployed would solve nothing. Instead, the unemployed needed access to natural resources and land, which were controlled presently by monopolies. Walter Wyckoff, his opponent, rejoined that the problem was not the monopoly of money or land, but rather the inability and lack of knowledge to use them properly.[16] Underlying both positions, however, was the assumption that land was a key to the solution of the problem. School gardens and vacant lot gardening movements were attempts in part to bridge the gap between urban and rural labor as Wyckoff and others saw it. In the major cities of the United States at the turn of the century, most unused parcels of land produced only weeds. This unused land had given birth to the idea that the unemployed could profitably cultivate it. Such city lot farming would, hopefully, satisfy Crosby's and Wyckoff's positions by providing work relief and by teaching thrift, independence, and agricultural methods. The charity organization reformers hoped that vacant lot gardening would influence the urban unemployed to seek a life out of the cities.

Vacant lot gardening was first initiated in Detroit to counteract the impact of Coxey's Army. Mayor Hazen S. Pingree of that city said that if Coxey's Army were given "the privilege to cultivate the vacant lots in our cities and have what they produce as a reward for their labor, we can stop this tramping instantly."[17] In 1894 Pingree introduced his "potato patch plan" by asking that open lands in and around Detroit be made available to the unemployed. Because the growing season was already underway, the city accepted donations of only about 430 acres, which were then divided into lots one-quarter to one-half acre each by a committee appointed by the mayor. *Lend A Hand* reported that Mayor Pingree employed 945 of "his tramps" on the acreage. According to the mayor's committee, however, only applications from men with families and widows were considered, and the term "tramps" was never mentioned.[18] But the whole program was immediately ridiculed, and the committee raised the required $3,600 for tools and seed only with the greatest of difficulty. One agricultural paper called the scheme a farmer's folly and jestingly wondered how well crops would grow after fertilization with "old tin cans and boots and shoes" dumped on the vacant lots. The joke was on the paper of course, because in the days before the horseless carriage, fertilizer was no problem at all—all that was needed was street sweepings.

In spite of the early criticisms of the program, when the season was over, Pingree and most of his critics considered the first year a success. Over 14,000 bushels of potatoes were harvested, as well as quantities of beans, turnips, and other vegetables. Some of the vegetables were even awarded a special prize at the state agricultural fair. In Pingree's view, the experiment demonstrated that 95 percent of the destitute were ready and willing to work, that large numbers of people could be supported by the plan, that a majority of citizens who owned vacant lots were willing to have them cultivated by the poor, thereby reducing taxes for support of the poor, and that the needy would be helped without demoralization.[19]

The project attracted much attention throughout the country, and, in 1895, about twenty cities and towns, including New York City, decided to try the scheme. The United States Department of Agriculture printed a pamphlet describing Pingree's program and distributed it to various charitable groups. The pamphlet pointed out that Detroit had about 400,000 unskilled laborers, mainly foreigners, and, when work failed, the situation became serious, if not dangerous. It explained the methods used in Detroit to set up the program and concluded:

> As nearly all our labor troubles are attended with violence largely due to the unemployed who sympathize with the strikers, and as uncertainty about financial legislation seems to threaten hard times for the winter, it behooves us now to provide for want. The idle man is the dangerous one.[20]

In New York City the vacant lot gardening program was initiated by the COS, the NYAICP, and the United Hebrew Charities. Representing the three groups were C. D. Kellogg, Robert F. Cutting, and Nathaniel S. Rosenau, who decided to offer the management of the program to the AICP. Accepting the offer, the AICP added Jacob H. Schiff, Thomas M. Mulry, Bolton Hall, Josephine Shaw Lowell, and Arthur W. Milbury to Kellogg, Cutting, and Rosenau to form the Vacant Lot Gardening Committee.

The first act of the committee was to distribute a flyer requesting donations of money and loans of fenced, vacant lots.[21] Initially, it thought that securing vacant lots in the city would be no problem; the postal census of 1893 had indicated that there were 17,329 lots (over 1,400 acres) within the city limits. But due to a poor response to the leaflet, the difficulty of growing crops between buildings, and other practical problems, the committee decided to turn down offers of vacant lots in the city and to seek larger parcels of land on Long Island. It secured three tracts totaling 138 acres in the vicinity of Long Island City and divided most of the acreage among eighty-four plot holders who earned just over sixty dollars each during the first season. Thirty-four applicants worked the remaining thirty-eight acres as a cooperative, and, after paying ten cents an hour for labor, profited just over fifty dollars. Of the total who had plots, only three earned nothing at all.[22]

The committee considered the experiment a resounding success. Rosenau noted that the participants learned how to work the soil and could see the opportunities open to them in farming. Arthur Milbury of the Industrial Christian Alliance agreed, observing that the scheme pointed up the anomaly of men living in poverty in cities "contiguous to which tens of thousands of acres of untilled soil lie ready to provide bountifully for every need of a teeming population."[23] J. W. Kjelgaard, the supervisor of the New York program, suggested that it strengthened the hope of avoiding a social crisis by employing the idle. The idle men, he asserted, were a threat to "ourselves and our children." But, he continued, "as long as United States soldiers will shoot rioters, we need not greatly fear insurrection, unless, indeed, a foreign war should leave a discontented soldiery of our own, on our hands." It was much better, he suggested, to place the unemployed on the soil and guide them until they became self-supporting. Then in a few years they would possess their own homes and "a citizen who owns his own home is always the best kind of citizen."[24] While the New York City reformers did not originate vacant lot cultivation, they did more than any other city to further Pingree's scheme by publishing instructions and by keeping extensive records of their own program.[25]

After the first season the committee made some changes in the original program. It reduced the amount of land allotted each applicant in favor of more intensive cultivation on smaller plots because it had increasing difficulty acquiring land on loan or in areas large enough to be suitable for economic cultivation. In addition it decided to exact some financial return from the gardeners, to keep the program on a philanthropic and, if possible, self-sustaining basis, and not to accept any public money from the city.[26]

During the life of this committee, Bolton Hall, a prominent New York City attorney, was its driving force, sharing the general view of the sponsors. He also was a supporter of the doctrines of Henry George. Writing in 1896 to Mayor Strong of New York City, Hall pointed out that one of the reasons for the increasing number of unemployed in New York City was a considerable discrimination in the tax assessment rate on vacant lands. While the owners were not profiting at the moment, they were withholding the land from the economy in expectation of large profits in the future. Hall suggested that taxes be raised on unimproved lands.[27]

When the original committee membership became less interested in vacant lot gardening as the panic declined, the Salvation Army expressed interest in continuing the program. Some cities even encouraged the Army to take over management of the program. In 1905, Hall secured use of about thirty acres from the Astor estate in the Bronx for the Salvation Army's vacant lot gardening program. The program did not flourish because the AICP and the Army had trouble finding applicants to work with the latter group in the Bronx.[28]

In an effort to save the program in 1906, the project was transferred from the Salvation Army to a new group formed by Hall and called the Vacant Lot Gardening Association. Composed of single-taxers and now entirely separate from the AICP, the association renewed the lease of land from the Astor estate but was unable to secure enough additional tillable land to make the program a success. In its first report, the association told landowners that it would be good policy to be more liberal in permitting use of their lands "in view of the widespread socialistic agitation."[29] Even this alarm was not enough to bring support to the faltering movement. In the 1908 and 1909 growing seasons, the Astor estate withdrew most of its land from the association. Thus, by 1909, the association was left with only one small plot of land, which six families used only for "tenting." In its final report, the association expressed the hope of buying 1,500 acres of land forty to fifty miles from New York City and also of receiving a donation of $75,000. Its ultimate dream was that the new farmers would show visitors how satisfying rural life could really be. In this way the scheme would "not only wean people from the Call of the Crowd and create work, but start an automatic movement out of the cities to 'God's Country.' "[30]

The vacant lot gardening movement failed for many reasons. Land was difficult to secure in and near cities without cost, and the growing conditions were not always good. Where the city gardeners were competent and lucky, they were successful because of their low planting costs and the ease of marketing their products. This embittered rural farmers, whose criticisms pointed out that vacant lot gardeners constituted unfair competition for other agriculturists.[31] The committee realized that the program was actually a matter of charity, and they sought to make it self-sustaining, which it was not and could not be. After the first year's experiment, the committee no longer provided seed and tools to the gardeners, but required payment for them. In addition, the reformers and their financial backers became disenchanted with the very small numbers of unemployed involved in the program, in relation to the total number of men out of work, and with the failure of the program to gain acceptance by the city population. Finally, even though the program caught the public imagination in the 1890s during the depth of the panic, the subsequent decrease in the number of tramps and unemployed reduced interest in it.[32]

While the COS and AICP actively supported the vacant lot gardening movement, they were content to be simply interested observers of the voluntary colonization program of the Salvation Army and the Jews. The Salvation Army was attracted to the vacant lot gardening movement in the United States after interest of the AICP had begun to wane because it fitted General William Booth's social scheme described in his book, *In Darkest England*. Booth had outlined a three-step program for the unemployed in England. He proposed the establishment of a city colony in which the unemployed would be exposed to uplifting influences and also receive temporary relief. The city colony would include such things as industrial homes where salvage (old clothes, papers, and furniture) was processed and lodging houses. The second step was the creation of a farm colony, where the unemployed would receive a knowledge of farming and be restored to health and good character. A few would then return to practice their own callings, but the rest would take the third step to form an overseas colony. The masses of unemployed would go to colonies, in places like Australia and Canada, for ultimate settlement. Vacant lot cultivation could serve as Booth's second stage in the the United States, "a stepping stone between the city and the farm creating a love of the land and a knowledge of how to handle it."[33] The American unemployed had no need to go "overseas" because plenty of land was available in the western United States.

The initial reaction to Booth's scheme by the London COS was not favorable because it ran counter to the principles of the British Poor Law. The New York COS, however, stated it would withhold judgment until able to examine the whole scheme carefully. One American commentator in *New England Magazine* found Booth's book impressive and agreed that cooperative colonies were the only hope for the unemployed. He further warned that if the surplus population were not removed from the cities, "a new social order will come to birth, either in the bosom of the old and living peacefully with it or perchance overthrowing and destroying it."[34]

The Salvation Army exploited this fear in 1897 when it attempted to put General Booth's social scheme into effect in the United States. The national commander of the Salvation Army, Frederick de L. Booth Tucker, asked what America was to do with "the ever increasing army of the unemployed who are reducing many of our cities to a state of siege or sweeping like a devastating swarm of locusts over some of our country districts?" His suggestion, echoing that of many others, involved the removal of the surplus population from the cities to the land. He urged a united effort and "utmost patriotism" to put such a plan into effect. This united effort, moreover, must take place through philanthropy and charity working through "voluntary participation," since the state should not monopolize the field.[35]

In its publications, the Salvation Army saw itself as the only organization that could successfully develop and manage colonization to ease class tensions. In 1897, an article in the *Conqueror* best expressed that self-image: "The poor and destitute look to us as deliverers and are interested in every move the Army makes—the rich look to us as the people able to deal successfully with the problem of the poor—the authorities look to us as valuable allies in the many difficult questions they have to meet." The Salvation Army saw this as its opportunity to form a link between "Plenty and Poor, between Country and City."[36]

To further this aim, the Salvation Army publicized its colonization scheme broadly in order to obtain sufficient funds. Booth Tucker made a point of discussing the relief of unemployment through his proposed farm colonies. "Society has sinned against itself," he asserted, "in ignoring the law that a man's home is a bond for his good behavior."[37] Money spent in placing the unemployed in competition with the employed or in training the jobless in idle habits through indiscriminate charity shattered family ties and increased the number of "homeless and hopeless men . . . to be prey to the anarchist and a menace to society." The remedy was to build cottages and to settle colonies of "happy, homeowning families, who would be a bulwark of strength to our nation." The Salvation Army plan would turn the "hobo" into a "homebo" or at least a "hopebo."[38] The Salvation Army reported that investigation of one group of 400 tramps in New York City indicated that nearly "to a man that if they were given such an offer as the farm colony they would gladly go at once and quit New York forever."[39]

Edward Devine, one of the COS policy-makers, was an open critic of the farm colony plan. He argued that plans for the farm colonies rested on the assumption that the flow of population from rural to urban areas was evil and that those incapable in the cities could best be handled by teaching them agricultural practices and then shipping them to the country. In his view, any such program could only dissipate valuable energy "in an attempt to prevent a movement of population which has shown itself to be world wide and to rest upon necessary economic changes." What had to be done was to train the unemployed and inefficient in the cities to enable them to fit into the urban economy.[40]

The Salvation Army ignored critics, however, and persisted in promoting its colonial ventures. Voluntary donations were supplemented with loans. In New York City, over $30,000 was raised at one Carnegie Hall meeting. In California, the San Francisco Chamber of Commerce joined with the Salvation Army to help underwrite the costs of the first farm colony, Fort Romie, in the Salinas Valley near the Bay of Monterey. Unfortunately, eighteen unemployed

families arrived at the same time a drought began at Fort Romie.
When the drought ended three years later, only one family remained.
After providing for irrigation, the Salvation Army selected new settlers
from the area around Fort Romie and the colony opened its second
phase in 1901.[41]

In April 1898, the Army opened its largest colony at Fort Amity,
located on prairie land in the Arkansas River Valley in eastern
Colorado. The initial colonists were primarily the urban unemployed,
although a few experienced farmers joined them. Due to the difficulty
of breaking up the native sod and preparing the soil, no crops were
grown the first year; however, once the soil was properly prepared,
the colony became somewhat self-sustaining. Fort Herrick, about
twenty miles from Cleveland, Ohio, was the site of the third Salvation
Army colony in the United States. The colony's 280 acres were a
gift to the Army, and about nine families were immediately settled
on the land. Their experience made clear, however, that the land
would not be sufficient to support them. Therefore, the Army moved
the families to other areas and used the colony for inebriates. In spite
of the early financial and other setbacks, the Salvation Army continued
to be enthusiastic and optimistic about its colonization program.

Two novels, published while the Salvation Army was establishing
its colonies, reflected public interest in the program and the enthusiastic hopes for its success. Lydia Platt Richard's *Ahead of the Hounds*
(1899) was the story of a young man, John Martingdale, who decided
to seek his first job in California by hitching a ride on a freight. In
a boxcar, Martingdale was confronted by a group of tramps embittered
toward society and its vagrancy laws that were in reality new fugitive
slave laws. They also blamed society for their present condition. A
"social earthquake" seemed to be their only means of salvation. After
a series of misfortunes involving these tramps, Martingdale became
one himself in the eyes of society. But at the end of the novel, Martingdale was reclaimed by society, and he saw the regeneration of
some of the tramps who rode with him that first night on the road.
One of the most vicious of all, a tramp called "Dynamite," took the
money he had stolen during his career and joined the "Volunteers
of America—The Salvation Army of Uncle Sam." He then made
retribution to society by purchasing 100,000 acres of land in Texas
with his ill-gotten gains and developed a farm colony for the unem-

ployed in conjunction with the Volunteers. He furnished the land and the money, and the Volunteers planned to "do the spiritual part and add character and dignity to the affair." That one of the most vicious tramps and most virulent opponents of society would find personal peace in the farm colony scheme is significant.[42]

Back to the Soil (1901), a novel by Bradley Gilman, is an account of an imaginary farm colony laid out in a manner to obviate the loneliness of country life. Gilman's plan, expressed through Colonel Royce, was to create a circular colony. The land would then be divided into wedges like a pie. All homes would be located at the apex of each wedge, and thus all farmhouses would be close to all others in the colony. This would end rural loneliness and increase the probable success of any farm colony. The model colony is a sustained success story in all aspects—financial, educational, religious, and political. In a review of the book, New York reformer Homer Folks found it stimulating and hoped that it would lead to experiments to induce some urban dwellers to return to the country. He had only one caveat—that with ideas like this "an ounce of actual experience is worth a ton of theory." To judge the merit of the farm colony scheme, impartial detailed reports would be needed from all groups experimenting with farm colonies, including the Salvation Army and the Jews.[43]

The Jewish farm colony program was also known to the reformers. The Hebrew Emigrant Aid Society had established a 1,100-acre colony in New Jersey in 1882. As pogroms intensified in Europe and Jewish immigration into the United States increased, Jews already settled in the United States became concerned. A number of organizations in New York City, including the Montefiore Aid Society, the United Hebrew Charities, and the Baron de Hirsch Fund, helped found an increasing number of colonies in New Jersey, Louisiana,. South Dakota, Oregon, Connecticut, Colorado, and Michigan. To aid untrained urban arrivals in rural settlements, the Jews established farm schools to help reclaim the ghetto unemployed and underemployed. Their program reinforced the "back to the soil" movement sweeping the nation. Joseph Krauskopf stated that the small farmer had health, a steady income, and was "sure footed." In short, the farmer was "the rock of the nation's salvation."[44] The Jews had one special motivation for the colony plan, alluded to by one author in *Jewish Charity* in 1904. Dispersal of Jews away from congested masses in New York

City was necessary "if this country is to be spared a Jewish question."[45]

The difficulty of obtaining funds for his own farm colony programs encouraged the Salvation Army national commander to make an offer to the Jewish colonies. In 1897, the Army had taken over the management of a colony of Armenians in Georgia for the Armenian Relief Committee, and thus it had a precedent. Booth Tucker proposed that the Army settle five thousand families and manage the colonies for the Jews for $500,000. This figure included transportation from Russia, if this was desired. To lessen Jewish fears of Salvationist proselytization, Booth Tucker proposed that rabbis be included in the groups of people to be colonized. His offer was not accepted, presumably because of the fear of proselytization. And perhaps the Jews' fears were not completely groundless.[46]

In 1904 Booth Tucker again stated that the Salvation Army was in the best possible position to manage colonies because it had the confidence of the working classes and the rulers. He regarded the Army as "the go-between in harmonizing the relationship between capital and labor." He then looked ahead: "Is it too much to expect that in the near future we shall be marching tens of thousands, or even hundreds of thousands, of men, women, and children from one quarter of the globe to the other?" The armies of colonists would pay interest on the investment and the capital could be used over and over again, "and from these settlers we shall be able in due time to recruit our Soldierhood and draw thousands of our best officers."[47]

In 1905, on the initiative of the Rhodes trustees in England, the British government sent an official commissioner, Henry Rider Haggard, to inspect and report upon the condition of the Salvation Army farm colonies. The Secretary of State for the Colonies told Haggard that if the Salvation Army was as successful as it seemed to be, some similar system might be applied in Britain to transfer urban populations of the United Kingdom to other parts of the British Empire. Haggard was instructed to pay special attention to the class of people recruited for the colonies, their training and agricultural success, the financing of the scheme, and the overall effect upon character and social happiness.[48]

Haggard was favorably impressed with the Salvation Army colonies at Fort Amity and Fort Romie. At each colony, he toured the facilities, interviewed Salvationists and colonists, and studied financial statements drawn up by independent appraisers. At Fort Romie, he found twenty colonists, most of them married, in excellent financial condition and apparently happy with their colony and its management. Although most of the settlers had no capital on arrival at the colony in 1901, they held an average equity of just over two thousand dollars by 1905. At Fort Amity, he found similar conditions with thirty-eight settlers, most married and working the soil. The settlers appeared satisfied and had accumulated an average equity of about eleven hundred dollars. He found no Salvationist infringement on the religious beliefs of the colonists.

Haggard found little to criticize in the Salvation Army management of the farm colonies once they were operating, and recommended colonization to England. He did fault the Army for some mistakes in founding the colonies, mistakes that had cost the Salvation Army about £10,000. The major financial loss at Fort Romie resulted from the first abortive settlement. Fort Amity had financial problems resulting from the time and effort required in initially developing the soil. In addition, to gather sufficient initial capital, the Salvation Army had borrowed money at high interest rates, which added a severe burden to the fiscal condition of the colonies. He also felt that the colonists should have shouldered a larger share of the expenses of the settlement. All these criticisms, however, were, in Haggard's view, remediable. Profiting from the Army's errors, he proposed that the British government guarantee a loan, which would ease the fiscal burdens. He also proposed that the government act as a watchdog over whatever management agency should be designated. Haggard favored the Salvation Army, and free land suitable for the venture was promised by the Canadian government.[49]

Haggard argued cogently for his plan and defended his choice of the Salvation Army as the management agency when he answered his critics in a later edition of his published report. He said that in the great cities, clamor and crisis arose every winter "with wild threats and violence appeased by ever increasing inroads" on public relief. Removing people to the soil was the only real solution. For additional support, he could point to President Theodore Roosevelt and Secretary of Agriculture James Wilson, both of whom thought Haggard's plan was admirable and workable if the various guarantees Haggard built into his plan were enforced. Needless to say, the Salvation Army was ecstatic with Haggard's support for its colonies and management. But the Haggard report marked the high tide of the Salvation Army's colonies in the United States. With Fort Herrick already a failure and Fort Romie only a marginal success, the Salvation Army abandoned Fort Amity in 1908, and all its land was sold.[50]

Although the back-to-the-land movement hit its peak during the first decade of the twentieth century and then declined, occasional attempts were still made by states and agencies outside New York to establish voluntary farm colonies. In 1914, a proposal to settle New York City's unemployed in New Mexico was ignored by Mayor John Purroy Mitchel. Among the more widely known programs was that of the California State Settlement Board under the leadership of Elwood Mead. Feeling that success in a colony program could be achieved only through group settlement, the board offered land in tracts of 5,000 acres or more to be divided by the colonizing group. Its program, however, was designed for men with some capital and not principally for the unemployed. In discussing the problems of demobilization, Walter Weyl wrote in the *New Republic* in 1918 that the unemployed returning soldiers would eventually find jobs if they did not "starve or go to jail or become tramps." Many proposed that discharged soldiers be settled on the land to preclude those possibilities.[51]

Voluntary farm colonies failed for many reasons. They did not fulfill the basic purpose of removing the unemployed from the cities. Although some unmarried, homeless unemployed were included in the programs, the colonizers found such men unsuitable. Even when the colonies were apparently successful, very small numbers of people were actually involved. To increase these programs significantly was financially unfeasible. The failure of some colonies had a depressing effect on the entire movement. The Salvation Army colonies, settled primarily by city dwellers, collapsed completely by 1908. Increasingly and ultimately discouraging for the colonizers was the reluctance of former city residents to remain in isolated areas, and the unprecedented growth of the cities which, in spite of overcrowding, were nonetheless maintaining all resident and homeless unemployed on at least a subsistence level.[52]

While the NYCOS observed the failure of voluntary farm colonies for those who wanted to work, it simultaneously favored and worked for compulsory farm colonies for those who would not work. In 1894 the society distributed a leaflet entitled *How to Help Homeless People*, designed in a question-and-answer format, to warn New York City residents against providing indiscriminate charity. The original draft of the leaflet asked an interesting question as to what could be done with tramps. The proposed answer suggested that the city detain tramps on a farm belonging to it and provide agricultural training. When the leaflet was ready to be printed, however, the COS was not ready to commit itself to the farm plan, which was then deleted from the publication.[53]

Nevertheless, many individuals worked to have a bill introduced into the New York State legislature authorizing such a compulsory colony. Edmund Kelly, author and founder of the City Club, which was dedicated to political reform, was one of the leading exponents for the colony in New York City. He worked closely with Josephine Shaw Lowell and others interested in the program. Convinced that voluntary programs would never succeed in returning incapable men to the land, Kelly helped draft and circulate a proposed bill among reformers and law enforcement officials for comments. The major criticism of the proposal came from Z. R. Brockway, superintendent of the New York State Reformatory at Elmira. He said that two-and-one-half-year fixed sentences had not proved sufficiently long enough to reform inmates at Elmira, and this would also prove true in a farm colony.[54]

While the supporters saw no way of materially increasing the maximum length of a confinement, they did change the sentence to ''indeterminate'' so the manager of a farm colony could vary the length of sentences at his discretion, depending on how well the tramps were reforming. The tramp, therefore, had an incentive to reform so that he would be released as quickly as possible. If he refused to work diligently, the manager could hold him at the farm until the maximum sentence had been served. In February 1897, a revised version of the reformers' bill, including indeterminate sentencing, was introduced into the state assembly. It provided for ''the establishment by the City of New York of a Farm Colony for the detention, reformation, and instruction of persons convicted of vagrancy, habitual drunkenness, and repeated disorderly conduct.''[55]

The Salvation Army highly praised the bill, which meshed neatly with its plans for placing the unemployed on the farms. At the colony the men would be "taught the best forms of agriculture" and would therefore qualify as farm laborers or as farmers in their own right. The measure passed the senate but was defeated in the assembly, largely due to the efforts of Assemblyman Daniel E. Finn of New York City. Finn opposed indeterminate sentencing as arbitrary and revolutionary in its application to American citizens.[56]

With the defeat of the bill and the end of the depression in the 1890s, the reformers temporarily lost interest in voluntary or compulsory farm colonies and concentrated on other matters. Two events then renewed their interest in compulsory colonies for the voluntarily unemployed; the first was a new wave of unemployment and tramping during the panic of 1907-1908 and the second was Kelly's publication of *The Elimination of the Tramp* (1908), which proposed a modified adaptation of the European forced labor colonies for the United States. Before publishing it, Kelly sent the book to Robert W. Hebberd, commissioner of public charities of New York City and member of the NYCOS, Robert F. Cutting, president of the NYAICP, and Robert W. DeForest, president of the NYCOS. All three wrote laudatory prefaces for the book, recommending the system be tried legally and fairly in the United States. With the support of these three powerful individuals and organizations, such a trial was a definite possibility.[57]

The idea of forced labor colonies was widely known in Europe, and the story of Count Rumford's eliminating vagrants in Bavaria was a story told and retold by reformers in articles about tramps. According to the story, Count Rumford was exceedingly troubled by the many vagrants in Bavaria. Finally he announced that on a specified date, every man not working would be confined to a labor colony. When the day arrived, few were without jobs. After the system had existed only a short while, Bavaria had no more vagrants.[58]

Kelly's book first discussed tramps in general and then summarized the experiences of European countries with forced labor colonies. He found that the Dutch and German colonies were not self-supporting and had largely abandoned all attempts to reform the inmates. Belgium's famed Merxplas was an industrial, rather than a farm, colony. The Swiss colony at Witzwyl became Kelly's model.

Witzwyl was divided into two sections, a forced labor colony and a free, or voluntary, one. When a tramp came before a magistrate, the magistrate could send him to the voluntary colony, which would leave no stigma on the tramp's future. If the vagrant refused to work, the colony's supervisor, with the concurrence of the magistrate, could transfer the offender to the forced labor colony. Kelly's plan for the United States was to offer each convicted tramp the choice of being sentenced to the forced labor colony or signing a contract for two months at the voluntary colony. Except for wearing institutional garb, those at the voluntary colony would hardly even know they were under contract. Any man running away would be charged with theft (of the colony garb), and all inmates would be so informed upon arrival. Kelly also suggested that the farms be kept small so as not to give much competition to regular farms.[59]

Kelly's book stirred up tremendous interest and numerous book reviews and articles appeared on his proposal. The two-phase operation of the compulsory farm colony was especially well received. Magistrates unwilling to sentence a tramp, and especially a young person, to prison or a forced labor colony would be apt to agree to the proposed voluntary commitment, realizing that if the defendant were a legitimate workman he would be released early. If the tramp refused to work, he would then in a sense go to a forced labor colony by his own hand.[60]

In 1908 a bill proposing a compulsory farm colony for tramps was drawn up by Kelly with the assistance of Robert Cutting, Robert DeForest, and representatives of certain railroads. The bill was defeated in the New York State legislature in 1908, 1909, and 1910 in spite of support by virtually all the New York reformers who wrote letters and made speeches in an attempt to influence legislators.[61] In 1911, the farm colony bill was again introduced. This time Alfred E. Smith, Democratic leader in the state assembly, and other public officials agreed to support the farm colony bill, and other legislators fell in line. The successful bill authorized an unpaid board of managers to secure land already owned by the state or to buy not less than five hundred acres. Supporters confidently announced that New York was now in the front rank of states that used modern methods in dealing with tramps. The law also reflected the reformers' recognition that there was a distinct difference between tramps and reputable unemployed workmen by stating that the law did not intend to label temporarily unemployed men as tramps.[62]

In spite of passage of the bill, the compulsory farm colony never went into operation. Under its terms, the board of managers was to select a suitable land site not later than March 1, 1912. Due to late passage of the law, most areas considered were under snow and could not be surveyed. Although the board requested $60,000 for a site to be selected and authority to draw up contracts not to exceed $500,000, none of this money was ever appropriated, and the farm colony existed only on paper.[63]

One reviewer of Kelly's book pointed out its most serious flaw. The tramp was not in an agricultural period of development but rather was "a sort of Ishmaelitish city-dweller."[64] To keep such a man on a farm would be a punishment rather than an opportunity. The scheme to remove all urban unemployed to the country was utopian, at the least.[65] The assumption that farm labor was always required met with increasing criticism after the panic of 1893. Richard T. Ely wrote to the Rev. Wilbur Crafts, who had complained publicly that, in spite of all the unemployed in New York City, it was impossible to find men to take jobs on farms. Ely pointed out that farmers had no trouble securing help even at harvest time, and when occasionally a few farmers could not find help, the newspapers exaggerated their failure. In addition, Ely said that the wages for an entire season could not match the transportation expenses from New York City to any distant point.[66]

The basic reason for the failure of all "back to the country" movements was simple—America was urbanizing. To send more men to rural areas, which could not support those already there, was ridiculous. Reformers supported programs to encourage farm boys to stay in rural areas and yet also supported programs to encourage the city poor to go to the country, when the simple economics of the situation was that rural areas were already saturated. Further, the rural life had little appeal or even opportunity for urbanites or the young. Josiah Strong, a Christian Socialist, asserted that moving 100,000 urban unemployed into the country and training them to be farmers would not relieve the overall economic conditions in the United States, because to do so would only put 100,000 farmers out of work. To avoid class division in society, the people had to be forged into one bond, one community of common industrial interests.[67]

While the New York reformers expressed faith in the rural ethic to solve urban problems when the panic of 1893 began, they soon observed the failure of back to the land programs to do so. They withdrew support from programs they were participating in and became open critics of other programs they observed. The only apparent exception to this increasing lack of faith in rural nostrums was their support for the state farm colony for tramps, which was truly designed for only a minority of the unemployed. The importance of all these rural experiments was to show the reformers that massive problems such as unemployment could not be solved by a rural panacea that did not exist. Although faith in the rural ethic was greatly weakened by 1908, no reformer suggested, nor did society as a whole believe, that perhaps there just was not enough work for everyone in America. The usual prescription was to make the laborer more efficient and then help him find a job. When it became apparent that efficient workmen could not find jobs, the reformers concluded that the task was to make the job-finding system more efficient.

NOTES

1. The chapter title was a slogan printed on the inside cover of the New York City Vacant Lot Gardening Association, *Report for the Season of 1906*, (n.p., n.d.).

2. Richard Hofstadter, *The Age of Reform* (New York, 1955), 25. The chapter on the place of the yeoman farmer in American thought, "The Agrarian Myth and Commercial Realities," is excellent. Other enlightening discussions on the subject are included in Marvin Meyers, *The Jacksonian Persuasion: Politics and Belief* (New York, 1960); Henry Nash Smith, *Virgin Land: The American West as a Symbol and Myth* (Cambridge, Massachusetts, 1950); and Leo Marx, *The Machine in the Garden: Technology and the Pastoral Ideal in America* (New York, 1964).

3. Smith, *Virgin Land*, 207.

4. Helene S. Zahler, *Eastern Workingmen and National Land Policy, 1829-1862* (New York, 1941), 35.

5. Roy Marvin Robbins, "Horace Greeley: Land Reform and Unemployment, 1837-1862," *Agricultural History* 7 (January 1933): 18, 41.

6. Quoted in Smith, *Virgin Land*, 254. Another Turner statement on the safety valve is in "Contributions of the West to American Democracy," *The Frontier in American History* (New York, 1920), 258; Walter Weyl, "Immigration and Industrial Saturation," NCCC, *Proceedings* (1905), 370.

7. Gene M. Gressley, "The Turner Thesis—A Problem in Historiography," *Agricultural History* 32 (October 1958): 227-249, is a summary of over two dozen historians' views of the Turner thesis. Another collection can be found in O. Lawrence Burnette, comp., *Wisconsin Witness to Frederick Jackson Turner, A Collection of Essays on the Historian and the Thesis* (Madison, 1961). See also Fred A. Shannon, *The Farmer's Last Frontier: Agriculture 1860-1897* (New York, 1945), chap. 15. In three articles, Joseph Schafer points out the psychological importance of the safety valve; and while Carter Goodrich has attacked Schafer generally, he does agree with the possible importance of the safety valve's psychological effect. Curtis Nettels, "Frederick Jackson Turner and the New Deal," in the Burnette volume accepts the psychological view and states the New Deal tried to fill the void.

8. Books and articles during the period 1890-1915 generally referred to the back-to-the-land or farm movement. The movement had three aspects: extolling rural values in the city, encouraging urban dwellers to settle on the land, and criticizing the inadequacies of the city. Most authors realized that America was already urban, or nearly so, bringing with it congestion, pollution, poverty, and class tensions. By appealing to the rural ethic to solve the city's ills, they were deluding themselves that the nation could return to the womb. For an example of the use of terminology of back to the land, see Harvey W. Wiley, *The Lure of the Land* (New York, 1915).

9. Charles Loring Brace, *The Dangerous Classes of New York and Twenty Years Work Among Them* (New York, 1880), 224-225.

10. *St. Vincent de Paul Quarterly* 1 (November 1895): 27; "Notes of the Month," *Charities Review* 2 (March 1893): 288; NYC YMCA, *Annual Report* (1895), 139; Five Points House of Industry, *Annual Report* (1910), 27.

11. Walter Augustus Wyckoff, *A Day with a Tramp and Other Days* (New York, 1901), 48-49, and his *The Workers: An Experiment in Reality: The East* (New York, 1897), 158. See also Bolton Hall, *A Little Land and a Little Living* (New York, 1908), 275.

12. Octave Thanet, "The Contented Masses," *Forum* 18 (October 1893): 204-215.

13. Owen Kildare, *My Mamie Rose: The Story of My Regeneration: An Autobiography* (New York, 1903), 155. For a detailed discussion of the subject see Peter J. Schmitt, *Back to Nature: The Arcadian Myth in Urban America* (New York, 1969).

14. NYAICP, *Inquiry into the Causes of Agricultural Depression in New York State* (New York, 1895), 18; Gould P. Colman, *Education and Agriculture: The History of the New York State College of Agriculture at Cornell* (Ithaca, 1963), 124.

15. Louise M. Greene, *Among School Gardens* (New York, 1910), 4. See also NYSBC, *Annual Report* (1912), 70, and Joseph Lee, *Constructive and Preventive Philanthropy* (New York, 1902), 215-216.

16. "Problem of the Unemployed," New York *Herald*, March 25, 1896, clipping in the Papers of Jacob A. Riis, The City College of the City University of New York.

17. R. F. Powell, "Vacant Lots vs Vagrancy," *Charities* 13 (October 1894): 25.

18. "A Record of Progress," *Lend A Hand* 14 (June 1895): 403; H. P. Pingree, "Mayor Pingree's Potato Patch Plan," *Public Opinion* 20 (January 23, 1896): 109. This is another example of the interchangeability of the terms "tramps" and "unem-

ployed" as discussed in chap. 2. Melvin G. Holli, *Reform in Detroit* (New York, 1969), 70-73.

19. Pingree, "Potato Patch Plan," 109; "A Record of Progress," 405.

20. United States, Department of Agriculture, Division of Statistics, *Report on the Experience of Detroit* (Washington, D.C., 1895).

21. NYAICP broadsheet requesting money and vacant lots for use in providing relief for the unemployed, March 1895, Russell Sage Collection, The City College of the City University of New York.

22. Committee on the Cultivation of Vacant Lots, "Minutes," April 22, 1895, Papers of NYAICP; Michael A. Mikkelson, "Cultivation of City Lots," *Forum* 21 (May 1896): 413-417.

23. NYAICP, "Cultivation of City Lots by the Unemployed," *AICP Notes* 1 (December 1895): 43-44.

24. J. W. Kjelgaard, *Cultivation of City Lots by the Unemployed* (New York, 1895), 14, 20, pamphlet located in the Russell Sage Collection.

25. Frederic W. Spiers, Samuel McCune Lindsay, and Franklin B. Kirkbridge, "Vacant-Lot Cultivation," *Charities Review* 8 (April 1898): 75, 81; *AICP Notes* 1 (December 1895): 3.

26. Committee on the Cultivation of Vacant Lots, "Minutes," October 15, 1895, February 24, 1896, Papers of NYAICP, Archives of the Community Service Society, New York City; *AICP Notes* 1 (April 1896): 57.

27. Bolton Hall to Edward P. Barker, May 13, 1896 with copy of an undated letter from Bolton Hall, R. W. Hebberd, and W. W. Locke to Mayor William Strong, Mayoralty Papers Prior to 1896, Municipal Archives, New York City. In *Things As They Are* (Boston, 1899), 112, Hall writes that vacant lot programs would succeed if only the unemployed had access to the land. This would bring "spiritual brotherhood" between the rich and poor.

28. "Editorial Comment," *Conqueror* 6 (April 1897): 89; "Editorial Comment," *Conqueror* 6 (May 1897): 113; Governor Hazen Pingree, "A Few Lines from the Governor's Own Pen," *War Cry*, March 27, 1897, 14; "Salvation Army Potato Patches, *War Cry*, May 27, 1905, 12; NYAICP, Relief Department, "Minutes," June 14, 1905; Vacant Lot Gardening Association of New York City, *Second Report: Season of 1907* (n.p., n.d.), 6.

29. Vacant Lot Gardening Association of New York City, *Report for Season of 1906* (n.p., n.d.), 3; Florence Kelly, "An Undertow to the Land," *Craftsman* 11 (December 1906): 32.

30. Vacant Lot Gardening Association of New York City, *Third Report: Seasons of 1908-09* (n.p., n.d.), 5.

31. See for example, Charles A. Robinson, "Pingree Potato Culture and His Effects on Business," *Arena* 19 (March 1898): 368-377; Bolton Hall, Letter to Editor, *Outlook* 54 (September 26, 1896): 578.

32. Spiers, "Vacant-Lot Cultivation," 104-105; Henry Rider Haggard, *The Poor and the Land* (New York, 1905), 139; NYCCCC, *Proceedings* (1910), 88; Robinson, "Pingree Potato Culture," 374.

33. William Booth, *In Darkest England, and the Way Out* (New York, 1890), 90-93. Frederick de L. Booth Tucker (national commander of the Salvation Army in the United States, 1896-1904), *Our Future Pauper Policy in America* (n.p., n.d.), 22, located at the Salvation Army Officers Training School in New York City; Frederick de L. Booth Tucker, "Farm Colonies of the Salvation Army," *Forum* 23 (August 1897): 759.

34. C. S. Loch, Bernard Bosanquet, and Canon Phillip Dwyer, *Criticisms on "General" Booth's Social Scheme: From Three Different Points of View* (London, 1891), 50-51; NYCOS, *Monthly Bulletin*, February 28, 1891, 3; William M. Salter, "Problem of the Unemployed," *New England Magazine* (N.S.) 4 (March 1891): 111; J. S. Rankin, "Come West with Your Unemployed," *Outlook* 49 (January 20, 1894): 154.

35. Frederick de L. Booth Tucker, "The Pauper Problem in America," *Charities Review* 6 (April 1897): 127, 132.

36. "Reflections and Forecasts," *Conqueror* 6 (March 1897): 56, 57.

37. Frederick de L. Booth Tucker, "The Proposed Colonization Scheme," *Conqueror* 6 (September 1897): 201.

38. Frederick de L. Booth Tucker, *The Social Relief Work of the Salvation Army in the United States* (New York, 1900), 32.

39. "Icy Hand of the Blizzard Brings Untold Suffering," *War Cry*, February 13, 1897, 4-5.

40. Edward T. Devine, "The Shifting and Floating Population," *Annals* 10 (September 1897): 158.

41. *The Farm Colonies of the Salvation Army* (New York, 1898) is a pamphlet designed to solicit funds for the movement. It is a summary of the beginning of the colonization and is quite optimistic in tone. United States, Department of Commerce and Labor, *Bulletin of the Bureau of Labor*, No. 48 (Washington D.C., 1903) is a summary of the Salvation Army Farm Colony program on a worldwide basis. The best contemporary document is Henry Rider Haggard's *The Poor and the Land: Being a Report on the Salvation Army Colonies in the United States and at Hadleigh, England with Schemes of National Land Settlement* (London, New York, and Bombay, 1905), which contains observations, interviews, and financial statements. See also Dorothy Roberts, "Fort Amity, The Salvation Army Colony in Colorado," *Colorado Magazine* 17 (September 1940): 168-174.

42. Lydia Platt Richards, *Ahead of the Hounds: A Story of Today* (Chicago, 1899).

43. Bradley Gilman, *Back to the Soil or From Tenement House to Farm Colony: A Circular Solution of an Angular Problem* (Boston, 1901); clipping of Homer Folk's review of *Back to the Soil* located in the Papers of Homer Folks, Columbia University School of Social Work.

44. New Jersey, Bureau of Statistics, *The Jewish Colonies of South Jersey: Historical Sketch of their Establishment and Growth* (Camden, New Jersey, 1901); Samuel Joseph, *History of the Baron de Hirsch Fund* (New York, 1935), 8-33; "Agricultural Colonies in the U.S.," *The Jewish Encyclopedia* (New York, 1901), I: 256-262; Philip R. Goldstein, *Social Aspects of the Jewish Colonies of South Jersey* (New York, 1921); Jacob

A. Riis, "Making a Way Out of the Slum," *Review of Reviews* 22 (December 1900): 689-697; Joseph Krauskopf, "Address," October 15, 1911, Papers of Lillian Wald, Columbia University; Joseph Krauskopf, "The National Farm School," *Jewish Charity* 4 (December 1904): 160.

45. M. V. Ball, "The Dispersion of the Immigrant," *Jewish Charity* 3 (April 1904): 168.

46. "Editorial Comment," *Conqueror* 6 (April 1897): 89; Frederick de L. Booth Tucker, "Settlement on the Land," *Jewish Charity* 3 (May 1904): 181-182.

47. Frederick de L. Booth Tucker, "Colonization and its Advantages to the Salvation Army," *International Staff Council Addresses* (New York, 1904), 304-306.

48. Haggard, *Poor and the Land*, xxxix.

49. All information is drawn from Haggard, *Poor and the Land*. See also Lamb, *The Social Work of the Salvation Army*, 109.

50. Haggard, *Poor and the Land*, xxix, 28; "Interesting Announcement," *War Cry*, November 4, 1905, 15.

51. J. H. Thain to Mayor John Purroy Mitchel, December 3, 1914, Papers of John A. Kingsbury, Library of Congress; Elwood Mead, "Farms for the Soldiers When They Come Back," *World's Work* 7 (November 1918): 66-67; Alvin Johnson, "Land for the Returned Soldier," *New Republic* 16 (September 21, 1918): 218-220; Walter Weyl, "Planless Demobilization," *New Republic* 17 (November 30, 1918): 125. See also Paul K. Conkin, *Two Paths to Utopia* (Lincoln, 1964), for a discussion of two other types of voluntary colonies.

52. *Bulletin of the Bureau of Labor*, No. 48, September, 1903, 1102; Jewish Agricultural and Industrial Aid Society, *Annual Report* (1909), 8.

53. NYCOS, Executive Committee, "Minutes," October 30, 1894, November 7, 1894; Papers of NYCOS, Archives of the Community Service Society, New York City; Edmund Kelly, "Compulsory Colonization," *Charities Review* 4 (November 1894): 78-86.

54. NYCOS, Executive Committee, "Minutes," December 23, 1895, Papers of NYCOS; Edmund Kelly, *Evolution and Effort* (1st ed., 1895, 2d ed. rev., New York, 1900), 162; Z. R. Brockway to Arthur W. Milbury, March 14, 1886, Papers of NYCOS.

55. State of New York, No. 728, Int. 650, February 9, 1897, copy in the Papers of Jacob A. Riis.

56. Editorial Comment," *Conqueror* 6 (April 1897), 89; Homer Folks, "The New York City Conference of Charities," *Charities Review* 6 (June 1897): 349.

57. Edmund Kelly, *The Elimination of the Tramp: By the Introduction into America of the Labour Coloney System Already Proved Effective in Holland, Belgium, and Switzerland, with the Modifications Thereof Necessary to Adapt This System to American Conditions* (New York and London, 1908).

58. For the historical background of the story see *Encyclopaedia Britannica*, 11th ed., XXIII, 850.

59. Kelly, *Elimination of the Tramp*, passim.

60. Frank M. White, "Eliminate the Tramp," *Harper's Weekly* 53 (February 6,

1909): 16-17; "Tramp Elimination," *Independent* 65 (September 3, 1908): 569-570; *International Socialist Review* 8 (May, 1908), 710-711; Orlando F. Lewis, "Concerning Vagrancy," *Charities and The Commons* 20 (September 5, 1908): 674-681.

61. Joint Application Bureau, "Minutes," December 9, 1907; NYCOS, Central Council, "Minutes," April 8, 1908, Papers of NYCOS; "Journal of Homer Folks (October 8, 1904-June 30, 1911)," entries for February 18, 19, 1908, Papers of Homer Folks; "A Brief for the Establishment of a State Farm Colony," 1911, Papers of Lillian Wald, New York Public Library; C. K. Blatchly, "State Farm for Tramps and Vagrants," *Survey* 24 (April 9, 1910): 87-89; *Railway Age Gazette* 45 (December 18, 1908): 1599; NCCC, *Proceedings* (1911), 79.

62. "Farm Colony Bill Urged on Governor Dix," *Survey* 26 (May 20, 1911): 284; Second Annual Conference of Mayors and Other City Officials of the Cities of New York State, *Proceedings* (1911), 162; "Tramp Farm Colony Assured in New York," *Survey* 26 (August 5, 1911): 633; "The Farm Colony for Tramps," *Independent* 71 (August 3, 1911): 270.

63. New York State, *Report of the State Industrial Farm Colony* (New York, 1912); NYCOS, *Annual Report* (1916), 116-117; NYSCCC, *Proceedings* (1913), 280.

64. Edward E. Hale, Jr., "Hobo in Theory and Practice," *Dial* 44 (May 16, 1908): 301-302.

65. Charles Sprague Smith (Peoples Institute) to Leonard Opdycke, March 19, 1909, Papers of NYAICP; Edward Ewing Pratt, *Industrial Causes of Congestion in New York City* (New York, 1911), 201; "The Week," *Nation* 86 (February 13, 1908): 140; William D. P. Bliss, ed., *The Encyclopedia of Social Reform* (New York and London, 1908), 1247.

66. Richard T. Ely to Rev. Wilbur F. Crafts, February 1, 1895, in Wilbur F. Crafts, *Practical Christian Sociology* (New York, 1895), 464-465.

67. Josiah Strong, "The Problem of the City," *Association Men* 33 (July 1908): 462, 463; Josiah Strong, *The Challenge of the City* (New York, 1907), 155. See Liberty Hyde Bailey, *The Country-Life Movement in the United States* (New York, 1911), 25-26.

5

"Connecting the Jobless Man and the Manless Job": Employment Bureaus and Labor Exchanges

IN THE 1890s the homeless unemployed in New York City had no efficient means of finding a job. To walk the streets in search of "help wanted" signs was tiring, discouraging, and seldom fruitful. If a man who had little money did not find work quickly, his physical appearance generally deteriorated so rapidly that no one would hire him because he looked like a tramp. Looking at newspaper advertisements was just as inefficient as applying directly to prospective employers. Vague job descriptions and overstated requirements for the number of men needed attracted many times the desired number of workmen to the place of interview, and those not hired wasted much time.

Commercial employment agencies were perhaps the most seductive and inefficient means of helping the job seeker. Posters on dreary windows advertised hundreds of positions: "Wanted": "Farm Hands," "1,000 Laborers For Railroad Work," or "500 Men For Woods in Wisconsin." The signs were only bait, however, for the jobs often did not exist. But once the agency collected the registration fee from a man, he did not recover it even if no job was found. The employment agencies rapidly gained a reputation for fraud and deceit, especially because of their treatment of the newly arrived immigrants and the illiterate. New York attempted to regulate the few honest agencies and to eliminate the dishonest ones through legislation in 1888 and 1891, but loosely written laws, coupled with poor enforcement, led to continued malpractice among agencies.[1]

The combination of the panic of 1893, which threw thousands out of work, and the widespread knowledge of the exploitation of the poor and unemployed by commercial agencies, led to increased philanthropic activity in the employment bureau field. The idea of aiding a man to find work was quite congenial to the New York reformers. In the fall of 1896, the NYAICP opened an employment bureau in conjunction with Cooper Union. By assisting men to help themselves, the AICP hoped that the employment bureau would ameliorate the conditions of "unrest and dissatisfaction" in the city.[2] Opening its doors during the heyday of the "back-to-the-land" movement, the new bureau's initial efforts were naturally directed toward placing its applicants in the country. The bureau posted circulars in 1,500 post offices and advertised in over 200 country papers within a 150-mile radius of New York City. The bureau expected double benefits: each man placed in the country would mean not only a job for the applicant but also one less man in New York City's labor market.[3] The Cooper Union Bureau learned quickly, however, that few jobs existed in the country for the city unemployed. When economic conditions were poor in the city, they were equally bad in the rural areas. In good times, however, the Cooper Union Bureau faced another problem: most of its applicants were not really suitable for the labor market because of a lack of training and discipline. Employers generally looked less favorably on applicants from philanthropic bureaus and offered them wages below the prevailing rate on the theory that the men, desperate and badly in need of a job, were probably not as competent as workers placed by commercial agencies. As the United States edged steadily out of the depression, the bureau had fewer applicants for work and fewer employers seeking workers, and, therefore, it recommended its own dissolution to the AICP. The AICP closed the Cooper Union Bureau in 1899.[4]

The Jews also operated a philanthropic employment agency during the panic of 1893. One of the first actions taken by the United Hebrew Charities of New York City after its organization was to establish a free employment bureau. The bureau became quite active after 1885, when a combination of increased unemployment in New York City and greatly increased Jewish immigration dictated a more intensive effort to place unemployed Jews. The bureau had more success than most of the other free charitable bureaus, placing three-fourths of its 3,000 applicants during the depth of the panic in 1893. But gradually the Jewish bureau encountered problems similar to those of other philanthropic bureaus. Administrators of the bureaus came to realize that, when economic conditions were good, skilled men found jobs on their own without difficulty. Men who did apply at the bureau during good times were not adequately prepared to compete on the labor market. In addition, men without the habit of discipline, which comes with steady work, often embarrassed the agency by accepting a job and then quitting after a short time. After such an experience, an employer rarely used the United Hebrew Charities Bureau a second time. The Jews felt that the ultimate solution required the prevention of unemployment, which was often "the first step toward chronic vagrancy." But the bureau was not organized to do preventive work, nor could it effectively place the applicants who asked for aid. Therefore, the United Hebrew Charities disbanded its bureau in 1904, turning over its functions to the B'nai Brith and the Industrial Removal Office.[5]

The YMCA, like the United Hebrew Charities, had always offered the services of an employment bureau. Its bureau charged a small fee and constituted an important part of the self-help philosophy of the YMCA. The YMCA proclaimed that looking for employment was an absolute duty in the eyes of God. Its bureaus had mixed success in placing men. The Twenty-third Street branch of the YMCA placed about one out of every two applicants between the years 1896 and 1898, while the Bowery branch placed only one applicant out of six during the same period. In 1902, the Bowery branch made one attempt at rural placement by purchasing a small farm in New Jersey to be used as an adjunct to its employment bureau. But it cost about $60,000 to place seventy-five men on the farm, and the Bowery branch dropped the experiment. After the failure of the Cooper Union,

United Hebrew Charities, and St. Vincent de Paul Society employment
bureaus, all because of the "taint of charity," the YMCA administrators eventually ruled that only members or prospective members
of the organization and not the "usual" unemployed could use its
employment bureaus, in an attempt to put their agencies on a more
commercial basis.[6]

While all philanthropic bureaus had the same problems in placing
men, those run by the rescue missions had particular difficulty because
employers considered their applicants to be the lowest class of men.
The wages offered were very low; the treasurer of the Bowery Mission
stated that he often sent men to work on farms at wages of five to
ten dollars per month when prevailing wages were twenty-five to thirty
dollars. The overall placement rate was low; one report estimated that
only one of six applicants found work. And the character of the work
available was often temporary and totally without prestige; one question on the Salvation Army application form asked whether the applicants were willing to carry advertising signboards through the streets.
McAuley's Water Street Mission in one annual report complained that
some men came to it just to seek employment, which was not its
principal interest. McAuley's Mission felt that the men who came to
it were drunkards and not trustworthy. It believed that its task was
to save men for Christ, not to find work for men, because "the Lord
has made a job for every saved drunkard, as soon as He sees it safe
for him to have it."[7]

In short, the philanthropic employment bureaus played only a
very small role in securing jobs for the unemployed. They did not
have the resources or, in a number of cases, the interest to run a
truly efficient bureau. The Salvation Army realized by the turn of the
century that its individual employment bureaus were not efficient and
attempted to set up an exchange of information among them in various
cities. The director of the Cooper Union Bureau came to much the
same conclusion. "Cooperation with other bureaus and exchange of
information were necessary to match the supply and demand for labor;
hopefully, the outcome of their services—jobs for the unemployed—would drive fewer men "by hunger and despair to become
tramps or lawbreakers."[8] But the philanthropic bureaus were unable
or unwilling to achieve this cooperation with each other during the
panic of 1893.

While most reformers favored philanthropic employment bureaus during this period, a few sought assistance for the unemployed through public bureaus. One of the earliest reformer exponents of a free public employment bureau in New York City was Jacob Riis. He said the need was brought forth to him one day when he read a story in a newspaper about an unemployed painter who committed suicide after failing to find work. At the time of the suicide, Riis was unable to find a painter for work he wanted accomplished. What was needed, he said, was to bring man and job together. He opposed a municipal bureau because of politics, but felt a state exchange would be acceptable. Riis received favorable comments on his proposal for New York, although some critics would have preferred a bureau run by voluntary associations.[9]

Finally, in the summer of 1896, a free public employment bureau opened in New York City, with five thousand dollars appropriated for its operation. Its purpose was to aid people to find jobs without paying a fee and also to reduce urban congestion, if possible, by diverting laborers to rural districts, but it had only marginal success. While the state legislature did authorize similar bureaus, it did not appropriate any money to develop an employment exchange. Hampered by politics in management and inadequate appropriations, the free bureau closed in 1906.[10]

The failure of the philanthropic and public employment agencies in New York City led to renewed activity in the area of regulating commercial agencies. In 1902 and 1903, Frances A. Kellor and a small staff studied the commercial employment bureaus of New York and other principal cities in behalf of the Women's Municipal League of New York City. Her study revealed that many employment agencies and intelligence offices (whose specialty was supplying domestics) for women were either careless or consciously cooperated with disorderly houses in sending girls to jobs that inevitably led to prostitution. In an atmosphere of white slavery, the more spirited girls were sent to employment agencies in strange cities to make them more pliable and more likely to remain in disorderly or "sporting" houses where the agencies ostensibly placed them as domestics.[11]

Miss Kellor was equally critical of employment agencies for men. She felt many of their practices were apt to weaken or break up the American home. Agencies were frequently located in saloons or

saloon hotels where despondent men could be lured to drown their
sorrows, or could be kept at the bar by promises of imminent work.
One of the most sinister practices involved cooperation between a railroad and a commercial agency. For example, one Chicago bureau
advertised that a railroad needed 4,000 construction laborers at a point
distant from the city. It gathered the men, charged them one dollar
each, and delivered them to a railroad station from where the hiring
railroad hauled the men to the construction site. Upon arrival, the railroad told the men that only 350 would be hired. With the large labor
surplus available in the remote area, the railroad then offered only
subsistence wages to those hired. The final result was that the unhired
had no money to pay for the return ticket and drifted into New York,
producing in Chicago "another batch of deserted wives, in New York
another set of tramps."[12]

Miss Kellor found that two-thirds of the 723 employment
agencies she visited resorted to dishonorable practices and fraudulent
methods at their worst and were grossly inefficient at their best. She
found that fees were too high and that, when non-English speaking
immigrants went to an agency that used only English, they were
cheated by their own padrones, or agents. In addition she found no
guarantees of job placement and many misrepresented contracts. Many
agencies operated at one location only for a short time and then moved
on to another to escape prosecution for fraud. The agencies were not
concerned about placing an individual in a permanent position,
because they received the same fee for placing a man in a temporary
position, which was easier to locate. Kellor's study led directly to
additional legislation for regulation of commercial agencies, but most
basic problems continued to exist, as later studies confirmed.[13]

A problem of special concern to New York City, but also of
importance nationwide, was the placement of the immigrant laborer.
The relationship between the massive influx of immigrants into New
York City and the unemployment there was not understood, yet
immigration was widely blamed for causing or at least increasing
unemployment. In good times, the immigrants were cursed for lower-
ing wages by their willingness to work for below-average rates. In
addition, when mass demonstrations of the unemployed developed in
the 1890s, the immigrants were widely condemned for participating
in or inciting them, because of their unfamiliarity with and hostility

toward American institutions.[14] The concern about the connection between immigration and unemployment was magnified in New York City since so many newly arrived immigrants remained there.

No group was more acutely aware of the increasingly unfavorable attitudes toward immigrants than the established Jews who acted to divert their co-religionists from the labor market. The Jews hoped to forestall any legislative action that would reduce or even end Jewish immigration into the United States. In 1891 Baron Maurice de Hirsch established a fund partly for the purpose of ameliorating the conditions of Jewish immigrants in America. At first, the directors of the Baron de Hirsch Fund, through its primary operating agency in the United States, the Jewish Agricultural and Industrial Aid Society, attempted to place Jews on farms. This attempt, like other back-to-the-soil movements, had only limited success. Thereafter, increasing importance was placed on a separate committee of the society called the Industrial Removal Office, which eventually became a separate and distinct organization in 1901.[15]

The IRO diverted few Jews to farm work but concentrated instead on finding positions for individuals in their own trades in the interior of the United States. From the inception of the program, "only such persons as had no employment or had employment of an unsatisfactory kind" were considered.[16] Removing these Jews from the ranks of the job-seekers in New York would, it was hoped, reduce friction generated against the Jews as a whole by unemployed gentiles. In doing its work, the office found that discouragement and anxiety made unemployed Jews "readily receptive of the gospel of unrest and dissatisfaction" preached to them at every turn.[17] This, too, caused considerable friction between native-born Americans and immigrants as a whole. The goal of the IRO was to distribute Jews throughout the United States to help them secure jobs and to strengthen their religious life. Hopefully the Jews would become "active, energetic, sober, industrious, and striving, strenuous, patriotic American citizens" rather than become discontent in New York City ghettoes.[18] In 1910 the manager of the IRO spoke with pride of the work of his agency, which had distributed some 50,000 Jews directly from New York City to more than 1,100 American cities and towns. Over 85 percent remained outside New York City. In addition, many more immigrants were attracted directly to locations where Jews already resided.[19]

In another attempt to reduce immigrant pressure in New York City, the Jews organized the Galveston Movement to divert Russian Jews from the East to the West through Galveston, Texas. Jacob H. Schiff inaugurated and financially supported the program partly to relieve congestion in New York City. This program achieved only modest success (about 2,000 Jews by 1910 and over 10,000 by 1914), however, because the Russian Jews feared to go to the American "hinterland" where kosher food was unknown and jobs were few.[20]

The Jews encountered an unexpected problem in their distribution from co-religionists in the interior who attempted to discourage the movement. Whenever possible, the IRO tried to match unemployed tradesmen with towns that needed help in specific trades, but more often it shipped unemployed Jews to cooperating communities in the hope that local Jews would aid their co-religionists find work. David Bressler, general manager of the IRO, pointed out that due to difficult individual cases, many communities expressed a reluctance to continue cooperation with his agency.

The most concerted action by interior communities against the activities of the IRO occurred in 1902 when Jews in the interior asserted that a transportation agreement applied to immigrants shipped West. Briefly, this agreement, accepted by the National Conference of Jewish Charities in 1900, stated that no charity organization in a city should provide a relief applicant free transportation to another place without the prior approval of a charity organization in the host city. If such approval were not secured, the sponsoring organization had to pay any expenses incurred in the care of the applicant along the way. Clearly this agreement was drawn up to prevent charitable groups from "passing on" their dependents from one community to another. It started a bitter argument in the National Conference. The final decision did not regard the distribution by the IRO as falling under the agreement. It emphasized that it was the duty of all Jews to help find employment for their brethren.[21] However, even after this decision had been reached, the IRO had to put continual pressure on interior cities and towns to seek employment for immigrants.[22] The program was continued because it did relieve the problem of a small percentage of the Jewish unemployed. It also provided a positive line of defense against anti-immigration policies.[23]

During the early 1900s the relationship between immigration and unemployment was explored by various investigations, commissions, and conferences. When the subject of restricting immigration was taken up by Congress in 1902, Edward Devine of the COS supported the curbs, believing that immigrants replaced American labor, diluted American citizenship, and created every year "a more and more serious menace."[24] The transfer of the Immigration Bureau to the United States Department of Commerce and Labor from the Treasury Department in 1903 gave formal federal recognition that immigration was largely a labor matter.[25] Agreeing with Devine in 1905, Walter E. Weyl wrote that unrestricted immigration was permanently depressing the working classes more than any other cause. He favored restriction as a solution to the problem.[26]

In 1905 the National Civic Federation held a conference on immigration in New York City. Frances Kellor wrote to the federation that although a woman could not address the conference, she wished someone would submit a resolution on distribution of immigrants. She felt a plan had to be worked out that was "governmental and industrial" rather than purely philanthropic. One central office for the proposed labor exchange, administered by the federal government, would be preferable, especially since agreements could be negotiated with foreign governments.[27] Her suggestion was brought up at the conference, which pointed out that the whole country was not interested in distributing the immigrants as Jews had already discovered. For example, while many industrialists favored increased foreign immigration into the South to provide a larger labor source, most Southerners did not. One Southerner warned that undesirable aliens might enter the South and if "their racial pride should not be higher than the Negro what a serious problem it would be for the South!"[28] One year after the conference a hope was expressed that the Immigration Bureau of the National Civic Federation might become a national employment agency, but it did not materialize.[29] The panic of 1907-1908 later intensified discussions on the relationship between immigration and unemployment.

In March 1907, securities plunged on the stock exchange in a warning of disaster. In October, security prices dropped a second time, and several banks associated with speculative issues failed. Within a month, a concerted effort between financiers and the United States Treasury Department averted the possibility of a major panic.

Nevertheless, a depressive effect spread over business, with a significant increase in unemployment in the principal cities of the nation and especially in New York City.[30]

After ten years of relative prosperity, the reformers did not look lightly on the advent of even a relatively minor panic and its attendant socialist activity. Large numbers of unemployed, particularly immigrant unemployed, seemed responsive to socialist and anarchist activity; class tension was increasing in the nation. The bombing incident at Union Square in New York City in 1908 brought the issue squarely before the New Yorkers. Some reformers denied that the Union Square meeting was in any way a demonstration of the actual unemployed, but was a carefully engineered demonstration by reckless socialists and attended only by interested bystanders. Accordingly the reformers insisted that no special public works or public relief should be started because this was exactly what the socialists wanted. Robert Hunter and other socialist leaders disavowed the action of the youthful anarchist, Silverstein, but were attacked in print for planting ideas subversive of law, justice, and order, which in turn helped create such advocates of violence. Using the occasion to attack the socialists, Arthur P. Kellogg questioned how many of the mob were involuntarily idle. In his view, most were not looking for work and, further, were not native Americans but recently arrived immigrants. Kellogg completed his attack on socialists and immigrants with a call for the suppression of speeches designed to inflame the mobs.[31]

While Kellogg preached suppression and the police commissioner requested $100,000 to establish a special police squad to deal with anarchists, Devine publicly disagreed with these proposals, emphasizing that while public meetings of the unemployed were unwise, they should not be suppressed. He asserted that because of a general apprehension over anarchism, the police had been allowed too much leeway in dispersing assemblages and that the people of New York were dangerously indifferent to the use of this arbitrary power. In Devine's opinion, "an unnecessary blow from a policeman in uniform" would do more "to disturb the mental equilibrium of an 'addlepated' embryonic anarchist than any address by Mr. Hunter or his associates."[32]

The accusations that "stunted foreign types," "Jewish faces," and, in general, recent immigrants participated in the Union Square demonstrations underlined the need to study immigration in all its aspects. In 1909, New York State Governor Hughes appointed a Commission on Immigration, which considered unemployment among recent immigrants. The commission recommended a clearinghouse or bureau to protect the alien from exploitation, and at the same time to "facilitate his development into intelligent and useful citizenship for the ultimate advancement of the state." It urged expanded cooperation among the state, federal, and philanthropic agencies "to expedite distribution and to minimize the evils of unemployment."[33]

The New York commission's findings generally agreed with those of the United States Immigration Commission of 1907, which recommended that a Division of Information be set up in the Bureau of Immigration to establish a system to distribute immigrants to sections of the country that could provide permanent employment. The division opened an office in New York City early in 1908 and used the post office as a means of gathering information on the availability of jobs.[34] The YMCA, Bowery Mission, and the Russell Sage Foundation, among others, supported the distribution of immigrants as a way to assimilate the foreign-born and to ease unemployment in urban areas.[35]

Meanwhile Robert Hebberd, New York City Commissioner of Public Charities, invited a number of individuals to a meeting, held in October 1908, to discuss necessary provisions to care for and employ the homeless unemployed in New York City during the coming winter. Almost all the participants were top leaders of New York's voluntarist societies. They elected Robert F. Cutting, chairman, and W. Frank Persons, secretary; Hebberd, Robert Bruere, and Edmund Kelly completed the standing committee. His committee was interested in preventing such mass demonstrations of the unemployed as had occurred the previous spring. In this connection, Jacob Schiff had a proposal for it. Schiff had previously given the connection between social unrest and unemployment much thought, but early in 1907 he had dismissed the possibility of unrest because of favorable economic conditions. However, with unemployment on the rise, he expressed concern to Robert W. DeForest, president of the COS, and suggested that the answer might be simply a more efficient employment bureau: "if such an organization be established on the proper lines, much undeserved misery could be prevented and also much of the existing social unrest removed.''[36] The solution to unemployment, he believed, lay in the organization of employment bureaus not by city or state agencies but by businessmen. The committee discussed his solution and then referred it to the standing committee for action. The committee, working very closely with the COS decided that Devine should make a thorough investigation of the proposal.[37] The Russell Sage Foundation bore the expense of the preliminary investigation and published the completed report in 1909.[38]

Devine's conclusion emphasized the desirability of an employment bureau and urged immediate action to secure one. He based his argument on a series of interviews with economists, industrialists, and public officials, who felt that most unemployment was simply due to maladjustment in the process of bringing a man and a job together. Professor Henry Seager cited as causes of maladjustments the irregular employment in many trades, new and failing businesses, immigration, and the failure to correctly identify skills so that workers might be properly placed. Other observers noted that maladjustment was particularly evident in New York City. Professor E. A. Ross of the University of Wisconsin stated that unemployment was often more local than usually assumed; therefore, it was only rational to help the unemployed leave New York to take advantage of the labor markets needing workers.[39]

Devine argued that existing institutions were not capable of distributing the unemployed through the nation. He cited Kellor's study to show the inadequacy of commercial bureaus, and he singled out the failure of philanthropic bureaus. Public bureaus, in his view, had not proved efficient or successful. Newspaper advertisements were not clear but were misleading in their descriptions of jobs. Trade unions were not large enough to take care of all workers seeking jobs. While his solution looked to private enterprise, Devine rejected the idea that it was the individual responsibility of all men to find work for themselves by tramping from place to place without any aid. Devine found that the practice was "expensive, time consuming, physically laborious, and mentally depressing.'' [40]

Devine made only one change in Schiff's proposal, suggesting that a fee be charged the worker rather than the employer so that the bureau would not be indebted to the latter. The bureau would be organized under a board of trustees drawn from the mercantile and industrial classes. Its trustees would establish an organization covering all parts of the United States in order to be in touch with all available employment opportunities. Although national in scope, its benefits, however, were to accrue primarily to New York City.[41]

In April 1909, the National Employment Exchange, embodying Schiff's and Devine's proposals, was incorporated in New York with a capital fund of $100,000 donated by New York's wealthiest citizens. In May the exchange opened its first branch, which specialized in placing unskilled labor.[42] Its first year seemed successful enough. The branch found jobs for over a thousand men, and two more branches were soon opened. The only unfavorable note was a loss of over ten thousand dollars during the first nine months of operation. Otto T. Bannard, wealthy New York banker and president of the exchange, was nevertheless optimistic and hoped for cooperation with other cities as soon as the new venture was well established in New York.[43] From a hopeful beginning, however, the National Employment Exchange declined steadily in effectiveness. By the third year of operation, it was charging employer and worker two dollars each for services, but even that amount, plus the interest on the $100,000 capital fund, did not cover expenses. The original capital rapidly dwindled as Bannard used it to meet current operating expenses. In an effort to make the exchange profitable, the trustees began reducing their activities in the area where the exchange was most needed. Harry L. Hopkins of the AICP's employment bureau reported in 1913 that although the exchange had been founded primarily for unskilled labor, it had not placed any such unemployed referred by the AICP. The exchange had assured Hopkins it would place 90 percent of all his unskilled applicants, but by 1915 it was directing itself exclusively to skilled and managerial areas.[44]

No one was more disillusioned with the experience of the exchange than Schiff himself. In a letter to Robert DeForest announcing his resignation as a trustee, Schiff pointed out that the exchange was founded as a social service and no one really expected any return on the $100,000; yet the drive to make a profit had caused the exchange to compromise with its original principles. The exchange was not national, but local. Most embittering to Schiff, it had shown prejudice against Jews. When Schiff confronted Bannard with his accusation, Bannard did not deny it, but said that if an employer did not want Jews, the exchange certainly had to comply with his request.[45]

The inability of the National Employment Exchange to deal effectively with unemployment was a dramatic failure for the proponents of voluntarism. The reformers, however, possibly had anticipated this from its inception. In the spring of 1909 the same New York reformers who applauded the opening of the exchange supported the passage of a bill requiring the establishment of a state committee to study unemployment. The reformers had found their own agencies unable even to assess the severity of the panic of 1907-1908, much less to deal with unemployment in all its aspects. Thus they turned to the public sector for action.

When the panic began in the fall of 1907, no one had accurate information on the number of unemployed, so, in December the United Hebrew Charities, the AICP, and the COS hired Frank J. Warne to study the situation in New York City. Warne estimated that unemployment in New York City and throughout the country was more severe than in any year since 1893-1894, but he was unable to offer more than an estimate of unemployment figures.[46] Nor could Mayor George B. McClellan of New York City who wrote Cutting to ask for data on the number of unemployed in New York. To give an estimated number, Cutting went to the Joint Application Bureau, which kept all records on the homeless unemployed for the AICP and the COS. In the spring of 1908, the director of the bureau had reported that its records had been kept in a "grossly inadequate manner." Not only were the figures inaccurate, but they could not be corrected by any information available. Statistics were duplicated on different pages of the same report. Errors in transcription and arithmetic were difficult to correct or notice, because all daily entries were not recorded.[47] These reports of faulty statistics had not stopped Cutting, however, from providing figures to the mayor.

The Central Council of the COS discussed the problem of statistics at a meeting in April 1908. The members were in substantial agreement that figures on unemployment seemed to be guesses, except for those prepared by trade unions. However, one letter received by Robert Bruere from an American Federation of Labor organizer indicated that the labor union was also not so certain of the accuracy of its figures.[48] Although unsure of their figures privately, publicly the NYCOS issued them with an air of professional superiority. After all, the COS council concluded, it had "as accurate knowledge of the subject as anyone could get."[49] But this did not stop the society in its quest for better information.

While doing the research for his study on unemployment, Warne had become convinced of the need for a broad study of unemployment in New York City as well as in the state and used his position as chairman of the Labor and Industry Committee of the Association of Neighborhood Workers to organize a subcommittee on unemployment. Warne and Gaylord White, with the new subcommittee, held a meeting on unemployment at the University Settlement in early February 1908 attended by about seventy-five persons from the major private and public relief agencies, including the COS. The committee formulated a plan, advising Governor Hughes to appoint a commission to investigate unemployment with the primary end in view of "remedial action in future emergencies," and circulated it to philanthropic groups like the AICP and the COS in March asking for suggestions. The AICP and COS were sympathetic to the proposal.[50]

Two days after the Union Square demonstration, a bill drawn up by Warne's committee was introduced in the state senate, and assembly hearings began shortly after. The *New York Times* noted that the anarchist bomb and "especially the meeting of the unemployed that preceded it . . . would be used as an argument in favor of the bill." The paper also reported that J. H. Hamilton of the University Settlement, Gaylord White of the Union Settlement, Edward Devine, Robert Bruere, Robert Hebberd, Dr. Stephen Wise of the Free Synagogue, Samuel McCune Lindsay of Columbia University, Charles Sprague Smith of the Peoples Institute, and J. L. Elliott of the Hudson Guild supported the bill's introduction and passage.[51]

Simultaneously Charles Sprague Smith, as managing director of the Ethical Social League, was planning a conference on unemployment. Early in 1908 a small group mailed out some 3,000 invitations to offer memberships in the league. The League proposed to hold conferences on vital social problems and to establish a speakers' bureau, which might stimulate a social awakening in the churches. Slightly over three hundred joined the league, and over a hundred were listed on the group's letterhead as members of its general committee. Reformers such as Robert Bruere, Robert DeForest, Robert Cutting,

Edward Devine, Bolton Hall, Edmund Kelly, James Reynolds, Jacob Riis, Jacob Schiff, Lillian Wald, and Mary Simkhovitch were listed, along with industrialists Cleveland H. Dodge and Andrew Carnegie; socialists Morris Hillquit, Samuel McCune Lindsay, and John Spargo; and such varied individuals as Nicholas Murray Butler, Rev. Daniel Greer, Dr. Charles H. Parkhurst, Lincoln Steffens, and Josiah Strong. Of this kaleidoscopic membership, Ralph Easley of the National Civic Federation wrote inaccurately and emotionally that the group was "a crazy quilt as 4/5 of them are radicals and socialists and the other 1/5 will not attend and will therefore have no influence. It is a radical bunch."[52]

In early March 1908, Smith wrote to Robert Bruere about the league's first planned conference on unemployment to find out facts about the present situation and look into the by-products of unemployment. He assured Bruere that it was not to be a radical conference, for the remedies proposed would in no way go "over into the question of such as would involve a complete reorganization of society, but remedies to meet immediate needs." Bruere agreed to meet Smith and go over the programs of the conference.[53]

On April 7, 1908, the Ethical Social League held its conference in New York City. It passed resolutions proposing that state and city officials undertake public works already authorized and urged the state legislature to organize state farms where vagrants from the cities could be committed. It also asked corporations and individuals to provide as much employment as possible and urged the governor and legislature "to institute a thorough inquiry into the causes of unemployment as shall lead to remedial legislation of a permanent character."[54]

Two days later, Governor Charles E. Hughes sent a special message to the legislature urging it to establish two different commissions, one to look into the distribution of immigrants, and the other, already being discussed in the legislature, to determine the number and condition of the unemployed and the means best adapted to restore them to productive activity.[55] The legislature took no action on establishing the latter commission in 1908. In April 1909, Hughes sent another message to the legislature requesting immediate passage of an act to establish a commission to look into employers' liability and the causes and effects of unemployment in the state. At the close of the session, the legislature passed the act creating such a commission, which was to be composed of three senators, four assemblymen, and six private citizens chosen by the governor. On June 22, 1909, the "Wainwright Commission" organized itself and elected state senator Jonathan M. Wainwright as chairman.[56]

In October the new commission secured the services of William M. Leiserson, honorary fellow in political economy at Columbia University, as its special investigator on unemployment. Leiserson came to Columbia from Wisconsin, where he had worked under the famed economist John R. Commons. Leiserson sent out thousands of questionnaires in an attempt to fathom the problem of unemployment in New York State. From over five thousand New York State employers, he sought information on how many men were employed at each place of business during each month in 1909, the greatest and the least number of men employed, where employers ordinarily secured their help, and whether the employers would favor the establishment of state employment bureaus or exchanges. He presented similar questions to over 2,300 trade union locals.[57] In addition, Leiserson traveled to Europe in the summer of 1910 with Assemblyman George A. Voss, chairman of the Subcommittee on Unemployment of the Wainwright Commission, to study the methods of dealing with unemployment in England, Belgium, Switzerland, and Germany. While in Europe, Leiserson spoke in Paris at the International Conference of Unemployment in September 1910. At the conference, Leiserson received additional data on European methods of dealing with unemployment.[58]

The influence of European practices on Leiserson was clear and, through him, on the commission's findings, which were published in 1911. Chairman Wainwright forwarded a copy of the completed report to Charles Miller of the *New York Times* and noted that the recommendation for the establishment of state labor exchanges was based on "the lines of foreign conclusion," mainly to establish a better medium of exchange between labor supply and labor demand.[59] Leiserson's ideas were influenced especially by the British and particularly William H. Beveridge, who had developed an interest in unemployment while working with Toynbee Hall, the first British social settlement, and the Mansion House Fund in 1903-1904.

The British government was deeply concerned with unemployment during the first decade of the twentieth century. In 1905, after almost two decades of debate, the British Unemployed Workmen Act recognized unemployment, officially for the first time, as evidence of an industrial maladjustment. From 1905 to 1909, the Royal Commission on the Poor Laws and Relief of Distress held hearings; the minutes required almost eleven hundred pages of indexing. While in spirit the commission was split, the majority and minority reports did agree on the need for some kind of insurance and a labor exchange system. Beveridge was an outstanding exponent of the labor exchange, and after observing the working of the German system, he returned to England and joined the Board of Trade. When the royal assent was given to the Labor Exchange Act of 1909, Beveridge became the director of Labor Exchanges. He published his famous work, *Unemployment, A Problem of Industry*, the same year.[60]

Beveridge pointed out that in England there had been a steady growth in the sense of public responsibility for the unemployed. Unemployment had to be studied in terms of a maladjustment between labor supply and the demand for labor, and any study should be of unemployment rather than of the unemployed. One positive feature of Beveridge's labor exchange program that appealed to those interested in unemployment was that it could reduce casual labor. Tramps could no longer claim that they could not find work; the exchange would find it for them. If a tramp did not take the work found for him, then the state could force him to do so or could confine him. All Beveridge's basic ideas appeared in the Wainwright Commission report.[61]

In its final report of 1911, the Wainwright Commission briefly addressed itself to the connection between immigration and unemployment. It found that the large and continual addition to the working population was among the most important causes of unemployment. The commission did not, however, propose restriction because it felt that the subject was not within the jurisdiction of the state, and thus the commission. Interestingly, Leiserson made no reference to immigration as a cause of unemployment in his preliminary report to the commission. Hourwich's study *Immigration and Labor*, which shows immigration declining during the depression periods, was not published until after the commission published its report. Very probably, Leiserson did not consider the possibility because of his background.

Born into a family of Russian Jews in Estonia, Leiserson personally suffered under the anti-Semitic policies of the Czar. His father disappeared under mysterious circumstances, and, in attempting to escape from Russia, Leiserson and his mother were captured and placed in a chain gang with thieves and murderers. By means of bribes, the family finally was able to leave Russia, arriving in New York's Lower East Side in 1890. Leiserson, obviously, was not likely to strengthen the case of the restrictionists. The final report, which pointed out a relationship between increased immigration and unemployment, but which made no recommendations, was possibly the result of a compromise between Leiserson and other members of the commission.[62]

The final report also asserted that unlimited opportunity for jobs in agricultural areas did not exist, confirming a view already held by most New York reformers; however, it did find limited opportunities in farm labor. First, some places in the state never had their total requirements for year-round labor filled, although admittedly these jobs were few. The commission also found a very large unsatisfied demand for farm labor during the harvest season. The reasons it offered for the scarcity of farm labor confirmed the findings of the country life movement: unsteady employment, low wages, long hours, monotonous work, and a limited social life. While the commission reported that improved transportation, telephones, and rural free delivery were relieving rural isolation, the social attractions and opportunities of the city were still too powerful. However, it asserted that if information about regular rural employment could be brought to the attention of the unemployed in the city, some of them would doubtless go to the country.[63]

In addition to finding some rural jobs available at all times, the commission also reported that some wage earners who were ready and willing to work could not secure employment. Commercial and philanthropic employment bureaus were unable to bring employers and workers together. Leiserson concluded, like Beveridge, that unemployment resulted largely from maladjustment, that is, the absence of an organization to coordinate the supply of labor and the demand for it. While almost all products had definite markets or exchanges, labor had none. Unnecessary idleness, then, could be largely eliminated through a system of state-wide, free, public employment offices that would collect information on the demand for labor and applications from those who desired work.[64]

By the time the Wainwright Commission published its report on unemployment in 1911, the tremendous interest in the subject had declined in direct proportion to the number of unemployed on the city streets. The legislature did not act on the commission's recommendations, and most reformers shifted their primary attention to other issues, such as those concerning the United States Commission on Industrial Relations. Only a few reformers carried their interest in unemployment into national politics.

New York reformers, including Frances Kellor, John Kingsbury, Paul Kellogg, and Homer Folks, advised the major parties to include social and industrial planks in their platforms written before the presidential election of 1912. The Republicans rejected their proposals, while the Progressives agreed to adopt a social and industrial plank. This Progressive plank, however, did not have the support of all charity organization reformers. Most, in fact, did not support legislation to prevent involuntary unemployment. They also did not support social insurance to protect against irregular employment. The Wainwright proposal for labor exchanges was not specifically included in the Progressive platform.[65]

While many New York settlement workers and some AICP officials campaigned for Roosevelt and the Progressives in 1912 (Lillian Wald and Robert Cutting were key exceptions), most reformers affiliated with the COS in policy-making positions did not. John Glenn approved of the social and industrial plank of the Progressive party, but supported Wilson. Otto T. Bannard, vice-president of the COS in 1912, was one of the leading Taft men in the East. The most influential of the COS leaders, Edward Devine, supported no candidate. He stated that it was "the first political duty of social workers to be persistently and aggressively non-partisan to maintain such relations with men of social goodwill in all parties as will insure their cooperation in specific measures for the promotion of the common good. . . ."[66]

During the period between the panics of 1893 and 1913-1915, the reformers continually sought more efficient means to help men find jobs. They realized that commercial, philanthropic, and most public employment bureaus failed in part because each bureau had access to only limited information about the availability of jobs. In short, the problem of unemployment transcended local boundaries and the limited information each bureau possessed.

The proposed reform was to connect employment bureaus in a network or labor exchange where more information on job opportunities could be collected and disseminated. When the reformer-financed and operated National Employment Exchange failed miserably to make a dent in the unemployment problem, in spite of wide publicity and a $100,000 investment, reformers decided that voluntarist activity in this area was not feasible. The Wainwright Commission's proposals for public employment exchanges, therefore, met with wide acceptance among reformers. However, since the report was published when economic conditions were relatively good, the proposals were not put into effect. By the depression of 1913-1915, the Wainwright Commission report was forgotten generally, and Jonathan Wainwright was bitter at this slight. Thus when Governor Glynn recognized the unemployment problem and called for public labor exchanges in 1914, Wainwright felt constrained to remind the public, and possibly Glynn as well, that his commission had emphasized the very thing three years before.[67]

NOTES

1. Thomas W. Hotchkiss (St. Bartholomew's Employment Bureau) to Miss Marion Moore, February 4, 1898, Papers of Jacob A. Riis, The City College of The City University of New York.

2. *Cooper Union Labor Bureau: A Study in a Free Labor Bureau* (New York, 1897), 2, 6.

3. Cooper Union Labor Bureau Committee, "Minutes," February 6, 1896, Papers of NYAICP, Archives of the Community Service Society, New York City.

4. Cooper Union Labor Bureau Committee, "Minutes," March 31, 1899, Papers of NYAICP; Edward T. Devine, *Report on the Desirability of Establishing an Employment Bureau in the City of New York* (New York, 1909), 112-113.

5. United Hebrew Charities of New York, *Annual Report* (1896), 29; "United Hebrew Charities Annual Report for Year Ending September 30, 1903," *Jewish Charity* 3 (November 1903): 47; David M. Bressler, "Free-Employment Bureaus," *Jewish Charity* 3 (January 1904): 93-94; "The Discontinuance of the Employment Bureau," *Jewish Charity* 3 (March 1904): 145.

6. G. A. Shumway, comp., "Historical Reference Book, 1852-1950," 139-144, typewritten manuscript, YMCA National Library, New York City; NYC YMCA,

Annual Report (1896), 47, (1897), 143-144, (January 1, 1902-April 30, 1903), 12-13; Devine, *Report*, 113; *Report of the* [New York] *State Executive Committee* (New York, 1910), 9.

7. New York State Commission appointed under Chapter 518 of the Laws of 1909 to Inquire into the Question of Employer's Liability and Other Matters, *Third Report: Unemployment and the Lack of Farm Labor* (Albany, 1911), 57, (hereafter cited as Wainwright Commission, *Report*); "The Struggle for Work," *War Cry*, March 6, 1897, 4-5; McAuley Water Street Mission, *Annual Report* (1896), 10.

8. Cooper Union Labor Bureau Committee, "Minutes," February 6, 1896, Papers of NYAICP; *Social Siftings* (Salvation Army) 1 (April 1, 1898): 3; "An Administrative Beehive," *Social News* (Salvation Army) 1 (February 1911): 7. Settlement houses were not successful in placing the unemployed. See Greenwich House, *Annual Report* (October 1908), 11.

9. Jacob A. Riis, "How to Bring Work and Workers Together in the United States," *Forum* 18 (September 1894): 122-128; Mrs. Mary J. Eastman to the Editor of *Forum* to be forwarded to Jacob A. Riis, December 12, 1894; Miss Frances G. Davenport to Jacob A. Riis, October 16, 1894, Papers of Jacob A. Riis. For information on the growth of public employment bureaus in the United States, see William D. P. Bliss, ed., *Encyclopedia of Social Reform* (New York, 1898), 1355; J. E. Conner, "Free Public Employment Offices in the United States," United States, Bureau of Labor, *Bulletin* No. 68 (January 1907), 1-115; Wainwright Commission, *Report*, 59-60; Charles E. Bartram, "Free Public Employment Offices," NCCC, *Proceedings* (1897), 207-211.

10. "Free Public Employment Offices in New York City," *Annals* 8 (1896): 424-426; John T. McDonough (New York State Bureau of Statistics of Labor) to Miss Marion Moore (Buffalo COS), September 17, 1897, Papers of Jacob A. Riis; New York State Bureau of Labor, *Annual Report* (1896), 1023-1028; Wainwright Commission, *Report*, 59-60.

11. Frances A. Kellor, *Out of Work: A Study of Employment Agencies, Their Treatment of the Unemployed and Their Influence upon Home and Business* (New York and London, 1904), chap. iv; Mary K. Ford, Review of Kellor's *Out of Work* in the Woman's Book Club Section of *Current Literature* 38 (March 1905): 237-239.

12. Kellor, *Out of Work*, 193.

13. Devine, *Report*, 12-13; Wainwright Commission, *Report*, 56; Bureau of Municipal Research, *What Should New York's Next Mayor Do?* (New York, May 10, 1909), 10.

14. Henry E. Pellew, "Out-Door Relief Administration in New York City, 1878," *Conference of Charities* (1878), 71; Walter Augustus Wyckoff, *The Workers; An Experiment in Reality: The West* (New York, 1898), 94-95; "America, Asylum for Whom," *Young Men's Era* 19 (August 31, 1893): 1026; Rev. Henry O. Dwight, ed., *The Encyclopedia of Missions* (New York, 1904), 302. An excellent summary of most arguments is Francis A. Walker, "Restriction of Immigration," *Atlantic Monthly* 77 (June 1896): 822-829.

15. Boris D. Bogen, *Jewish Philanthropy* (New York, 1917), 27-31; Jewish Agricultural and Industrial Aid Society, *Annual Report* (1909), 8-12; *The Jewish Encyclopedia*

(New York, 1904), VI: 411-412. See also Moses Rischin, *The Promised City; New York's Jews, 1870-1914* (Cambridge, Massachusetts, 1962), 51-75.

16. Jewish Agricultural and Industrial Aid Society, *Annual Report* (1904), 19.

17. David M. Bressler, "The Removal Work, Including Galveston," Sixth Biennial Session of the National Conference of Jewish Charities in the United States, *Proceedings* (1910), 113.

18. David M. Bressler, "The Removal Office," *Jewish Charity* 3 (June 1904): 216; Simon Wolf (president of the Independent Order of B'nai Brith), "The Removal Work," Third Biennial Session of the National Conference of Jewish Charities in the United States, *Proceedings* (1904), 141.

19. Bressler, "The Removal Work," 114, 119.

20. Ibid., 123-131.

21. Max Herzberg, "Report of the Committee on Transportation," Second Biennial Session of the National Conference of Jewish Charities in the United States, *Proceedings* (1902), 222-240. Jeffrey R. Brackett, *The Transportation Problem in American Social Work* (New York, 1936), explains the origin of the Jewish transportation agreement and its subsequent adoption by the National Conference of Charities and Correction.

22. A. M. Sakolski, "The Expansion of Removal Work," *Jewish Charity* 5 (December 1905-January 1906): 67. For specific examples, see David M. Bressler to Paul Karger, Columbus, Ohio, March 12, 1908, to S. G. Kusworm, Dayton, Ohio, January 18, 1912, Papers of Industrial Removal Office, American Jewish Historical Society, Waltham, Massachusetts.

23. Bressler, "The Removal Work," 141, 144, 154, 162.

24. Edward T. Devine to Samuel M. Jackson, February 1, 1902; Charles Cox (Treasurer of New York, Chicago, and Illinois Railroad) to Edward T. Devine, January 30, 1902, Edward T. Devine to Charles F. Cox, February 1, 1902, Papers of NYCOS, Archives of the Community Service Society, New York City.

25. Don D. Lescohier and Elizabeth Brandeis, *History of Labor in the United States, 1896-1932* (New York, 1935), III: 21.

26. Walter E. Weyl, "Immigration and Industrial Saturation," *University Settlement Studies Quarterly* (July 1905): 61-73.

27. Frances A. Kellor to Nathan Bijur, November 28, 1905, and to Ralph Easley, December 6, 1905, Papers of National Civic Federation, New York Public Library.

28. National Civic Federation Immigration Conference, "Minutes," December 6, 7, 8, 1905, 216, 238, quotation opposed to the immigrants by George Sheron (Kentucky), 219-220. See also Ralph Easley to Frederick P. Fish, July 28, 1905, Papers of National Civic Federation.

29. S. A. Haight to Charles S. Hamlin (NCF), August 13, 1906; George B. Edwards to Ralph Easley, June 8, 1906: Papers of National Civic Federation.

30. Leah Feder, *Unemployment Relief in Periods of Depression* (New York, 1936); Hornell Hart, "Fluctuations in Unemployment in Cities of the United States, 1902-1917," *Helen S. Trounstine Foundation Studies* 1 (May 15, 1918): 57, points out that 4 million individuals employed in September 1907 were unemployed in January 1908.

31. "The False Teachers and Their Dupes," *New York Times*, March 30, 1908,

6; Arthur P. Kellogg, "Traffic Squad at Union Square," *Charities and The Commons* 20 (April 4, 1908): 9, 12.

32. "A Review of the World," *Current Literature* 44 (May 1908): 467; NYCOS, *Annual Report* (1908), 12-13; Edward T. Devine, "Public Meetings and the Police in New York," *Charities and The Commons* 20 (April 4, 1908): 2.

33. New York State Commission on Immigration, *Report of the Commission of Immigration* (New York, 1909), 140-141; A. P. Kellogg, "Traffic Squad at Union Square," 12; Jason F. Jackson to Mary Richmond, March 21, 1908, Papers of Mary Richmond, Columbia University School of Social Work.

34. Lescohier and Brandeis, *History of Labor*, III: 22; Wainwright Commission, *Report*, 59. John Higham, *Strangers in the Land: Patterns of American Nativism* (New York, 1963), 130, interprets the establishment as a victory for the antirestrictionists. The Jews clearly set the precedent for this line of defense with the Industrial Removal Office.

35. "Suggestions to Trustees," Russell Sage Foundation, *Confidential Bulletin*, no. 1 (1907), 109; "The Poor in Our Cities," *Christian Herald* 31 (March 25, 1908); NYC YMCA Bowery Branch, *Annual Report* (1908); Lillian Wald to Dr. Henry VanDyke (Princeton University), July 8, 1908, Papers of Lillian Wald, New York Public Library.

36. Jacob H. Schiff to Lillian Wald, June 10, 12, 1907, Papers of Lillian Wald, Columbia University; Jacob H. Schiff to Robert W. DeForest, October 1, 1908, in *Jacob H. Schiff: His Life and Letters*, ed. Felix Adler (Garden City, New York, 1928), I: 361.

37. "Minutes," of a special meeting called to consider what to do about homeless men during the winter of 1908-09, October 22, 1908, Papers of NYAICP; NYCOS Central Council, "Minutes," November 11, 1908, Papers of NYCOS; Edward T. Devine to Robert Bruere, November 5, 1908, Papers of NYAICP.

38. Devine, *Report*: Edward T. Devine, "Employment Bureau for the People of New York City," *Annals* 33 (March 1909): 225-238, summarizes his full report.

39. Devine, *Report*, 7-11, 85.

40. Ibid., 12-29.

41. Ibid., 3.

42. "A Social Service Employment Bureau," *Survey* (May 1, 1909): 162. A large number of those donating to the NEE were wealthy Jewish friends of Schiff, most of them described in Stephen Birmingham, *Our Crowd* (New York, 1967).

43. National Employment Exchange, *Annual Report for Year Ending September 30, 1910* (New York, 1910), 6-8, 11, 15, 16.

44. Ibid., 1911, 9; 1912, 6, 21; 1915, 7, 10; Harry L. Hopkins, "Memorandum: Annual Report of Employment Bureau," January 8, 1913, Papers of NYAICP.

45. Otto T. Bannard to Jacob H. Schiff, March 16, 1916; Jacob H. Schiff to Robert W. DeForest, March 27, 1916: Papers of Jacob H. Schiff, American Jewish Archives, Cincinnati, Ohio.

46. William H. Allen (General Agent, NYAICP) to Miss F. M. Painter, January 24, 1908, Papers of NYAICP; Frank Julian Warne, "The Unemployed in New York City," *Charities and The Commons* 19 (February 8, 1908): 1584-1586.

47. Mayor George B. McClellan to R. F. Cutting, February 25, 1908, Papers of NYAICP; Charles K. Blatchly to Frank Persons, May 18, 1908; Lilian Brandt to Edward T. Devine, October 17, 1908; Lilian Brandt to W. F. Persons, October 28, 1908; Orlando F. Lewis to Frank Persons, October 22, 1908; Charles K. Blatchly to Frank Persons, November 2, 1908, Papers of NYCOS.

48. NYCOS Central Council, "Minutes," April 8, 1908, Papers of NYCOS; Herman. Robinson (general organizer of AFL) to Robert Bruere, February 19, 1909, Papers of NYAICP.

49. NYCOS, *Annual Report* (1908), 23-27; NYCOS Central Council, "Minutes," April 8, 1908, Papers of NYCOS.

50. NYCOS Central Council, "Minutes," February 5, March 11, 1908, Papers of NYCOS; Frank J. Warne to NYAICP, March 5, 1908; William H. Allen to Frank J. Warne, March 10, 1908, Papers of NYAICP; Wainwright Commission, *Report*, 174-175.

51. "Bill to Aid Unemployed," *New York Times*, March 30, 1908, 2.

52. Fred R. Conant (secretary to the Executive Committee of the Ethical Social League) to the Members of the General Committee of the Ethical Social League, June 29, 1908, Papers of Lillian Wald, Columbia University. (Miss Wald was a member of the General Committee). Ralph Easley (secretary, NCF) to D. A. Tomkins, Charlotte, North Carolina, March 3, 1908, Papers of National Civic Federation. For a survey of the Ethical-Social Movement, see Howard B. Radest, *Toward Common Ground* (New York, 1969).

53. Charles Sprague Smith to Robert Bruere, March 6, 1908; Smith to Bruere, March 12, 1908; Bruere to Smith, March 18, 1908, Papers of NYAICP.

54. "Statements and Resolutions by the Ethical Social League," April 7, 1908, Papers of NYAICP; "Out of Work in New York," *Charities and The Commons* 20 (April 18, 1908): 92-93.

55. *Public Papers of Charles E. Hughes, Governor for 1908* (Albany, 1909), 44.

56. Ibid., 1909 (Albany, 1910), 186; Herbert Hillel Rosenthal, "The Progressive Movement in New York State, 1906-1914" (Ph.D. diss., Harvard University, 1955), 178.

57. Wainwright Commission, *Report*, 1, 2; Jonathan Wainwright to New York State Employers, August 10, 1910, to Trade Unions, August 10, 1910, Papers of Jonathan M. Wainwright, New York Historical Society; J. Michael Eisner, *William Morris Leiserson: A Biography* (Madison, 1967) provides a useful sketch of Leiserson's career. However, Eisner devotes only three pages to Leiserson's work with the Wainwright Commission.

58. Dr. L. Varle (Le President du Fonds de Chomage gantois) to Jonathan M. Wainwright, July 25, 1910, Papers of Jonathan M. Wainwright; Wainwright Commission, *Report*, 1; William Leiserson, *The Fight Against Unemployment in the United States, Rapport No. 15, Conference Internationale du Chomage, September 18-21*, 1910 (n.p., n.d.).

59. Jonathan M. Wainwright to Charles Miller, *New York Times*, November 2, 1911, Papers of Jonathan M. Wainwright.

60. Roy Lubove, *The Struggle for Social Security, 1900-1935* (Cambridge, Mas-

sachusetts, 1968), 150-153; A. C. C. Hill, Jr., and Isador Lubin, *The British Attack on Unemployment* (Washington, D.C., 1934), 18-26, 30-32; William H. Beveridge, *Unemployment: A Problem of Industry* (New York, 1909).

61. Beveridge, *Unemployment*, 2-3. William H. Beveridge, "Unemployment and Its Cure," *Contemporary Review* 93 (April 1908): 392, 397.

62. Wainwright Commission, *Report*, 7, 8, 12, 13; William M. Leiserson, "Unemployment-Report to the Commission on Employers Liability and Causes of Industrial Accidents, Unemployment, and Lack of Farm Labor," 1910-1911, Papers of William M. Leiserson, State Historical Society of Wisconsin; Eisner, 7; Isaac Hourwich, *Immigration and Labor* (New York, 1912).

63. Wainwright Commission, *Report*, 10, 11.

64. Ibid., 8, 56-58, 68-69.

65. Paul U. Kellogg, "The Industrial Platform of the New Party," *Survey* 28 (August 24, 1912): 668-670; Irwin Yellowitz, "The Origins of Unemployment Reform in the United States," *Labor History* 9 (Fall 1968): 338; Walter I. Trattner, "Theodore Roosevelt, Social Workers, and the Election of 1912: A Note," *Mid-America* 50 (January 1968): 64-65; John A. Kingsbury, "Does Roosevelt Know What Social and Industrial Justice Means?" typed manuscript, 1912, Papers of John A. Kingsbury, Library of Congress; Kirk Porter and Donald Bruce Johnson, comp., *National Party Platforms, 1840-1960* (2d ed., Urbana, 1961), 175-183, includes the complete Progressive party platform.

66. Allen F. Davis, "Settlement Workers in Politics, 1890-1914," *Review of Politics* 26 (October 1964): 505; Trattner, "Theodore Roosevelt," 67-69; Edward T. Devine, "Politics and Social Work," *Survey* 29 (October 5, 1912): 9; Kellogg, "The Industrial Platform," 669.

67. *New York Times*, March 10, 1914, 9.

6

The Recognition of Unemployment

in New York

THE DEPRESSION of 1913-1915 began quietly in the fall of 1913, and conditions steadily worsened until war orders revived industry two years later. Unemployment was extensive and demanded the attention of New York reformers, city officials, and the public in general.[1] In January 1914, Mayor John Purroy Mitchel of New York City called a meeting attended by, among others, reformers Edward Devine, Walter Weyl, Frances Kellor, and Lillian Wald to discuss the unemployment situation. His letter of invitation to the participants suggested the far-reaching impact that concern with unemployment was to have during this depression. The letter, signed by John A. Kingsbury, commissioner of public charities and former AICP official, stated that "the Mayor appreciates that the problem of unemployment is not a temporary one, and he hopes to deal as soon as possible, with the more serious question of the permanent irregularity of unemployment."[2]

All participants at the meeting agreed that the number of involuntarily unemployed was far greater than in the previous winter when Harry Hopkins of the NYAICP had conducted a survey of the unemployed in New York City and had estimated 325,000 as being out of work. Hopkins had called his estimate conservative and pointed out that the time-worn platitude that "anyone can find work if he really wants it" was not warranted by the facts. Edward Devine of the COS said conditions in the winter of 1913-1914 were especially severe for single men usually employed in common labor. While the Municipal Lodging House had provided beds for 37,000 homeless between November 1912 and January 1913, during the same three months one year later it housed 93,000. At the close of the meeting, the representatives of private agencies pledged their support to whatever measures the mayor considered necessary to handle the unemployment situation.[3] This alliance between private and public relief agencies in New York was the first open acknowledgment by voluntarist groups that the primary responsibility for unemployment must lie with the public sector.

The first major demands of the unemployed were for jobs and shelter. During the first week of February 1914, a delegation of homeless unemployed, led by the director of the Bowery Mission and others, pleaded with the mayor to provide both. While the mayor agreed to do everything possible to provide work, he felt that sufficient shelters were available in the city. However, in late February a mob of 700 homeless unemployed entered the Second Avenue Baptist Church demanding shelter. The mob told the Reverend Pierce that they had nowhere to sleep and that leaders of an unemployment demonstration at Union Square encouraged the homeless unemployed to break into stores and take food to satisfy their hunger and to seek out churches to sleep in. For the next three nights after the Second Avenue Baptist Church incident, the mobs slept in three different churches with permission. Reactions to this situation were varied. The state committee of the Socialist party chided the New York City Socialists for letting the leadership of the unemployed fall into the hands of "freaks," while a self-proclaimed "cool-headed, far-seeing scientist" (a consulting engineer) wrote Mayor Mitchel that the demonstrations were "evidence of the volcano beneath us."[4]

Acting on requests from concerned churchmen, the police commissioner ordered the police to watch out for mobs of unemployed moving about the city seeking shelter. On March 4, the police confronted the unemployed. About five hundred homeless unemployed led by a youthful leader of the IWW, Frank Tannenbaum, stood before St. Alphonsus Roman Catholic Church in a light snowfall. The rector of St. Alphonsus, Father John Schneider, sent for the police. While

Tannenbaum went to the rectory to request permission to spend the night in the church, which was refused, the mob entered the church. Tannenbaum went to the church and told the men that they were not welcome, and one of the parish priests requested all who were not regular members of the congregation to leave. Men had started to leave when a photographer from the New York *World* took a picture with a flashbulb which exploded. Fearing a gunshot, the unemployed and police panicked and a riot ensued. The police sealed the church and arrested 190 men and one woman. Tannenbaum was charged with inciting to riot and subsequently sentenced to one year in prison by a judge who gave a talk at the trial on the worthlessness of men who were unemployed in a country filled with opportunity and overflowing with prosperity. Others who were convicted with Tannenbaum and had soft hands received six month sentences while those with calloused hands—presumably the genuinely unemployed—received fifteen days.[5]

John Haynes Holmes of the Church of the Messiah in New York City asserted that the true measure of the Tannenbaum affair was that it had "forced ninety millions of people in the United States to know that there is a question of the unemployed and to ask what can be done about it."[6] Holmes said the churches should accept the homeless unemployed—and many clergy agreed. In Holmes' view, most clergy objected to the movement because the homeless unemployed were in a mob represented by a leader and because the call for help was phrased more as a demand than a request. Among others, *America*, the prestigious Roman Catholic weekly, the *Christian Herald*, and the *Presbyterian* of Philadelphia opposed Holmes and supported the action taken by St. Alphonsus. The Rev. Charles H. Parkhurst, famed Presbyterian minister, in the New York *Evening Journal* spoke of the IWW members as traitors, public enemies, and fomenters of unrest. He hoped that the insurgents throughout the nation would heed New York's hardening policy toward the IWW.[7] By 1914, the IWW had become a household word, if an unpleasant one. John A. Kingsbury asserted that the city's homeless unemployed were like a "disorganized army" without able leadership but nevertheless "a source . . . of danger to the community in which it exists." The great fear was that the IWW would assume leadership for this headless horde of unemployed and this would be fraught with danger for the state.[8] Such fear of the unemployed had a great "effect on the public mind."[9]

In New York City, however, the unemployed continued to meet night after night in the public squares at the lower end of Manhattan. One formal meeting called by New York's Socialist party was supposed to feature Mayor Mitchel. When he did not appear, IWW members stoned the platform and took over the meeting.[10] In April 1914, an assassin attempted to kill Mayor Mitchel but his shot hit a member of Mitchel's party instead. When the would-be assassin was arrested, a New York magistrate reported to the mayor that the assassin had been present at an IWW meeting of the unemployed where a "young Jewess" had preached that the only redress for grievances was through violence. The magistrate hoped that the event would lead to drastic measures against the IWW.[11]

The American Federation of Labor agreed and completely disavowed the actions of the IWW as unrepresentative of organized labor. One book written earlier in defense of the AFL had termed the legitimate trade union "a social safety valve," while a horde of undisciplined laborers would mean "a series of revolutions." Samuel Gompers was a key member of the National Civic Federation, which worked to instruct public opinion "as to the real meaning of socialism and anarchy, and as to the necessity of combating them if our American political system and its underlying economic institutions are to be preserved."[12]

The National Civic Federation collected money for this work from New York's leading businessmen and financiers. Ralph Easley of the federation stated in 1914 that "the forces of destruction" which had already given New York a "taste of their revolutionary methods will seek this opportunity [mass unemployment] to preach their doctrines of class hatred." Therefore, he asked his contributors, such as Andrew Carnegie, to increase their donations; "saving the country" was expensive. Easley defended trade unions, but supported repression of the IWW demonstrators. In a letter to Mayor Mitchel he wrote that when a policeman confronted a member of a revolutionary group in the street, he was "not expected to pull out of his pocket a copy of the Constitution of the U. S. and read it carefully before he knocks the stuffing out of him."[13]

The Merchants Association of New York City agreed with Easley's philosophy, and it hoped for greater protection from unrest through the operation of the National Guard. The association urged businessmen to encourage employees to join the guard and to provide incentives because of the "proper protection of life and property and therefore of the development of commerce and industry of the whole state" which resulted. It believed the existence of a "well-equipped and adequate National Guard" was an "important element of insurance."[14]

Two tremendous bomb blasts in October reminded New Yorkers that violence, often attendant with unemployment, was just beneath the surface. One bomb went off in St. Patrick's Cathedral and the other at the rectory of St. Alphonsus Parish, both on October 13, the anniversary of the death of Ferrer, the Spanish anarchist. The police immediately connected the blast with the IWW expulsions from St. Alphonsus during the previous spring; as the New York *Sun* put it, the police put two and two together and "spelled IWW." Alexander Berkman and Joseph J. Cohen, an IWW spokesman, both acknowledged that members of their organization had probably set the blasts. Cohen bragged that many would be pleased by the blast at St. Alphonsus because of the rough treatment accorded Tannenbaum there. Berkman asserted that the blasts were, in a sense, a demonstration of the unemployed and promised more demonstrations and mass meetings of unemployed each night. He emphasized that a definite movement was "now underway to organize the unemployed."[15]

The number and complexion of the unemployed was crucial because, as in the past, it was an indicator of potential unrest as well as of the amount of aid required. Throughout the winter, a number of surveys was conducted by various groups, including the National Civic Federation, Metropolitan Life Insurance Company, New York City Police Department, and the United States Bureau of Labor Statistics. The studies indicated that between 398,000 and 500,000 were unemployed in New York City alone.[16] While most of the unemployed were family men, as many as one-third were considered homeless. Reflecting changed ideas on unemployment, all the homeless unemployed were not regarded as tramps. Even those on bread lines were usually considered victims of circumstances. In spite of changed theory, the unemployed feared to go to the Municipal Lodging House lest they be sentenced as vagrants, and instead slept in saloons. On one trip through the Bowery, Frank Persons of the COS found an average of nineteen sleeping at each bar. When Persons complained, Police Commissioner Arthur Woods asked where they would go if he drove them out.[17]

Some proposed that not only the churches but also the National Guard armories should house the homeless. However, with radical agitators haranguing bread lines night after night in an effort to get support for demonstrations, the churches and armories were reluctant to do so. Charles Stelzle of the Labor Temple stated that those in authority, while sympathetic to the miseries of the unemployed, "were afraid that the gathering together of great masses of unemployed men in buildings stored with arms and ammunitions, might result disastrously should radical leadership be developed."[18]

Jefferson Davis, self-styled "king of the hoboes" or "Emperor of the Knights of the Road," had another suggestion for housing the homeless. "Jeff" Davis first came to the attention of the New York reformers as a result of testimony given before the United States Industrial Commission. He had founded the Itinerant Worker's Union in 1908, chartered under the laws of Indiana as "The Hoboes of America." While Davis was in Seattle in the winter of 1913-1914 as a delegate to an AFL conference, mass unemployment broke out. Seattle police put tremendous pressure on the homeless unemployed, jailing hundreds on vagrancy charges. Davis secured the assistance of a lawyer, and, within a week, Seattle freed nearly 500 of the convicted "vagrants." In order to give the men a place to stay, Davis and his right-hand man Henry Pauly convinced a real estate agent to rent them a building on a one-month trial basis. The Hotel de Gink was born. During the winter, Davis and Pauly housed over 2,000 men, barred the IWW from the premises, and provided the men with work clearing tree stumps and razing old buildings. By the end of the winter, Seattle's officials expressed their appreciation to Davis for reducing vagrancy, the number on relief rolls, and IWW threats.[19]

Davis asked New York City officials for a city-owned building to be converted into a Hotel de Gink in New York. While observing that he could not have tree stumps pulled for the City of New York, Davis guaranteed to cut down police work with respect to vagrancy and to eliminate the city's "IWW question." The IWW, he asserted, flourished on discontent and idleness, which he hoped to eliminate through his proposed hotel. City Chamberlain Henry Bruere found a condemned building for Davis to use and raised a small amount of money to begin the experiment. But leaders of the COS termed the scheme fantastic and objected that its "picturesque characteristics" would be widely publicized and draw even more unemployed into New York City. However, Frank Persons realized that the city officials acceded to Davis' request in an attempt to forestall threatened demonstrations by the homeless unemployed and the IWW, and he, therefore, reluctantly tolerated the experiment. Although the men slept on bare floors and cooked over canned heat, the Hotel de Gink maintained itself in orderly fashion for some months until it closed down in the summer of 1915.[20]

While a program like that of Davis' might give some relief, city churches contended that the best way to end unemployment was to find jobs for men. To do this, they formed the Religious Citizenship League, composed principally of clergymen and trade union representatives. In a meeting on unemployment, the league listened to Harry Hopkins of the AICP, C. A. Andrews of the American Association for Labor Legislation, Paul Kennaday of the New York Socialist party, and other speakers. After the talks, the league resolved to find and create as many jobs as possible.[21] Therefore, in October 1914, it began working through the New York Federation of Churches to organize an interdenominational employment bureau. In the organizational letter sent to all the clergy in New York City, the federation pointed out that "the problem of unemployment, and the consequent danger that the needy and unemployed may be misled and troubled by the IWW and other agitators" was serious. This was especially true now, the letter continued, because "Miss Kellor and other experts" were convinced that the IWW would be more active than at any other time in the history of New York City.[22] The federation sponsored such programs as "Unemployment Sunday" and "Be A Good Neighbor" and suggested reading lists and scriptural passages for clergy to use in their sermons.[23]

Most churchmen did not delude themselves, however, that the churches could handle the problem of unemployment without help from the public sector. Reverend W. D. P. Bliss of the Religious Citizenship League pointed out that the problem of the unemployed could be met only through cooperative action and that the league also planned to promote suitable legislation in the interest of the unemployed. The city and state had to cooperate by providing work, penal colonies for those unwilling to work, and free labor exchanges.[24] While some clergymen attacked the league for its emphasis on the social sphere and particularly its emphasis on the labor exchange idea rather than the Trinity, an increasing number concluded that the unemployed should be helped and unemployment ended. One clergyman reminded his readers that "the right to work" was a motto of the French Revolution and that a perusal of IWW literature indicated the same concern. Thus the clergy should help find work for those desiring it. However, one Episcopalian priest, the Rev. Floyd Appleton, stated that the church should enter the field of unemployment relief only to "supplement the work of the state." John Haynes Holmes asserted the inevitable conclusion that socially conscious clergy were beginning to acknowledge that the churches were confronted "by a problem infinitely bigger than they can handle—a problem so big indeed that no institution short of society itself can hope to cope with it."[25]

One measure of growing public interest in the problem of unemployment was the increase in the number of articles published on unemployment. This change in public attitude was noted by William Hard, a member of the editorial staff of *Everybody's Magazine* in 1912. By using as a yardstick the number of magazine articles published on unemployment in what he termed "important American magazines," he found that from 1900 to 1904 eight articles were published, while from 1905 to 1909 sixty-four appeared. He found, and correctly so, not only the number significant, but also the fact that unemployment "emerged from its original concealment in such magazines as *Municipal Affairs* and the *American Journal of Sociology* into open appearance in the weeklies and monthlies of large circulation."[26] A bibliography on unemployment compensation published by the Industrial Relations Counselors, Inc., in 1928 charted the dramatic increase in the number of articles published on this subject between 1892 and 1915. Comic paper jokes about "Weary Willy" the tramp, which had begun in the 1890s, declined in number and public interest, indicating the change in public attitudes toward the homeless unemployed.[27] Articles on unemployment, not surprisingly, climbed sharply in number in depression years. More significant was the number published in nondepression years. And this increasing interest was reflected in the actions taken against unemployment in 1914 and 1915.

Generally, the actions taken in the depression of 1914-1915 were broadly based, reflecting the necessity of cooperation between public and private agencies and recognizing the need for government action on unemployment. In February 1914, the American Association for Labor Legislation held the First National Conference on Unemployment in New York City. Founded in 1906 by social scientists, the association had first concentrated on industrial hygiene but in 1912 formed an American Section of the International Association on Unemployment, which had been established in 1910. One of the bylaws of the section was "to combat unemployment and its consequences, to organize studies, to give information to the public, and to take the initiative in shaping improved legislation and administration, and practical action in times of urgent need."[28]

Attending the conference in 1914 were delegates from twenty-five states who listened to speeches and debated the issues of unemployment in the United States. The conference recommended that a Bureau of Distribution be formed in the United States Department of Labor with the authority to establish employment exchanges throughout the country, to act as a clearinghouse for information, and to aid in the distribution of labor. It urged that free municipal and state employment bureaus be established to become part of the federal network and recommended further study on unemployment, including preventive actions, such as the regularization of industry and unemployment insurance. The recommendations, on the whole, were received favorably in the press. The more conservative journals, such as *Nation*, asserted that the regularization of industry should be left to employers and that the question of insurance was dangerous. But it did support the establishment of labor exchanges.[29]

The reason that even *Nation* could accept the employment exchange principle was its tie with the idea of self-help and the notion of job availability in the United States. No one was giving the unemployed anything—except the opportunity to work at a job that already existed. The Wainwright Commission had proposed exchanges in 1911, but an earlier exponent who had more impact on the conference's proposal was Frances Kellor, whose interest in the exchanges was a result of her interest in immigrants and her studies of private employment bureaus. She had proposed a system of distributing immigrants to the National Civic Federation in 1905, but no action was taken at that time.

During the period 1905-1915 one can easily discern Miss Kellor's maturing ideas on the nature of unemployment by her prescription for community responses. Her study of employment bureaus published in 1905, *Out of Work*, proposed and succeeded in securing regulatory legislation against private bureaus in New York, but the legislation had no significant impact in reducing unemployment. Ten years later, her revised study dealt with the employment bureau in the larger context of national unemployment. She realized that local bureaus must be connected with similar agencies elsewhere to be truly efficient, and therefore, federal operation of the program was a necessity. She reported that although trade unions had few immigrant members, they still reported 13 percent were unemployed in 1913, which meant that immigrants were not the only ones without work. And of 2,000 men investigated in the Municipal Lodging House, she noted that only 9 percent had been in the city less than a year; the average time of residence was thirty-two years. She did not attribute the increasing disorder to the immigrants: the causes were deeper and not so easily explained.[30] In 1913 as an official of the Progressive party, Miss Kellor had prepared a bill for labor exchanges, which was promoted by the North American Civic League for Immigrants. Her proposal for a Bureau of Distribution was submitted to Congress in the same year. While the proposed bill dealt primarily with immigrants, it also covered the unemployed in general.[31] The problem, as she saw it, was that America had never really attempted to analyze the causes and factors of unemployment except to devise "remedies only for those aspects wherein there is a menace to law and order, or inconvenience to a community because of large numbers of unemployed, or suffering so sharp that it can not be disregarded." Miss Kellor reemphasized her view that unemployment was not solely a municipal problem, but involved the larger units of state and nation. In short, unemployment was a national problem and should be considered as such.[32]

The federal labor exchange program, combined with distribution of immigrants, gained wide support among clergy and reformers, but especially among the Jews. Jews, who had helped pioneer the idea of distribution, regarded the developing general support for a federal labor exchange with mixed emotions. In 1912, they realized that their philanthropy, as generous as it was, no longer was sufficient to relieve the unemployment and destitution of all Jews; however, they continued to give relief in small amounts, though often not sufficient, to all applicants because of the "fear of arising anti-Jewish prejudice."[33] Outside help was needed and acceptance of public labor exchanges could serve as a vehicle for distributing Jews. On the other hand, they feared Jews would not secure sufficient attention from the federal government. In a letter to the editors of the *New Republic*, the secretary of the IRO criticized John Andrews and others for discussing labor exchanges without reference to the Jewish program or without the aid of interested Jews. Probably the Jews hoped to be included in the planning and operation of any federal exchange program by virtue of their expertise (which was impressive) in placement work. At the management level, they could then coordinate the exchanges with the work of the IRO.[34]

One necessary adjunct to the Kellor and Wainwright Commission plans was the establishment of free state and municipal bureaus, which would interlock within the federal system. New York City's Mayor Mitchel opened a central employment exchange in February 1914. Mitchel wrote that "while it is not a function of government directly to provide employment for those out of work, the establishment of free labor agencies where employers may obtain workers and the unemployed may obtain work is a well recognized government function." The agency, he stated, was modeled after similar ones in Massachusetts, Ohio, Germany, and England.[35] Leiserson came to New York in 1914 to act as an advisor to the bureau, and he suggested that the state take control of the agency to link it with other agencies in the state.[36]

The City Club of New York distributed in March 1914 a report on labor exchanges. Regarding the municipal exchange in New York City as a promising first step, the report recommended that a statewide exchange be established within the New York Department of Labor in a newly created Bureau of Employment. Mitchel agreed because unemployment could not be dealt with adequately on the municipal level. A method of intra- and interstate cooperation of exchanges, supervised or run by the federal government, was required.[37]

Within a week after the publication of the City Club report and two days after the IWW confrontation with the police at St. Alphonsus, Governor Glynn of New York sent a message to the state legislature recommending that a Bureau of Employment be created in the Department of Labor to operate labor exchanges. In his message, Glynn asserted that unemployment was "always present in a greater or lesser degree in our industrial system" and that steps had to be taken to deal with it. In 1914, Wainwright called upon the legislature to support the governor's proposal. By 1915, both city and state had opened free employment bureaus.[38] The whole New York system, however, was doomed to fail without federal connection.

One attempt to create such a federal system occurred in April 1914 when Congressman Victor Murdock introduced into the House of Representatives a bill to create a Bureau of Employment in the United States Department of Labor. This bureau would have the responsibility to create a system of free labor exchanges and to investigate and issue licenses for all bureaus involved in interstate business. It would also issue reports on employment opportunities. Murdock's proposal was essentially Kellor's draft, and he quoted her at length in his introductory speech. While the proposal never was enacted, it brought the idea before the legislators, who eventually established the United States Employment Service in 1918.[39]

In addition to the labor exchange proposals, another indicator of the recognition of public responsibility for unemployment was the mayors' committees for unemployment, which sprang up in cities across the nation. The committees were formed to provide relief for the unemployed and to reduce the effects of unemployment as much as possible. Chicago had begun one as early as 1912 in the form of a commission that recommended free state employment bureaus. During the depression, the Chicago committee attempted to increase cooperation between private and public agencies, improve the administration of Chicago's free employment bureau, and reduce the incidence of unemployment by modifying industrial management.[40]

In New York, Mayor Mitchel appointed a committee in the summer of 1914 to advise him on unemployment problems. In a series of informal meetings at the Midday Club, private and public relief agency representatives discussed the problem posed by the coming winter. After a few such meetings, Henry Bruere suggested that "bankers, employers, and others who would be definitely and vitally interested in the problem confronting the City for the coming winter" be added to the Midday group to form an official mayor's committee. The AICP agreed to the idea, because this plan would preclude "the organization of a Mayor's Committee which might not be representative."[41]

Henry Bruere then submitted a formal proposal to the mayor to establish the official mayor's committee, stating that it would gather facts about unemployment, develop a system of labor exchanges, organize emergency relief where and when necessary, and encourage industry to consider means of preventing periodic unemployment. Bruere's proposal rejected the philanthropic approach to unemployment and instead integrated the efforts of public officials, reformers, and businessmen. His proposal was acceptable to the COS.[42]

Upon releasing to the press information on the formation of the committee, Henry Bruere received an immediate inquiry from the watchdog of conservatism, Ralph Easley of the National Civic Federation. The public release had stated: "Unemployment is a chronic problem in N. Y. C. under present conditions of industrial organization." Easley asked Bruere exactly what type of industrial organization he was proposing. Bruere answered that he had nothing in mind other than to increase the awareness and cooperation within the present organization "to the point of constructive and comprehensive consideration of the employment problem as a business problem." But Easley was apparently not satisfied with Bruere's reply, because he wrote Samuel Gompers that Robert Bruere of the AICP was "an out and out radical socialist" and that while Bruere's brother Henry had not proclaimed himself a socialist he was "all the more dangerous on account of that fact."[43]

In December, Mayor Mitchel officially created the Mayor's Committee on Unemployment and selected Judge E. H. Gary, chairman of the board of United States Steel, to head it. In a letter to Gary, Mitchel said that the committee should work carefully to effect maximum cooperation from businessmen and to find out "to what extent can this condition [unemployment] which grows acute now and again, but which is a persistent chronic condition be minimized by the cooperative effort of businessmen."[44] The mayor appointed about eighty others to the committee, including the leaders of all the important philanthropic agencies in the city, as well as businessmen, economists, and public officials. Some reformers joined the mayor's committee with reservation, acknowledging the need for such public-private action, but fearing a large dispersal of indiscriminate relief.[45] The membership of the committee was soon criticized. Socialists opposed Gary because of his identification with the "wrong-side" of labor-management relations. Conspicuously absent were radical and conservative labor leaders. And the National League on Urban Conditions Among Negroes complained to Lillian Wald that, while Negroes were prominent among the unemployed, none was appointed to the mayor's committee.[46]

In accord with original proposals, the committee worked closely with business. In January 1915, Mayor Mitchel, Gary, and Bruere attended a meeting of the Merchants Association of New York City to explain the program. The chairman of the Members' Council of the Association explained to the meeting why the committee was organized to consider unemployment at its meeting. "Nothing," he began, was "so productive of social revolution, intemperance, physical demoralization, and poverty as unemployment."[47] And in the United States, "the public mind has not until recently been seriously awake to the existence of such a problem as unemployment." The public was also beginning to realize that unemployment was not a temporary problem associated only with a depression; it was always in evidence. The individual, the city, and the state could not afford to let it be said "that the devil *only* finds something for idle hands to do." Public demonstrations were the only method available for the unemployed to express grievances and "meetings such as this, and the Mayor's Committee" were an attempt to let the unemployed know that "their problem is being considered."[48]

When the mayor spoke, he pointed out that "probably" the unemployed existed every winter. It was just that the city had previously ignored them. Henry Bruere agreed and hoped that all would discard "fatalistic shortsightedness which makes us neglectful of preparation against disaster in time of prosperity and pessimistic when disaster overwhelms us." In short, more planning was needed to preclude the problem of unemployment. Judge Gary asserted that at least part of the adverse conditions was the fault of businessmen. Carelessness in management, indifference to the rights of others, and public welfare in general had brought much criticism of the businessman and some legislation unfavorable to him. The improvement of business morals, conduct, and management would result in more cooperation between all classes of people in the country.[49]

While the mayor's committee did not originally intend to provide large sums of direct relief to the unemployed in the form of doles, it did require money to provide workshops, school lunches, and publicity. The mayor asked George W. Perkins, financier and retired partner of J. P. Morgan & Co., to collect $200,000 discreetly from New York's leading citizens because he feared that an unsuccessful public campaign might cause the citizens to become dispirited. Eventually most of the money was raised, but with some difficulty.[50]

New York reformers actively worked within the mayor's committee to assure that no large relief funds would be collected counter to the original purposes of the committee. They recognized that some relief was necessary, but saw it as more of a palliative in order to prevent a curative that would reorder capitalism. As in 1908, the reformers participated in a "Confidential Emergency Winter Exchange" run by Mary Richmond of the Russell Sage Foundation. Charity organization societies in twelve cities exchanged information each week on the methods each used in combating indiscriminate relief in their respective cities. Mary Richmond stated the fear of the reformers that some groups would use the industrial crisis to form demonstrations, "to organize processions of the unemployed and to force on the government some scheme." Working in conjunction with the mayor's committee in New York and other cities, the reformers hoped to ameliorate the condition of the unemployed while blocking broad relief measures and forestalling "excessive" governmental measures to aid them. Reports of the successes in other cities were sent to Persons and then forwarded by him to Bannard of the mayor's committee. In this way, Bannard was aware of what the representatives of the other societies were doing on mayors' committees to retard government action. In spite of Persons' and Bannard's efforts, however, the committee did hold a Bundle Day (distribution of used clothing), although no huge relief fund was collected.[51] Although some of these actions were negative, there were positive aspects to the reformer membership on the committee.

From the inception of the mayor's committee Mitchel had stressed that the city had "a moral responsibility toward its citizens who are involuntarily unemployed . . . though able and anxious to work."[52] Support of the mayor's committee by the reformers was in part a tacit admission of this position although tempered by their participation in the public sphere, and it also reflected their changing ideas regarding tramps and unemployment. Studies by Barnes, Solenberger, the Municipal Lodging House, and others had altered significantly the picture of the unemployed. In the studies, the homeless unemployed were seen not as tramps but principally as unwelcome by-products of the industrial system.

The shift in reformer views on the causes of unemployment can be seen in the writings of Edward Devine, the chief policy-maker of the COS. In 1904, Devine wrote in the *Principles of Relief* that "it may be assumed that employment is to be found in ordinary times if there is ordinary persistence in seeking it." He was uncertain, however, and wrote in the *Practice of Charity* (1904) that he did not know the "extent to which industrial displacement and psychological defects respectively are the real causes of homelessness and lack of regular employment."[53] In a later book, *Misery and Its Causes* (1909), Devine wrote that

> in contrast with the idea that misery [defined by Devine as poverty and pauperism under which he includes the homeless unemployed] is moral, the inexorable visitation of punishment for immoral actions and the inevitable outcome of depraved character, I wish to present the idea that it is economic, the result of maladjustment, that defective personality is only a half-way explanation, which itself results directly from conditions which society may largely control.[54]

The depression of 1914-1915 brought persons of influence such as Devine into closer accord with the earlier "radical" views of unemployment expressed by Henry George, Governor Lewelling, and others. The mayor's committee report of 1916 was at once a public acknowledgment that unemployment was a permanent problem, a summary of contemporary thought about unemployment, and a proposed outline of future actions to be taken against unemployment. Unemployment as an endemic problem in American society was recognized in the formation of the committee. More significant was the committee's recommendation to the mayor that he form a permanent committee on unemployment. This particular recommendation was especially significant because, when the report was published in January 1916, the depression had abated and war orders were rapidly reducing the ranks of the unemployed. Edward Devine and Lillian Wald from the original committee were appointed to the permanent one, which also included reformers Herbert Croly, Frederic C. Howe, and Mary van Kleeck.[55]

The first recommendation of the mayor's committee was another statement in favor of public employment exchanges that had been recommended in virtually every study on unemployment between 1910 and 1916. The report stated that the exchanges could be expected to organize the labor market and to reduce unemployment by keeping workers informed of job opportunities. In this manner, unemployment in seasonal industries and casual labor could be reduced to a minimum. In preventing unemployment, however, the prime function of the public employment exchanges would be to prevent seasonality by working with industry and by finding employments which dovetailed with the work of those engaged in seasonal trades. For example, plants making Christmas cards in the fall could make stationery in the spring. In short, the exchanges would encourage regularization of industry so that men would be hired on a full-time basis. To do this effectively, the United States Secretary of Labor would have to insure cooperation among the city, state, and federal governments.[56]

The report admitted that while public employment exchanges could do much to reduce unemployment they could not create employment. When the total volume of employment slipped below certain levels, as in the winter of 1914-1915, the exchanges would be helpless. In such a situation, the state should act to create employment. Reformist contributions to the report agreed with its position. To look back at voluntarist attitudes regarding public employment in previous depressions is to see what a tremendous change had taken place. In the panic of 1873, reformers had warned their volunteers that rather than allow public works to be used to aid the poor, they should "tolerate any wrong and let any suffering go unrelieved rather than give countenance to it."[57]

During the panic of 1893 the reformers postulated the view that public works were an acceptable means of reducing unemployment if the projects were already planned, funding approved, and contracts had only to be let earlier than originally conceived. Jacob Riis, for example, favored this position but denied the implication that the city was obliged to do so. The city *could*, but not necessarily *should*. Charles Kellogg of the COS said that "the argument that the State or City is duty bound to provide employment is socialistic, and should be discouraged."[58] Governor Flower agreed and stated to do so would cause no end to "official paternalism" and "corruption, socialism, and anarchy" would naturally follow.[59] In 1908, following the IWW demonstrations in New York City, COS and AICP officials not only accepted the idea of hastening public works expenditures but actually petitioned public officials to do so in another step toward the belief that the state should do something for the unemployed.[60]

In the depression of 1913-1915 AICP officials even made a small experiment with work relief. The program involved paying unemployed men the current wage rate for unskilled labor to make improvements on two publicly owned areas—the New York Botanical Gardens and the Bronx Zoological Park. The AICP reported the experiment was successful and stated that it should be adopted "with modifications on a larger scale by urban communities in times of unusual unemployment." Interestingly, the two directors of the work relief program were William Matthews, who later directed the Emergency Work Bureau in New York from 1930 to 1933, and Harry L. Hopkins, who subsequently directed the Works Progress Administration during the New Deal.[61] The reformers were learning to recognize that the unemployed wanted jobs, not charity.

Suggestions were also made that the induction of the unemployed into the armed forces would help ease economic problems. Professor F. H. Giddings of Columbia University proposed to the New York State Conference of Charities and Correction in 1914 that conscripting the unemployed would not only provide them employment, but the army could give men manual training so that upon discharge the men could more easily find employment. One industry representative in an interview with *Railroad Trainman* applauded the plan of the so-

I Asked You for Bread

and You Gave Me a Stone

New York *Evening Mail*, January 23, 1915

called citizen soldiers. Frances Kellor considered military training to relieve unemployment as a legitimate "public works" project, but not all agreed with her position. While some argued the training would make the men "moral," others argued that "it would be dangerous to give military training to the riffraff and vagrant classes who are already in sort of revolt against society." One journalist thought it would be "dangerous to teach such men how to organize and fight."[62]

The mayor's committee favored planning public expenditures to compensate for decreased private employment during business depressions; it also favored diverting a certain percentage of yearly appropriations into a contingency fund. It did not, however, envision mass expenditures of this money for relieving the unemployed whenever an economic lull occurred. Rather the money would be used to initiate projects, which would be awarded on regular contracts as opposed to direct relief of the unemployed. In addition to standard public works such as road building, the committee suggested producing equipment for the armed forces, making post office additions, and compiling historical documents.[63]

The committee's final recommendation was that the subject of unemployment insurance should be brought "forcibly to the attention of the leaders of opinion in industry, politics, and government."[64] New York reformers were greatly influenced by the European experience in the matter of social insurance initiated by Bismarck in the 1880s. The Russell Sage Foundation had commissioned a special study on the European system of insurance and published it in 1911. Edward Devine, in one of his Kennedy Lectures at the New York School of Philanthropy, mentioned insurance as a probable necessity in times of depression. Following Devine, both Henry Seager in 1910 and Isaac M. Rubinow in 1912 lectured to budding social workers on social insurance and the need for unemployment insurance.[65]

By 1915 most reformers supported the idea of some form of unemployment insurance tied with the public employment exchange. The official bulletin of the COS in 1915 advocated insurance along with exchanges and urged its 7,000 members to demand that these ideas be put into practice. John A. Kingsbury stated that after exchanges were established and industry was made as stable as possible, the nation should establish insurance for those "able and willing to work" and "yet unable to find it." Mary Richmond found the idea had "appeal." If the exchange could not find a job for a man who wanted one, then the unemployed was entitled to insurance.[66] While the Wainwright Commission report on unemployment had recommended trade union unemployment insurance, it had not recommended public unemployment insurance. However, Leiserson, who had written the report, became convinced of the necessity of public unemployment insurance by 1915.[67]

Reformers did not learn easily to accept the preeminence of the public sector in areas formerly considered to be the province of voluntarism. They were staunch defenders of capitalism and feared what they considered socialistic encroachment by the state. When studies commissioned by them pointed out the responsibility of society for unemployment they were caught in a dilemma. They lacked resources to solve the problem, yet were reluctant to give up their self-assumed responsibility to the state. For example, when William Nolan, the social secretary at the Municipal Lodging House, stated that he thought government ownership of the railroads would help relieve seasonal unemployment, Johnston DeForest wrote a letter marked "confidential" to "Persons of the COS" complaining that Nolan "missed his mark, in fact it doesn't seem to me that he has any good idea of the mark at which he ought to be aiming, nor has he any good idea of certain COS fundamentals." Nolan's contract was not renewed by the COS.[68]

Another example was the debate over widowed mothers' pensions. The United Hebrew Charities in New York had long financially supported widows with families in accordance with the general Jewish philosophy of relief. The non-Jewish New York reformers opposed the pension because to them it was a form of outdoor relief. An executive meeting of the COS in 1912 decided on formal opposition, but decided to wait until the probable attitudes of other societies could be ascertained before publicizing its opposition. One writer noted that, even when organized charity realized a problem could be attributed to society as a whole, organized charity was unwilling to act "beyond prevailing public opinion," functioning almost as "politicians" with ears to the ground.[69]

When formal hearings were held on the Widow's Pension Bill, the NYCOS sent Lawrence Veiller, Otto Bannard, and Robert DeForest to testify and lobby against the proposed bill. When it seemed that the bill would pass in spite of its opposition, the COS decided against further public opposition because no statement by the society would be useful and, if it did oppose the bill, it would "stand alone." The AICP openly supported the bill.[70]

Otto Bannard's testimony before the Commission on Widowed Mothers' Relief explained the COS opposition. He stated that the pensions presented "the strongest sentimental appeal . . . for this entering wedge towards state socialism." The cry was not for alms but "the right to share." Subsequent steps, he prophesied, would be old age pensions, free relief to the unemployed, and "the right to be given work."[71] The plan, he stated, "is not American; it is not virile." The passage of the widowed mothers' relief bill, the New York State Child Welfare Law of 1915, was "a watershed in the history of American social welfare."[72]

The idea of the right of individuals to secure government assistance gained slow acceptance in American society. That right New York reformers had long opposed but they eventually accepted it in the mayor's committee report. In its argument for unemployment insurance, the report stated that insurance was "preferable to any form of relief in that it comes as a right and not as a grant conditional on the good will of a benevolent organization." The inference was clear. If a man received insurance as a right because he had no work, then employment was a right as well.[73]

In spite of the hope held by the mayor's committee and by the New York reformers in 1915, public interest in solving the problem of unemployment declined. The advent of World War I and steadily decreasing unemployment greatly hastened the growth of apathy on the subject of unemployment. The mayor's committee failed to consolidate its gains and relaxed its efforts, thus leaving the community unprepared to meet the next unemployment crisis, "except for the fact that a set of principles and policies had been formulated." The contribution of the era was posed in 1915 by Frances Kellor:

> Unemployment has taken its place among the questions with which we shall deal with increasing sympathy and intelligence: it has been transferred from the province of charity to that of industrial organization. Where one citizen was listed as its foe, a hundred now stand ready. The preliminary educational work has been done, we have now but to

organize the forces at work, seek the causes, and institute remedies.[74]

While Miss Kellor was perhaps overly optimistic, she did place unemployment in its proper framework. Unemployment was not solved between 1873 and 1916, but it was finally recognized as a problem to be solved in the United States. By exhausting voluntarist methods of dealing with the unemployed and by encouraging studies of unemployment, the New York charity organization reformers played a major role in the discovery of unemployment in New York —and America. Organizing the forces at work, seeking the causes, and instituting remedies for unemployment would prove to be difficult, if not impossible, but at least the war on unemployment had begun.

NOTES

1. David Moses Schneider and Albert Deutsch, *The History of Public Welfare in New York State* (Chicago, 1941), 205; New York State Commission Appointed under Chapter 518 of the Laws of 1909 to Inquire into the Question of Employer's Liability and Other Matters, *Third Report: Unemployment and the Lack of Farm Labor* (Albany, 1911), 14-15.

2. John A. Kingsbury to Henry Seager, Paul Kennaday, Frederick Underwood, president of Erie R.R., Edward Carpenter (NEE) et al., January 27, 1914, Papers of John A. Kingsbury, Library of Congress.

3. Harry Hopkins, "Report of the Question of Unemployment in New York City," January 8, 1913, typescript, Papers of NYAICP, Archives of the Community Service Society, New York City; "Proceedings of a Hearing Held on Unemployment at the Mayor's Office, January 29, 1914," 9, 13, 47, 75, Mayoralty Papers of John Purroy Mitchel, Municipal Archives, New York City.

4. "Urge $50,000 for Immediate Aid of City's Homeless," *New York Call*, February 7, 1914; "Unemployed Army Raids East Side Church Demanding a Place to Spend the Night but is Chased Away by Police Reserves," *New York Call*, February 28, 1914; "Half a Hundred Jobless Sheltered in 14 St. Labor Temple . . .," *New York Call*, March 1, 1914; Harry L. Slobodin to Julius Gerber, March 4, 1914, Papers of Socialist party, New York City, Tamiment Library, New York University; H. F. Stimpson to Mayor J. P. Mitchel, March 2, 1914, Mayoralty Papers of John Purroy Mitchel.

5. St. Alphonsus Parish, New York City, Annals (a log kept by a chronicler), March 4, 1914; "Churches, the City, and the Army of Unemployed in New York," *Survey* 32 (March 28, 1914): 793-794; "Tannenbaum Guilty Is Jury's Verdict," *New York Call*, March 28, 1914; "The Catholic Church and the Unemployed," *International Socialist Review* (April 1914): 608-609; *New York Times*, April 9, 1914, 5.

6. John Haynes Holmes, "Tannenbaum in the Large," *Survey* 32 (April 23, 1914): 94.

7. Ibid., 94; John A. Ryan, "The Unemployed and the Churches: A Reply," *Survey* 32 (June 27, 1914): 342-343; "What Churchmen Think of the Invasion of Their Sanctuaries by the Unemployed," *Current Opinion* 56 (May 1914): 367-368.

8. "Industrial Workers of the World: Formation of the Movement and the Guerilla Style of Organization and Warfare Developed by this Labor Army Which Does Not Ban Even the Tramp from its Ranks," New York *Evening Post*, November 9, 1912. Graham Adams, Jr., *Age of Industrial Violence, 1910-1915: The Activities and Findings of the United States Commission on Industrial Relations* (New York and London, 1966), discusses much of the violence investigated by the commission. Adams poses the possibility (p. 38) that the labor violence and developing class tensions were instrumental in securing congressional approval of the Commission on Industrial Relations. John A. Kingsbury, "Our Army of the Unemployed," *Review of Reviews* 49 (April 1914): 433; "Jobless Armies," *Literary Digest* 48 (January 31, 1914): 190-192. Jim Tully, "The Hoboes of America," *America as Americans See It*, ed. Fred J. Ringel (New York, 1932), 320, calls the hoboes the "midwives" of the IWW.

9. W. Frank Persons, "Memo," to Bailey Burritt, October 24, 1914, Papers of NYAICP; Frances H. MacLean, "Our Many Illiads," *Survey* 11 (November 1, 1913): 141.

10. *New York Call*, March 15, 20, 1914; B. de P. Cruger (secretary to Mayor Mitchel) to Julius Gerber, March 23, 1914, Papers of Socialist party.

11. Robert Gibson, Jr., to B. de P. Cruger, April 18, 1914; James J. McInerny (Justice of Court of Special Sessions, New York City) to Mayor Mitchel, April 29, 1914. At least one immigrant group disavowed and deplored the assassination attempt. See French and Canadian Democratic Club of New York City, "Resolutions," April 17, 1914, Papers of John Purroy Mitchel, Library of Congress.

12. Herbert N. Casson, *Organized Self-Help: A History and Defence of the American Labor Movement* (New York, 1901), 39, 62, 68-69; Ralph Easley to Samuel Gompers, April 28, 1914, Papers of National Civic Federation, New York Public Library; "Memorandum: Concerning the policy to be pursued by the Department of Industrial Economics of the National Civic Federation" (n.p., n.d.), Papers of Seth Low, Columbia University.

13. New York *Tribune*, November 30, 1941; Ralph Easley to Andrew Carnegie, March 31, 1914, to Mayor Mitchel, May 13, 1914, Papers of National Civic Federation, New York Public Library.

14. "Urge Service in State Guard: The Association Requests Employers to Give it Their Unreserved Support: It Insures Stable Conditions," *Greater N.Y.* 3 (May 11, 1914): 3.

15. St. Alphonsus Parish, New York City, Annals, October 14, 1914; New York *Herald*, October 14, 1914, 1; New York *Sun*, October 15, 1914, clippings in the Annals concerning the incident at St. Alphonsus.

16. National Civic Federation, "Inquiry into Business Conditions and Unemployment," November 12, 1914, Papers of National Civic Federation; Haley Fiske (vice-

president of Metropolitan Life Insurance Co.) to Mayor J. P. Mitchel, February 2, 1915, Mayoralty Papers of John Purroy Mitchel; New York City Police Department, "Report of the Police Department Committee on Distress and Unemployment," Winter of 1914-15, New York City Police *Bulletin*, supplement (September 1915); Schneider and Deutsch, *History of Public Welfare*, 205; Karl de Schweinitz to Mary Richmond, March 24, 1915, Papers of NYCOS, Archives of the Community Service Society, New York City.

17. "Thanksgiving at the Bowery Mission," *Christian Herald* 37 (December 16, 1914): 1185; W. Frank Persons and C. C. Burlingham to Police Commissioner Arthur Woods, December 8, 1914; "Whiting in Disguise Tours the Bowery," New York *Sun*, January 9, 1915, clipping, Papers of NYCOS.

18. "Minutes of the Executive Committee (New York Socialist party) Unemployment Conference," February 7, 1914, Papers of Socialist party; Mayoralty Papers of John Purroy Mitchel; *New York Call*, March 27, 1914; Charles Stelzle, *A Son of the Bowery: The Life Story of an East Side American* (New York, 1926), 230-231.

19. John A. Fitch, "Class Fighters and a Hobo Who Solved a Problem," *Survey* 32 (September 5, 1914): 558-560; *New York Times*, April 6, 1968, 40; New York *Globe and Commercial Advertiser*, December 30, 1914, 1, 11; Ida M. Tarbell, "The Golden Rule in Business," *American Magazine* 78 (December 1914): 27-28.

20. New York *Globe and Commercial Advertiser*, December 30, 1914, 11; "Reminiscences of Henry Bruere," 118-120, Columbia Oral History Project; Frank Persons to Mary Richmond, January 15, 1915, Papers of NYCOS; "Reminiscences of Martin C. Ansorge," 55, Columbia Oral History Project.

21. "To Aid 320,000 Jobless Men," New York *Globe and Commercial Advertiser*, February 5, 1914; Frank J. Bruno, notes on "Meeting of the Religious Citizenship League to Consider the Question of Unemployment," February 6, 1914, Papers of NYCOS; W. D. P. Bliss to Mayor J. P. Mitchel, February 18, 1914, Executive Secretary of Mayor Mitchel to W. D. P. Bliss, March 17, 1914, Mayoralty Papers of John Purroy Mitchel; *New York Call*, February 7, 21, 1914.

22. New York *Evening Mail*, October 7, 1914; Jonathan C. Day (superintendent of Labor Temple) to W. F. Persons, October 15, 1914, Papers of NYCOS; Form letter of George William Douglas (Chairman of Committee on Economic Conditions), November 21, 1914, Papers of NYAICP.

23. Charles Stelzle (executive secretary of the Inter-Church Employment Committee of the N.Y. Federation of Churches) to W. F. Persons, January 15, 1915, Papers of NYCOS; "Unemployment Sunday Bulletin," Russell Sage Collection, The City College of the City University of New York; "Unemployment Relief in New York; How the Churches are Meeting the Problem," *Congregationalist and Christian World* 100 (January 7, 1915): 24.

24. "Churches, the City, and the Army of the Unemployed in N. Y.," 794; *New York Call*, February 11, 1914; A Christian Pastor, "Should the Church be a Legislative Force?" *Christian Herald* 37 (April 22, 1914): 427.

25. Henry A. Atkinson, "The Unemployed Man and the Church," *Persistent Public Problems: Unemployment; Social and Industrial Righteousness*, ed. Arthur O. Taylor

(Boston, 1916), 244; Floyd Appleton, *Church Philanthropy in N.Y.: A Study of the Philanthropic Institutions of the Protestant Episcopal Church in the City of New York* (New York, 1906), 81; Holmes, "Tannenbaum in the Large," 95. Christian Socialists were among the first religious leaders to look to the state for aid in the unemployment problem. For examples see Washington Gladden, "Relief Work—Its Principles and Methods," *Review of Reviews* 9 (January 1894): 39, and "What to do With the Workless Man," *Ohio Bulletin of Charities and Correction* 5 (June 30, 1899): 16; Walter Rauschenbusch, *Christianizing the Social Order* (New York, 1912). Even missions began to look to the government for help. See Ballington Booth, "One Experience of an Unemployed Man," *Volunteer's Gazette*, February 29, 1908, 8; Gertrude Atherton, "The Church and the Workingman," *Christian Herald* 37 (December 16, 1914): 1195.

26. William Hard, "Unemployment as a Coming Issue," *American Labor Legislation Review* 2 (1912): 93. Hard does not name the "important magazines" in his article.

27. Linda H. Morley, *Unemployment Compensation: A Chronological Bibliography of Books, Reports, and Periodical Articles in English* (New York, 1928), iv. See also "Awakening of Public Interest," *American Labor Legislation Review* 5 (1915): 495-501; Hard, "Unemployment as a Coming Issue," 95.

28. Roy Lubove, *The Struggle for Social Security, 1900-1935* (Cambridge, Massachusetts, 1968), 30-31; William Hard, "Report of the Committee on Unemployment," *American Labor Legislation Review* 3 (1913): 138.

29. "First National Conference on Unemployment," *Survey* 31 (March 7, 1914): 693; "The Jobless Man and the Manless Job," *Outlook* 106 (March 14, 1914): 568; "Unemployment," *Nation* 98 (March 5, 1914): 229-230.

30. Frances A. Kellor, *Out of Work* (New York, 1915), 5, 111-112. Another defense of the immigrant is Isaac A. Hourwich, *Immigration and Labor* (New York and London, 1912), chap. 6.

31. Wainwright Commission, *Report*, 12; North American Civic League for Immigrants, *Bi-Monthly Bulletin*, no. 2 (December 1913-January 1914), 1, 2, 7-10.

32. Kellor, *Out of Work* (1915), 392-393; Frances A. Kellor, "Organizing to Fight Unemployment Effectively," *Survey* 31 (February 14, 1914): 611, "The Way Out of Unemployment Situation," *Survey* 31 (February 21, 1914), 634-639, "Is Unemployment a Municipal Problem?" *National Municipal Review* 3 (April 1914): 366-370, and "The Crying Need for Connecting Up the Man and the Job," *Survey* 31 (February 7, 1914): 542.

33. NYCOS, *Annual Report* (1915), 12; Ray C. Risley to John A. Kingsbury, May 12, 1913, Papers of NYAICP; Ray Livingston, *The Ways of the Hobo* (Erie, Pennsylvania, 1915), 59; O. H. Pannkokf, "Unemployment A National Problem," *Christian Herald* 38 (January 27, 1915): 101; Harry F. Ward, *Poverty and Wealth* (New York, 1915), 32; Rauschenbusch, *Christianizing the Social Order*, 452; "Our Duty to the Unemployed," *Literary Digest* 47 (November 29, 1913): 1067; Harry S. Lewis, *Liberal Judaism and Social Service* (New York, 1915), 130.

34. Boris D. Bogen, *Extent of Jewish Philanthropy in the United States* (n.p., n.d.),

4; David M. Bressler to S. Essy, September 23, 1912, Papers of the Industrial Removal Office, American Jewish Historical Society, Waltham, Massachusetts; NYCCCC, *Proceedings* (1912), 13; NYAICP, Employment Department, "Report," May 1913, Papers of NYAICP; Adolphus S. Solomons (secretary, IRO) to Prof. Charles R. Henderson, March 17, 1914, A. Caminetti, Commissioner General of Immigration, Washington, D.C., March 17, 1914, and Editors of *New Republic*, December 30, 1914, Papers of Industrial Removal Office.

35. Mayor J. P. Mitchel to NYC Board of Aldermen, March 24, 1914, Mayoralty Papers of John Purroy Mitchel; "Municipal Plans for the Unemployed," *Survey* 31 (February 14, 1914): 633-635; *New York Call*, February 11, 1914; *New York Times*, February 14, 1914, 8.

36. "Report" of a Special Committee on the City Agency to the Mayor, March 3, 1914, Mayoralty Papers of John Purroy Mitchel.

37. City Club of New York, Public Employment Exchanges, *Report of the Committee Appointed by the Trustees on December 17, 1913, to Inquire into the Need of Public Employment Exchanges in New York* (New York, 1914) 6; Mitchel statement to the Press, February 10, 1914, Mayoralty Papers of John Purroy Mitchel; *New York Call*, February 11, 1914; *New York Times*, February 25, 1914, 14.

38. *New York Times*, March 7, 1914, 5; J. Mayhew Wainwright, "Letter to Editor," *New York Times*, March 10, 1914, 9.

39. Victor Murdock, *Speech in the House of Representatives, May 1, 1914*, reprint (Washington, 1914), Russell Sage Collection. Darrell Hevenor Smith, *The United States Employment Service, Its History, Activities, and Organization* (Baltimore, 1923), 1-57, sketches the history from its beginning with the Division of Information established in 1907. Smith pays scant attention to the pre-1916 period when the theoretical framework for the Employment Service, as well as many of its municipal and state links, were established.

40. Leah Hannah Feder, *Unemployment Relief in Periods of Depression: A Study of Relief Methods Adopted in Certain American Cities, 1857 Through 1922* (New York, 1936), 237-241. The portion of the Chicago report pertaining to public employment agencies was submitted as a doctoral dissertation to the University of Chicago. Edwin H. Sutherland, *Unemployed and Public Employment Agencies* (Chicago, 1914).

41. Mitchel Scrapbook, Vol. IV, August 13, 1914, Mayoralty Papers of John Purroy Mitchel; "Memo of Informal Conference at the Midday Club," September 23, 1914, "Memorandum of Conference Held at the Midday Club," September 28, 1914, 2 (Bruere quotation), Papers of NYAICP; Homer Folks' *Journal 1912-1919*, on meeting dates, Papers of Homer Folks; NYAICP Executive Committee, "Minutes," October 15, 1914. Presumably a nonrepresentative committee would be one in which the NYAICP was not represented and one in which "radicals" would be members.

42. "Memorandum on the Conference on Unemployment Held at the Midday Club," October 26, 1914, Papers of NYAICP; Henry Bruere, "A Proposal in Reference to Unemployment in the Winter of 1914 for Consideration by His Honor, the Mayor of the City of New York," New York, November 1914, 3, Papers of NYCOS. The pro-

posal was submitted on October 15, 1914. NYCOS Executive Committee, "Minutes," November 18, 1914. See also "Reminiscences of Henry Bruere," 121, Columbia Oral History Project.

43. Clippings and Correspondence From the Office of the Mayor of the City of New York, Vol. CVII, New York Public Library Annex; Ralph Easley to Henry Bruere, November 18, 1914, Henry Bruere to Easley, November 28, 1914, Easley to Samuel Gompers, December 7, 1914, Papers of National Civic Federation.

44. Mayor J. P. Mitchel to E. H. Gary, December 2, 1914, Mayoralty Papers of John Purroy Mitchel.

45. Robert W. DeForest to Mayor J. P. Mitchel, December 4, 1914, Otto T. Bannard to Mayor J. P. Mitchel, December 4, 1914, Mayoralty Papers of John Purroy Mitchel.

46. "The Right to Starve," *International Socialist Review* (March 1915): 522; Ruth S. Baldwin (chairman of National League on Urban Conditions Among Negroes) to Lillian Wald, December 2, 1914, Lillian Wald to Paul Wilson, December 3, 1914, Mayoralty Papers of John Purroy Mitchel.

47. *Greater New York* (Bulletin of the Merchants' Association of New York) 4 (January 25, 1915): 2.

48. Ibid., 3.

49. Ibid., 4, 11, 5-6.

50. John Purroy Mitchel to George W. Perkins, January 25, 1915, Mayoralty Papers of John Purroy Mitchel; George W. Perkins to Jacob H. Schiff, April 5, 1915, Papers of Jacob H. Schiff, American Jewish Archives, Cincinnati, Ohio; Ralph Easley to Seth Low, February 5, 1914, Papers of National Civic Federation.

51. Mary Richmond to Emergency Winter Exchange (EWE), November 27, 1914, Papers of NYCOS; "Special Number on the Coming Winter," *Charity Organization Bulletin* (N.S.) 5 (November 1919): 125, 130; Frank W. Persons to EWE, December 14, 1914, Persons to EWE, February 24, 1915, Persons to Otto T. Bannard, December 22, 1914, Papers of NYCOS.

52. New York Unemployment Committee to Mayor John P. Mitchel, April 7, 1915, Mayoralty Papers of John Purroy Mitchel; Frances A. Kellor, "Unemployment in American Cities: The Record for 1914-1915," *National Municipal Review* 4 (July 1915): 427.

53. Edward T. Devine, *Principles of Relief* (New York, 1904), 153, and his *Practice of Charity*, 174.

54. Edward T. Devine, *Misery and Its Causes* (New York, 1909), 11.

55. New York City, Mayor's Committee on Unemployment, *Report* (New York, January, 1916), 91, 5, 109 (hereafter cited as Mayor's Committee, *Report*); The American Association for Labor Legislation and the United States Industrial Commission (1915) also recommended public employment exchanges, regularization of industry, and unemployment insurance. In addition the AALL recommended public works. See John Andrews, "The Prevention of Unemployment," NCCC, *Proceedings* (1915), 539-555, and Bryce M. Stewart et al., *Unemployment Benefits in the United States: The Plans and Their Setting* (New York, 1930), 8.

56. Mayor's Committee, *Report*, 96, 45-47.

57. Ibid., 51; SCAA, *Handbook for Visitors to the Poorhouse* (New York, 1877), 52.

58. "Relief of the Unemployed: Charity or Work," *Current Literature* 15 (February 1894): 118-119; *New York Times*, August 23, 1893.

59. *Public Papers of Roswell P. Flower, Governor, 1893* (Albany, 1894), 351.

60. Mayor George B. McClellan (New York City) to Robert W. DeForest, April 8, 1908, Papers of George B. McClellan, New York Historical Society; Robert F. Cutting to F. C. Stevens, Commissioner of Canals and Public Works, April 6, 1908, Papers of NYAICP.

61. E. H. Gary to Mayor Mitchel, January 4, 1915, Mayoralty Papers of John Purroy Mitchel; NYAICP, *Annual Report* (1915), 12-14, 26-28; William H. Matthews, *Adventures in Giving* (New York, 1939), 106-110; Bailey Burritt, "Outline of Remarks on Occasion of Testimonial Dinner to Mr. Harry Hopkins," June 22, 1933, Papers of NYAICP.

62. "Make Hoboes Soldiers," *Utica Daily Press*, November 14, 1914, Papers of John A. Kingsbury; "A Million Men Out of Work," *Railroad Trainman* 32 (February 1915): 177; Frances A. Kellor, "Unemployment in Our Cities," *National Municipal Review* 4 (January 1915): 75.

63. Mayor's Committee, *Report*, 53-54.

64. Ibid., 93-94.

65. Lee K. Frankel and Miles M. Dawson, *Workingmen's Insurance in Europe* (New York, 1911); Devine, *Misery and Its Causes*, 137; Henry Rogers Seager, *Social Insurance: A Program of Social Reform* (New York, 1910), chap. 4; I. M. Rubinow, *Social Insurance with Special Reference to American Conditions* (New York, 1913), 441-455.

66. NYCOS, *Charity Organization Bulletin*, no. 74, June 2, 1915; Kingsbury, "Our Army of the Unemployed," 439; Mary Richmond to unknown addressee, March 30, 1907, Papers of Mary Richmond. Other reform writings which acknowledged insurance for unemployment by 1916 include Charles B. Barnes, "The Function of Public Employment Offices," NCCC, *Proceedings* (1915), 504; John B. Andrews, "American Cities and the Prevention of Unemployment," *American City* 14 (February 1916): 121; Kellor, "Unemployment in Our Cities," 75; and Robert Bruere, "Reanchoring the Home," *Harper's Magazine* 124 (May 1912): 924.

67. Wainwright Commission, *Report*, 13; J. Michael Eisner, *William Morris Leiserson: A Biography* (Madison, 1967), 36.

68. William J. Nolan, "Report," of the activities of the Social Secretary at the MLH for March 1913 to Charles K. Blatchly (superintendent, JAB), April 4, 1913; Johnston DeForest to W. F. Persons, April 12, 1913, Papers of NYCOS.

69. M. D. Waldman, "The UHC of N. Y.," February 24, 1914, lecture delivered at the New York School of Social Work, at American Jewish Historical Society; "Pensioning Widows," *Jewish Charity* 4 (January 1905): 113-114; "Notes" for a hearing on Widow's Pensions, November, 1913, Papers of Mary Richmond; Frederick T. Hill to Robert F. Cutting, February 7, 1912, Papers of NYCOS; NYCOS Executive Commit-

tee, "Minutes," November 12, 1912; Hutchins Hapgood, "Organized Charity—The Conservative Viewpoint," New York *Globe and Commercial Advertiser*, March 7, 1913, clipping in Papers of NYCOS.

70. Isaac Russell to W. F. Persons, December 26, 1914, Papers of NYCOS; NYAICP Board of Managers, "Minutes," January 21, 1915; NYCOS Executive Committee, "Minutes," February 3, March 17, 1915; Chris Morton, "Vested Rights in Charity," *The Masses*, February, 1915, 11.

71. "Vested Rights," 11.

72. Lubove, *Struggle for Social Security*, 103, 101.

73. Mayor's Committee, *Report*, 69.

74. Kellor, "Unemployment in American Cities," 428.

Epilogue

BETWEEN 1870 and 1915, the term "tramp" underwent a gradual metamorphosis. In the beginning of this period, the charity organization reformers regarded as tramps not only all the homeless unemployed, but most of the resident unemployed as well. Since the great American dream indicated that everyone could work and rise to the top, one who did not work was an outcast—a tramp. The reformers did not ask why a man was not working, but assumed that personal failure was the reason. Thus the reformers' remedies were directed at the tramp himself in the form of vagrancy laws and forced labor.

During the 1890s the term "tramp" applied less broadly. The reformers began to revise slowly their assumption that most homeless unemployed were voluntarily out of work and, therefore, tramps, and they began to recognize that a sizable number were involuntarily unemployed. Since homeless wanderers seemed a threat to established order, the reformers hoped to return as many of them as possible to work and, presumably, to a commitment to American captialism. To aid in this task the reformers developed new institutions to separate the voluntary from involuntary tramps and sought new methods to keep men from taking to the road in the first place.

The reformers and society did come to realize that a certain measure of social dislocation was necessary and even desirable in an industrial state. By the panic of 1907-1908 a man who moved in search of work was often called a "hobo" in recognition of this belief. Most of the great masses of involuntarily unemployed persons in depression periods after 1908 were not labeled with derisive terms, but were referred to only as "the unemployed." The attempt to establish employment exchanges sought two results: to find jobs for all the unemployed, even in depression years, and to end the apparently confused wandering of men seeking work in good times as well as bad.

After 1900 social welfare reformers began to realize that voluntarism alone was incapable of solving societal problems like unemployment and that the public sector had to assume the responsibility for measures of prevention, amelioration, and solution. Because of the trend in emphasis, the reformers worked first in liaison with other groups and then with the governmental agencies themselves. They used their agencies to lobby for legislation, accepted appointive positions in government, and served as unofficial advisers to public officials. New York reformers such as John A. Kingsbury, Walter Weyl, Herbert Croly, and Harry Hopkins were indeed successful in such efforts.

Tramps did not disappear after 1915, of course, but Charlie Chaplin's portrayal of the tramp on the silver screen in 1915 became more firmly fixed in the public mind than a shadowy conspirator in battered clothing seeking the overthrow of society. The vision of the tramp became increasingly romantic and less terrifying. When huge numbers of tramps appeared in America after 1929, they were viewed differently than they had been in depressions before 1915. Almost everyone in the 1930s accepted most tramps as products of the depression and thus treated them with more sympathy, and the government accepted responsibility for them. The United States Employment Service, virtually defunct in 1919, expanded rapidly in the 1930s.

Since World War II "tramps" have seemingly almost disappeared in the United States. But one can see the prototypes of the nineteenth century tramps if one looks carefully. They draw welfare checks or unemployment compensation so do not usually beg on the streets. They live in old folks' homes or in private homes by the grace of old age pensions, social security, and medicare, however meager the benefits. They reside in mental institutions and hospitals for chronic diseases. They have been trained to overcome handicaps of missing limbs, senses, and low mental capacities. Federal, state, and local governments work steadily, although with only some success, in attempting to reduce alcoholism and drug addiction.

Many tramps on the Bowery in New York or on similar streets of other urban cities are running from parents that do not understand them, from unwanted wives and families, or from themselves. Others flock to the Bowery because alcoholism, narcotics, and disease have reduced them to chronic vagrancy. It is rarely necessary for a man to tramp because of economic displacement in order to keep from starving. Most of these men do not tramp, but remain part of the hard-core unemployed living off welfare checks and food stamps, moving only to states with more liberal welfare laws. Treatment of tramps today goes on continually. Operation Bowery in New York City treats alcoholics. Missions such as McAuley's Water Street Mission and the Bowery Mission treat tramps with interlocking doses of professional medical and psychological care and religious guidance.

This reassessment of the tramp challenged stereotypes held by reformers and society at large. Popular and journal literature had suggested that the tramp could not and would not work even if work were offered. The only work generally offered, of course, was of a menial nature, which others would not perform. The tramp's presumed laziness and wanderlust were regarded as hereditary and not easily changed by environmental conditions. He also did not take baths and appeared satisfied to remain dirty. Laws and legal practices established in the 1880s to punish the "won't works" with jail sentences for being "without visible means of support" institutionalized society's distaste for the tramp. These laws were infringements of personal liberties; in a sense, they were black codes against labor. By 1969, however, a series of court decisions, including *Lazarus vs. Faircloth* and *Goldman vs. Knecht*, found these laws unconstitutional. These decisions in part recognized the need for the mobility of labor in an industrial state, which did not maintain full employment at all times. But recognition did not come easily. Unfortunately, the reason America looked closely at the tramp to identify him and his problems was the fear that the unemployed might challenge the very foundations of society. Only then was the tramp studied and attempts made to incorporate him into the American dream.

A Selective Bibliography

MANUSCRIPTS

THE MOST valuable collections for this study were the papers of the New York Charity Organization Society and the New York Association for Improving the Condition of the Poor located in the Archives of the Community Service Society in New York City. In addition to all the printed reports for the two organizations, the holdings also include minutes of the Executive Boards and minor operating committees such as the Woodyard Committee. Also located in the archives are extensive correspondence files of both groups containing letters of New York reformers, such as Edward T. Devine, Robert W. DeForest, and Robert F. Cutting who have left no personal collections of papers elsewhere.

Although no manuscripts are included in the Russell Sage Collection at The City College of the City University of New York, the very large (4,000 shelf feet) collection is invaluable because of its holdings of organizational and public reports and other fugitive material. Also at City College are the uncataloged papers of Jacob A. Riis, useful in regard to the closing of the police station lodging and the opening of the Municipal Lodging House in the 1890s. This collection has virtually no outgoing correspondence, but has many letters from Josephine Shaw Lowell to Riis on the subject of the homeless unemployed.

For reconstructing the position of the city government regarding the homeless unemployed, the mayoralty papers located at the New York Municipal Archives were useful. Unfortunately the collections are huge and poorly indexed with no indexes of the correspondence. The Mayoralty Papers prior to 1896 is a collection containing papers of many administrations filed by subjects. The most useful information for this study was found in files marked ''Charities and Corrections.'' The Gilroy Papers had items pertaining to relief of the unemployed in 1894 and, although the Mitchel Papers deal with unemployment and the Mayor's Committee on Unemployment, they were not as strong as one might expect.

The Mary Richmond Papers at the Columbia University School of Social Work were particularly useful for the period when she was associated with the Charity Organization Department of the Russell Sage Foundation. The Homer Folks Papers at the Columbia School of Social Work were of only limited use because the correspondence files for the period 1904-1917 are missing.

The several hundred cubic feet of papers of the Industrial Removal Office and the Baron de Hirsch Fund are now located at the American Jewish Historical Society at Waltham, Massachusetts. At the time I was doing my research, the papers were completely uncataloged and in packing cases, and so were of only limited use for this study. However, I sampled the collection and there is sufficient material for doctoral dissertations and/or masters' theses.

The John A. Kingsbury Papers at the Library of Congress had little unpublished material on unemployment and the Mayor's Committee on Unemployment. Although the collection is huge (12,000 items), many folders are missing and the correspondence seldom deals with policy matters. The Mitchel Papers shed little light on the principal problems related to unemployment.

The collection of Lillian Wald Papers at Columbia was especially interesting because it contains pre-1915 Jacob H. Schiff letters, which do not exist elsewhere. The Schiff letters deal primarily with personal conflicts he had with Riis and Devine. There are also some Frances Kellor letters in this collection. This Wald collection supplements the Lillian Wald Papers at the New York Public Library, which are weak prior to 1915.

The Wainwright Papers at the New York Historical Society are disappointingly weak on the Wainwright Commission. Virtually all material in the collection concerns procedural and routine decisions and operations. The National Civic Federation Papers at the New York Public Library proved to be of only marginal value because they do not deal directly with the problem of the unemployed. The Socialist party Collection at the Tamiment Library was useful for showing the party's view of New York's unemployment problem.

Of the reminiscences used at the Columbia University Oral History Project, Henry Bruere's was most valuable because of his discussions of Jeff Davis, the "King of the Hoboes," and the Mayor's Committee on Unemployment. William H. Allen's comments were too colored by later events to be of much historical use in this study.

Although consulted, the Paul U. Kellogg and *The Survey* papers at the Social Welfare History Archives Center at the University of Minnesota had few papers prior to 1915. The same criticism holds true for the papers of the Kelly Family and Charles Stelzle at Columbia University. The George B. McClellan Family collection and the Jacob A. Riis Papers at the Library of Congress contain little of a policy nature and, therefore, were of little use in this study.

McAuley Water Street Mission, the Salvation Army Eastern Territorial Headquarters, the YMCA National Library, and the State Communities Aid Association (State Charities Aid Association), all of New York City, have only a very small amount of manuscript material. The Bowery Mission, St. Vincent de Paul Society, and the Volunteers of America have virtually no historical material of any kind prior to 1916. The principal printed documents for these three organizations are located at the New York Public Library.

Papers of Homer Folks
   Columbia University School of Social Work, New York City

Mayoralty Papers of Thomas Gilroy
   Municipal Archives, New York City

Papers of Baron de Hirsch Fund
   American Jewish Historical Society, Waltham, Massachusetts

Papers of Richard Holz
   Salvation Army, Eastern Territorial Headquarters, New York City

Papers of Industrial Removal Office
    American Jewish Historical Society, Waltham, Massachusetts

Papers of John A. Kingsbury
    Library of Congress, Washington, D.C.

Papers of Samuel M. Lindsay
    Columbia University, New York City

Papers of Seth Low
    Columbia University, New York City

Mayoralty Papers of Seth Low
    Municipal Archives, New York City

Papers of John Purroy Mitchel
    Library of Congress, Washington, D.C.

Mayoralty Papers of John Purroy Mitchel
    Municipal Archives, New York City

Papers of the National Civic Federation
    New York Public Library, New York City

Papers of New York Association for Improving the Condition of the
    Poor
    Archives of the Community Service Society of New York City

Papers of New York Charity Organization Society
    Archives of the Community Service Society of New York City

Mayoralty Papers of New York City prior to 1896
    Municipal Archives, New York City

Papers of Mary Richmond
    Columbia University School of Social Work, New York City

Papers of Jacob A. Riis
The City College of the City University of New York

St. Alphonsus Roman Catholic Church
St. Alphonsus Parish, New York City

Papers of Jacob H. Schiff
American Jewish Archives, Cincinnati, Ohio

Mayoralty Papers of Smith Ely (1877-1878)
Municipal Archives, New York City

Papers of the Socialist party (NYC)
Tamiment Library, New York University, New York City

Papers of James G. Phelps Stokes
Columbia University, New York City

Mayoralty Papers of Robert A. VanWyck (1898-1902)
Municipal Archives, New York City

Papers of Jonathan M. Wainwright
New York Historical Society, New York City

Papers of Lillian Wald
Columbia University, New York City

Papers of Lillian Wald
New York Public Library, New York City

OFFICIAL REPORTS AND PROCEEDINGS OF PRIVATE AND PUBLIC AGENCIES

Since a wide variety of public and private agencies were interested in the tramp and in unemployment, the annual reports, bulletins, and proceedings of these organizations contain useful information. Ordinarily these official publications carried "official" views of its agency, stressing the actions that took place rather than the motivations behind the actions. Therefore, they have to be used with care and supplemented by other sources.

Most useful private agency reports included those of the New York Charity Organization Society (NYCOS), *Annual Reports*, 1884-1916; New York Association for Improving the Condition of the Poor (NYAICP), *Annual Reports*, 1874-1915; New York State Charities Aid Association (SCAA), *Annual Reports*, 1876-1896; New York State Board of Charities (NYSBC), *Annual Reports*, 1884-1916; Bowery Mission and Young Men's Home, *Annual Reports*, 1881-1886; McAuley's Water Street Mission, *Annual Reports*, 1896-1915; New York City Young Men's Christian Association (NYC YMCA), *Annual Reports*, 1895-1914; New York City Vacant Lot Gardening Association, *Annual Reports*, 1906-1909; Jewish Agricultural and Industrial Aid Society, *Annual Reports*, 1904-1909. Most of these reports can be found in one or more of three locations in New York City: the Archives of the Community Service Society of New York City, the Russell Sage Collection at The City College of the City University of New York, and the New York Public Library.

Of public agency reports, most useful were the New York City Police Department, *Annual Reports*, 1894-1915, and the New York City Department of Public Charities, *Annual Reports*, 1903-1915. The New York Municipal Reference Library and the New York Public Library hold these reports.

Often more useful than reports of single agencies were proceedings of joint meetings of reformers and/or public officials. Papers relating to tramps and unemployment were occasionally delivered at these conferences, and the printed discussions following the papers occasionally proved enlightening. Most useful papers were sponsored by: the National Conference of Charities and Correction (NCCC), 1874-1916; New York State Conference of Charities and Correction (NYSCCC), 1900-1915; New York City Conference of Charities and Correction (NYCCCC), 1910-1916; and Conference of Mayors and Other Officials of the Cities of New York State, 1911-1912.

Andrews, John B. "The Prevention of Unemployment." NCCC, *Proceedings* (1915), 539-555.

Bressler, David M. "The Removal Work Including Galveston." Sixth Biennial Session of the National Conference of Jewish Charities in the United States, May 17-19, 1910, *Proceedings* (Baltimore, 1910), 111-140.

Bull, W. L. "Trampery: Its Causes, Present Aspects, and Some Suggested Remedies." NCCC, *Proceedings* (1886), 188-206.

Devine, Edward Thomas. "The Value and Dangers of Investigation." NCCC, *Proceedings* (1897), 193-199.

Gladden, Washington. "What to do With the Workless Man." *Ohio Bulletin of Charities and Correction* 5 (June 1899): 10-17.

Hunter, Robert. "The Relation Between Social Settlements and Charity Organization." NCCC, *Proceedings* (1902), 302-314.

Kellogg, Charles D. "Charity Organization in the United States." NCCC, *Proceedings* (1893), 52-93.

————. "The Situation in New York City During the Winter of 1893-94." NCCC, *Proceedings* (1894), 21-30.

Kingsbury, John A. "Rehabilitation of the Homeless Man." NYSCCC, *Proceedings* (1914), 29-38.

Lowell, Josephine Shaw. "The Economic and Moral Effects of Public Outdoor Relief." NCCC, *Proceedings* (1890), 81-91.

————. "Poverty and its Relief: The Methods Possible in the City of New York." NCCC, *Proceedings* (1895), 44-54.

McCook, J. J. "The Tramp Problem: What It Is and What to Do With It." NCCC, *Proceedings* (1895), 288-302.

Warner, Amos G. "Our Charities and Our Churches." NCCC, *Proceedings* (1889), 36-41.

SPECIAL STUDIES AND INVESTIGATIONS

Devine, Edward T. *Report on the Desirability of Establishing an Employment Bureau in the City of New York.* New York, 1909.

Kellor, Frances Alice. *Out of Work: A Study of Employment Agencies: Their Treatment of the Unemployed and Their Influence Upon Home and Business.* New York and London, 1904.

————. *Out of Work: A Study of Unemployment.* New York, 1915.

Laubach, Frank Charles. *Why There are Vagrants: A Study Based on an Examination of One Hundred Men.* New York, 1916.

New York City. Mayor's Committee on Unemployment. *Report.* New York, 1916.

New York State. Commission Appointed Under Chapter 518 of the Laws of 1909 to Inquire Into the Question of Employer's Liability and Other Matters. *Third Report: Unemployment and the Lack of Farm Labor.* Albany, 1911.

Solenberger, Alice Willard. *One Thousand Homeless Men: A Study of Original Records.* New York, 1911.

NEWSPAPERS

Newspapers proved very useful on many occasions in preparing the manuscript. The *New York Times* and the *New York Call* were used most often, but almost all other New York City newspapers were checked regarding specific events. Many newspaper sources cited in the text were from clippings in manuscript collections. The *Christian Science Monitor* and the Newburyport (Massachusetts) *Daily Herald* also provided useful information.

PERIODICALS (Contemporary)

Articles on tramps were fairly common during depression periods in the latter half of the nineteenth century. Articles on unemployment multiplied between 1893 and 1916, reflecting increased public concern in this area. The New York social welfare reformers were prolific writers and published articles often on all phases of reform, including that of the "discovery" of unemployment in the United States. Principal forums for social welfare reformers included *Charities Review*, 1891-1901; *Commons*, 1896-1905; *Charities*, 1897-1905; *Charities and The Commons*, 1906-1909; and the *Survey*. Other periodicals surveyed, which occasionally published articles by the reformers, include: *American City, American Labor Legislation Review, American Magazine, Annals of the American Academy of Political and Social*

Science, Arena, Atlantic Monthly, Chautauquan, Forum, Independent, Jewish Charities, Jewish Charity, Lend A Hand, Nation, National, Municipal Review, North American Review, Outlook, and *World To-Day.*

Religious publications commenting on tramps and unemployment included those of the Volunteers of America (*Volunteer's Gazette*), Salvation Army (*Conqueror, Harbor Lights, War Cry*), and Young Men's Christian Association (*Association Men, Empire State, Young Men's Era*). Other religious periodicals include *American Hebrew, Catholic World, Christian Herald, Congregationalist and Christian World,* and *St. Vincent de Paul Quarterly.*

The *American Agriculturist, American Rural Home,* and *Rural New Yorker* all published editorials giving rural views of the tramp. The *Railroad Trainman* had many articles on the problems with tramps on the railroad. Other periodicals with occasional articles on tramps and unemployment include: *Century, Contemporary Review, Cosmopolitan, Current Literature, Current Opinion, Dial, Harper's Magazine, Harper's Weekly, Literary Digest, Masses, New England Magazine, Popular Science Monthly, Public Opinion, Scientific American,* and *Scribner's Monthly.*

"A Review of the World." *Current Literature* 44 (May 1908): 461-468.

Adams, C. E. "Real Hobo: What He Is and How He Lives." *Forum* 33 (June 1902): 438-449.

Andrews, John B. "American Cities and the Prevention of Unemployment." *American City* 14 (February 1916): 117-121.

"Awakening of Public Interest," *American Labor Legislation Review* 5 (1915): 495-501.

Blatchly, C. K. "State Farm for Tramps and Vagrants." *Survey* 24 (April 9, 1910): 87-89.

Bogen, Boris D. "The Jewish Tramp." *Jewish Charities* 1 (November 1910): 3-5.

Booth Tucker, Frederick de L. "Settlement on the Land." *Jewish Charity* 3 (May 1904): 181-182.

Bressler, David M. "The Removal Office." *Jewish Charity* 3 (June 1904): 213-217.

[Brewer, W. H.] "What Shall We Do With Our Tramps." *New Englander* 37 (July 1878): 521-532.

Bruere, Robert. "Reanchoring the Home." *Harper's Magazine* 124 (May 1912): 918-924.

Butler, Rosalie. "Separation of Charities and Correction." *Charities Review* 2 (June 1893): 164-170.

Devine, Edward Thomas. "Public Meetings and the Police in New York." *Charities and The Commons* 20 (April 4, 1908): 1-3.

————. "The Shifting and Floating Population." *Annals* 10 (September 1897): 149-164.

Dodge, William E. "The Value of Property Depends on the Character of Young Men." *Association Men* 26 (March 1901): 189.

Ely, Richard T. "Unemployed." *Harper's Weekly* 37 (September 2, 1893): 845.

Fitch, John A. "Class Fighters and a Hobo Who Solved a Problem." *Survey* 32 (September 5, 1914): 558-560.

"Five Months' Work for the Unemployed in New York City." *Charities Review* 3 (May 1894): 323-329.

Flower, B. O. "Plutocracies' Bastilles; or Why the Republic Is Becoming an Armed Camp." *Arena* 10 (October 1894): 601-621.

Flynt, Josiah. "The American Tramp." *Contemporary Review* 60 (August 1891): 253-261.

————. "How Men Become Tramps." *Century* (N.S.) 28 (October 1895): 941-945.

Forbes, James. "The Tramp; or Caste in the Jungle." *Outlook* 98 (August 19, 1911): 869-875.

Glenn, John M. "Cooperation Against Beggary." *Charities Review* 1 (December 1891): 67-72.

Hale, Edward E. Jr. "Hobo in Theory and Practice." *Dial* 44 (May 16, 1908): 301-302.

Hard, William. "Unemployment as a Coming Issue." *American Labor Legislation Review* 2 (1912): 93-104.

Holmes, John Haynes. "Tannenbaum in the Large." *Survey* 32 (April 23, 1914): 94-95.

"Icy Hand of the Blizzard Brings Untold Suffering." *War Cry* (February 13, 1897): 4-5.

"The Jobless Man and the Manless Job." *Outlook* 106 (March 14, 1914): 568.

Kellogg, Arthur P. "Traffic Squad at Union Square." *Charities and The Commons* 20 (April 4, 1908): 9-12.

Kellor, Frances Alice. "The Crying Need for Connecting Up the Man and the Job." *Survey* 31 (February 7, 1914): 541-542.

————. "Unemployment in American Cities: The Record for 1914-1915." *National Municipal Review* 4 (July 1915): 420-428.

Lowell, Josephine Shaw. "Methods of Relief for the Unemployed." *Forum* 16 (February 1894): 655-662.

McCook, John J. "Increase of Tramping: Cause and Cure." *Independent* 54 (March 13, 1902): 620-624.

————. "Some New Phases of the Tramp Problem." *Charities Review* 1 (June 1892): 355-364.

————. "Tramp Census and Its Revelations." *Forum* 15 (August 1893): 753-766.

Millis, Harry A. "The Law Affecting Immigrants and Tramps." *Charities Review* 7 (September 1897): 587-594.

"Once More The Tramp." *Scribner's Monthly* 15 (April 1878): 883.

Riis, Jacob A. "How to Bring Work and Workers Together in the United States." *Forum* 18 (September 1894): 122-128.

Roosevelt, Theodore. "Municipal Administration: New York City Police Force." *Atlantic Monthly* 80 (September 1897): 289-300.

Swift, Morrison I. "Tramps as Human Beings." *Outlook* 52 (August 31, 1895): 342-343.

"The Unemployed: What Shall Be Done with the Worthy Poor?" *Outlook* 48 (December 30, 1893): 1229-1230.

Warne, Frank Julian. "The Unemployed in New York City." *Charities and The Commons* 19 (February 1908): 1584-1586.

"What Churchmen Think of the Invasion of Their Sanctuaries by the Unemployed." *Current Opinion* 56 (May 1914): 367-368.

CONTEMPORARY BOOKS

Books written by reformers and other concerned individuals about various phases of social welfare and unemployment proved useful in this study. Occasionally they provided the only link between seemingly unrelated correspondence. Devine's books were especially useful because the gradual change in his outlook on charity and relief could be documented.

Bellamy, Edward. *How to Employ the Unemployed in Mutual Mainte-nance*. Boston, 1893.

Booth, William. *In Darkest England, and the Way Out*. New York, 1890.

Booth Tucker, Frederick de L. *The Social Relief Work of the Salvation Army in the United States*. New York, 1900.

Brace, Charles Loring. *The Dangerous Classes of New York, and Twenty Years' Work Among Them*. 3d ed. New York, 1880.

Brown, Edwin A. *"Broke," The Man Without a Dime*. Chicago, 1913.

Brown, Mary Wilcox. *The Development of Thrift*. New York, 1899.

Campbell, Helen. *Darkness and Daylight: or Lights and Shadows of New York Life*. Hartford, Connecticut, 1896.

Devine, Edward Thomas. *Misery and its Causes*. New York, 1909.
————. *The Practice of Charity, Individual, Associated and Organized*. New York, 1904.

Dugdale, R. L. *"The Jukes": A Study in Crime, Pauperism, Disease, and Heredity*. New York, 1877.

George, Henry. *Progress and Poverty*. New York, 1955.
————. *Social Problems*. New York, 1934.

Greene, Maria Louisa. *Among School Gardens*. New York, 1910.

Haggard, Sir Henry Rider. *The Poor and the Land: Being a Report on the Salvation Army Colonies in the United States and at Had-leigh, England with Scheme of National Land Settlement and an Introduction*. New York and Bombay, 1905.

Hourwich, Isaac Aronovich. *Immigration and Labor: The Economic Aspects of European Immigration to the United States*. New York and London, 1912.

James, William. *The Varieties of Religious Experience*. New York, 1908.

Kelly, Edmund. *The Elimination of the Tramp: By the Introduction into America of the Labour Colony System Already Proved Effec-tive in Holland, Belgium, and Switzerland with the Modifications Necessary to Adapt the System to American Conditions*. New York and London, 1908.

Lamb, Edward Gifford. *The Social Work of the Salvation Army*. New York, 1909.

Lee, Joseph. *The Tramp Problem*. Boston, 1905.

Lewis, Orlando Faulkland. *Vagrancy in the United States*. New York, 1907.

Lowell, Josephine Shaw. *Public Relief and Private Charity*. New York, 1884.

Nearing, Scott. *Social Adjustment*. New York, 1911.

Pinkerton, Allan. *Strikers, Communists, Tramps, and Detectives*. New York, 1878.

Rauschenbusch, Walter. *Christianizing the Social Order*. New York, 1912.

Riis, Jacob A. *How the Other Half Lives*. New York, 1957.

———. *The Making of an American*. New York, 1947.

Sargent, Charles Edward et al. *Our Home: or Influences Emanating From the Hearthstone*. Springfield, Massachusetts, 1899.

Stelzle, Charles. *A Son of the Bowery: The Life Story of an East Side American*. New York, 1926.

Stewart, William Rhinelander, compiler. *The Philanthropic Work of Josephine Shaw Lowell*. New York, 1910.

Strong, Josiah. *The Challenge of the City*. New York, 1907.

Taylor, Arthur O., editor. *Persistent Public Problems: Unemployment, Social and Industrial Righteousness*. Boston, 1916.

Wayland, Francis. *A Paper on Tramps Read at the Saratoga Meeting of the American Social Science Association Before the Conference of State Charities: September, 1877*. New Haven, 1877.

TRAMP SELF-PORTRAITS

Between 1890 and 1920, numerous men became tramps and then returned to tell the real story of tramp life. In this study only the most representative and, more important, most widely circulated ones were used. Josiah Flynt and Walter Wyckoff were both known to the New York reformers and participated occasionally on their committees and surveys. Leon Livingston, who used the pen name "A-No. 1," published lurid unhappy accounts of tramp life to discourage new recruits. Jack London's accounts are descriptive and written with a sense of pride for his chosen profession. The books listed below represent the best examples of the many works of this type.

Flynt, Josiah [Josiah Flynt Willard]. *Tramping With Tramps: Studies and Sketches of Vagabond Life.* New York, 1899.

Livingston, Leon Ray [A-No. 1] *The Curse of Tramp Life, by A-No. 1, the King of the Hobqes: A True Story of Actual Tramp Life Written by Himself.* Cambridge Springs, Pennsylvania, 1912.

————. *The Ways of the Hobo.* Erie, 1915.

London, Jack. *The Road.* New York, 1907.

Wyckoff, Walter Augustus. *A Day With a Tramp, and Other Days.* New York, 1901.

————. *The Workers: An Experiment in Reality: The East.* New York, 1897.

————. *The Workers: An Experiment in Reality: The West.* New York, 1898.

SECONDARY WORKS

BOOKS

Numerous books dealing with urban life, unemployment, and reform provided valuable background material. Robert Bremner's book is a basic starting place for overall scope and method. Smith's book and Hofstadter's section on the agrarian myth are superb. Wyllie and Fine provide basic background for nineteenth-century ideas. Watson, Warne, and Bruno clarify the intricacies of the charity organization movement and make research easier. And what these men did for private welfare agencies, Schneider and Deutsch did for public ones. Bruce's and McMurry's work on depression violence were vivid and enlightening. Feder's book was very useful, and Mills' provided interesting thoughts, as well as research leads.

Abell, Aaron I. *The Urban Impact on American Protestantism, 1865-1900.* Cambridge, Massachusetts, and London, 1943.

Adams, Graham Jr. *Age of Industrial Violence, 1910-1915: The Activities and Findings of the United States Commission on Industrial Relations.* New York, 1966.

Allsop, Kenneth. *Hard Travellin': The Hobo and His History.* New York, 1967.

Bloomfield, Maxwell H. *Alarms and Diversions: The American Mind Through American Magazines, 1900-1914*. The Hague and Paris, 1967.

Bogen, Boris D. *Jewish Philanthropy: An Exploration of the Principles and Methods of Jewish Social Service in the United States*. New York, 1917.

Bonner, Arthur. *Jerry McAuley and His Mission*. Neptune, New Jersey, 1967.

Brackett, Jeffrey R. *The Transportation Problem in American Social Work, Including an Account of the Origin and Development of the Transportation Agreement*. New York, 1936.

Bremner, Robert Hamlett. *From The Depths: The Discovery of Poverty in the United States*. New York, 1956.

Brissenden, Paul Frederick. *The I.W.W., A Study of American Syndicalism*. New York, 1919.

Bruce, Robert V. *1877: Year of Violence*. Indianapolis, 1959.

Bruno, Frank John. *Trends in Social Work as Reflected in the Proceedings of the National Council of Social Work, 1874-1946*. New York, 1948.

Community Service Society of New York. *Frontiers in Human Welfare*. New York, 1948.

Davis, Allen F. *Spearheads for Reform*. New York, 1967.

Feder, Leah Hannah. *Unemployment Relief in Periods of Depression: A Study of Relief Measures Adopted in Certain American Cities, 1857 Through 1922*. New York, 1936.

Fine, Sidney. *Laissez Faire and the General Welfare State: A Study of Conflict in American Thought, 1865-1900*. Ann Arbor, 1956.

Haller, Mark Hughlin. *Eugenics: Hereditarian Attitudes in American Thought*. New Brunswick, 1963.

Hayter, Earl W. *The Troubled Farmer, 1850-1900: Rural Adjustment to Industrialism*. DeKalb, Illinois, 1968.

Hill, Arthur Cheney Chilton Jr. and Lubin, Isador. *The British Attack on Unemployment*. Washington, D.C., 1934.

Hofstadter, Richard. *The Age of Reform: From Bryan to F. D. R.* New York, 1955.

Hyndman, Henry Mayers. *Commercial Crises of the Nineteenth Century*. New York, 1967.

Joseph, Samuel. *History of the Baron de Hirsch Fund.* Philadelphia, 1935.

Lescohier, Don Divance and Brandeis, Elizabeth. *History of Labor in the United States, 1896-1932.* New York, 1935.

Lewis, Harry Samuel. *Liberal Judaism and Social Service.* New York, 1915.

Lubove, Roy. *The Struggle for Social Security, 1900-1935* Cambridge, Massachusetts, 1968.

McMurry, Donald LeCrone. *Coxey's Army, A Study of the Industrial Army Movement of 1894.* Boston, 1929.

Mills, Frederick Cecil. *Contemporary Theories of Unemployment and Unemployment Relief.* New York, 1917.

Mott, Frank L. *A History of American Magazines, 1885-1905.* Cambridge, Massachusetts, 1957.

Pollack, Norman. *The Populist Response to Industrial America: Midwestern Political Thought.* Cambridge, Massachusetts, 1962.

Porter, Kirk H. and Johnson, Donald Bruce, compilers. *National Party Platforms, 1840-1960.* 2d edition. Urbana, 1961.

Schneider, David Moses, and Deutsch, Albert. *The History of Public Welfare in New York State.* Chicago, 1938-1941. 2 vols.

Smith, Darrell Hevenor. *The United States Employment Service: Its History, Activities, and Organization.* Baltimore, 1923.

Smith, Henry Nash. *Virgin Land: The American West as Symbol and Myth.* Cambridge, Massachusetts, 1950.

Watson, Frank Dekker. *The Charity Organization Movement in the United States, A Study in American Philanthropy.* New York, 1922.

Warner, Amos Griswold. *American Charities.* 3d ed. revised. New York, 1919.

Wisbey, Herbert Andrew, Jr. *Soldiers Without Swords: A History of the Salvation Army in the United States.* New York, 1955.

Wyllie, Irvin G. *The Self-Made Man in America: The Myth of Rags to Riches.* New Brunswick, 1954.

ARTICLES

Cherry, George L. "American Metropolitan Press Reaction to the Paris Commune of 1871." *Mid-America* 32 (January 1950): 3-12.

Gutman, Herbert. "Protestantism and the American Labor Movement: The Christian Spirit in the Gilded Age." *American Historical Review* 62 (October 1966): 74-101.

Leonard, Frank. " 'Helping' The Unemployed in the Nineteenth Century: The Case of the American Tramp." *Social Service Review* 40 (December 1966): 429-434.

Nichols, William W. "A Changing Attitude Toward Poverty in the *Ladies' Home Journal*: 1895-1919." *Mid-Continent American Studies Journal* 5 (Spring 1964): 3-16.

Rezneck, Samuel. "Patterns of Thought and Action in an American Depression, 1882-1886." *American Historical Review* 61 (January 1956): 284-307.

————. "Unemployment, Unrest, and Relief in the United States During the Depression of 1893-97." *Journal of Political Economy* 61 (August 1953): 324-345.

Seelye, John D. "The American Tramp: A Version of the Picaresque." *American Quarterly* 15 (Winter 1963): 535-553.

Spence, Clark C. "Knights of the Tie and Rail-Tramps and Hoboes in the West." *Western Historical Quarterly* 2 (January 1971): 5-19.

Steeples, Douglas W. "The Panic of 1893: Contemporary Reflections and Reactions." *Mid-America* 47 (July 1965): 155-175.

Trattner, Walter I. "Theodore Roosevelt, Social Workers, and the Election of 1912: A Note." *Mid-America* 50 (January 1968): 64-69.

Yellowitz, Irwin. "The Origins of Unemployment Reform in the United States." *Labor History* 9 (Fall 1968): 338-360.

DOCTORAL DISSERTATIONS AND MASTERS' THESES

While some articles and portions of books have dealt with tramps, Hoffman's "The American Tramp" is the only scholarly study that deals entirely with tramps. It is, however, a rather superficial study

212

without well-thought out conclusions. Skolnik's excellent study is a massive one, dealing with the attempts by reform elements to "infiltrate" New York City politics. Speizman's work is a handy guide to nonreformer attitudes toward charity and relief.

Auble, Arthur G. "The Depressions of 1873 and 1882 in the United States." Ph.D. dissertation, Harvard University, 1949.

Carey, John J. "Progressives and the Immigrant, 1885-1915." Ph.D. dissertation, University of Connecticut, 1968.

Hoffman, Victor, "The American Tramp, 1870-1900." Master's thesis, University of Chicago, 1953.

Kuhlman, Frieda M. "A Study of Varying Trends in the Treatment of the Poor." Master's thesis, New York School of Social Work, 1937.

Lloyd, Gary A. "Social Work Concepts of the Causes and 'Treatment' of Poverty: 1893-1908." Ph.D. dissertation, Tulane University, 1965.

Rosenthal, Herbert Hillel. "The Progressive Movement in New York State, 1906-1914." Ph.D. dissertation, Harvard University, 1955.

Scannell, Ruth. "A History of the Charity Organization Society of the City of New York from 1882-1935." Master's thesis, New York School of Social Work, 1938.

Skolnik, Richard. "Crystallization of Reform in New York City, 1890-1917." Ph.D. dissertation, Yale University, 1964.

Speizman, Milton D. "Attitudes Toward Charity in American Thought." Ph.D. dissertation, Tulane University, 1962.

Index

213

"Dynamite" (tramp), 120-121

Easley, Ralph, 150, 173
East Side Relief Committee, 95-97
Elimination of the Tramp, The (Kelly), 126
Elliot, J. L., 149
Elmira Reformatory, 125
Ely, Richard, 38, 59, 128
"Emergence of Class Consciousness, The," editorial, 68
Emergency Work Bureau of New York, 178
Employment bureaus and agencies, 135-155
  fraudulent practices of, 140
  Salvation Army and, 46, 116-126
Environment, tramping and, 91-92
Ethical Social League, 149-150
Evans, George Henry, 109
Everybody's Magazine, 168

Farm colonies
  establishment of, 119-121
  failure of, 124-125
  in New York City, 125
  Salvation Army and, 119-120
Federal Bureau of Labor, 24, 143, 169
Federal labor exchange program, 170-171
Ferrer, Francisco, 165
Finn, Daniel E., 126
Fires, setting of by tramps, 12
First National Conference on Unemployment in New York City, 169
Fitzgerald's Army, 43
Flower, Benjamin O., 46
Flower, Roswell P., 38, 178
Flynt, Josiah, 39-42, 60
Folks, Homer, 66, 121, 154
Food, processing of, 9-10
Forbes, James, 58, 72
Forced labor colonies, Europe, 126

Fort Amity, farm colony at, 120-124
Fort Herrick, Salvation Army colony at, 120, 124
Fort Romie, farm colony at, 119-120, 122-124
Forum, 69, 111
Frank Leslie's Illustrated Newspaper, 17
French Revolution, 42, 45, 168
Frick, Henry C., 68
Frick, H. C., Coke Company, 45
Frontier, Turner's thesis on, 110
Frye's Army, 43

"Gallus Mag," 85
Galveston Movement, 142
Gardening, school, 112-113
  see also Vacant lot gardening
Garland, Hamlin, 28, 41
Gary, E. H., 173-174
George, Henry, 36-37, 116, 176
Gerry, Eldridge T., 94
Ghettos, Jewish workers in, 141
Giddings, F. H., 178
Gilman, Bradley, 121
Gilroy, Thomas F., 93
Glenn, John, 59, 154
Glynn, Martin H., 155, 172
God, tramps and, 84
Goldman, Emma, 43
Gompers, Samuel, 38, 164, 173
Gould, E. R. L., 66
Grady, James, 56
Great Britain
  Salvation Army colonies in, 122
  unemployment in, 152
  see also British Poor Law
Great Depression, 110
Greeley, Horace, 110
Greenback Labor party, 38
Greenwich Village, Salvation Army in, 90
Greer, Rev. Daniel, 150
Gurteen, Rev. S. Humphreys, 25